THE AFGHAN INTEL CRISIS

THE AFGHAN INTEL CRISIS

SATELLITE STATE – WAR OF INTERESTS AND THE BLAME GAME

MUSA KHAN JALALZAI

Algora Publishing
New York

Library of Congress Cataloging-in-Publication Data —
Names: Jalalzai, Musa Khan, author.
Title: The Afghan intel crisis : satellite state, war of interests and the
    blame-game / Musa Khan Jalalzai.
Description: New York : Algora Publishing, 2017. | Includes bibliographical
    references.
Identifiers: LCCN 2017005270 (print) | LCCN 2017010236 (ebook) | ISBN
    9781628942705 (soft cover : alk. paper) | ISBN 9781628942712 (hard cover :
    alk. paper) | ISBN 9781628942729 (pdf)
Subjects: LCSH: Intelligence service—Afghanistan. | Military
    intelligence—Afghanistan. | Interagency coordination—Afghanistan.
Classification: LCC JQ1765.A55 I65 2017 (print) | LCC JQ1765.A55 (ebook) |
    DDC 958.104/78—dc23
LC record available at https://lccn.loc.gov/2017005270

Printed in the United States

Table of Contents

Preamble

In a modern state system, a state without a proper mechanized intelligence is not only unimaginable, it is impossible for such a state system to exist; and if one were to be found, it could be likened to a human body without a nervous system. The primary purpose of intelligence being utilized is to facilitate the conduct of daily internal and external affairs of the state, mostly military related and war conditions. From the 17th, 18th and 19th centuries, its usage slowly increased and states started using it as a mechanism for power consolidation and expansionist ideas. At the end of the 19th century and beginning of the 20th century, the shape and functionality of intelligence completely changed. In the first two stages mentioned above, mostly it was in the service of states run by monarchs, tyrannical leaders and unelected leaders, but in its present and as we say third stage, today's intelligence services being highly sophisticated and modern, have become equally dangerous and brutal with unverified and weak sources of information not only causing much damage globally but to the detriment of innocent lives, especially due to the intelligence of military warfare, a cost which is unjustified.

It is predominantly used by elected democratic powers of the world to control the state function, mainly their foreign relations, economic deals, military pacts, arms deals and elections. Electoral outcomes "need" to be managed due to the uncertainty of the results and unpredicted candidates winning, a possibility which cannot always be stopped before the election due to legal and procedural complications, and the outcomes not be according to requirement and demands of the state and national security. Former President Barack Obama and President Donald Trump are the best examples, if we listen to their speeches and promises during their campaigns, and thereafter the actions and subsequently the results after their nomination and receiving the first intelligence briefing, clearly shows a 180-degree turnaround in their policies they had to follow what they were briefed because that was the actual line of policy, not the one which they were preaching during their campaign.

In the case that the elected leaders do not follow the instructions they have been given, they are then stopped by intelligence agencies using different methods. In some countries, the intervention is so obvious and direct such as Russia, China, Egypt and most of the third world states, however, it is also happening in the first world the so called "pioneers" of democracy but it is action with a difference, it is so subtle they do it in way to be as smooth as possible so it should not be felt easily by the masses in order to complete the process and achieve its objectives too.

In the case of a nuclear state, it is the intelligence services that predict and control the unpredicted. So nowadays, the world has more or less become a surveillance society always under observation and controlled by the secret eagle eyes of the unknown, and the intelligence being in the service of the government of the time acting as a guarantor of the state and controlling the government, providing direction so as to ensure it is acting as it should be. However, this is not the case when it comes to the United States of America, a leading super power of the world. Quite frankly it's the opposite, its intelligence agencies (CIA, FBI, CIB, NSA, and so on) not only influence the internal politics of the country but they make policy decisions and instruct on military and its actions, politics, foreign policies and foreign relations, economic and trade agreements. It's the intelligence agencies that control the government and safeguard the state rather than government who should have the intelligence at their disposal.

Using intelligence is not a new phenomenon, mankind has used these tactics for centuries, and it has been used by human beings against one another in different shapes and scales; small and large, under innumerable prefaces and not limited to; religion, military, economic (Trade) and politics. In modern history from the beginning of 19th century to the end of the Cold War in 1980-90s the world was divided into two major poles (WARSAW and NATO) KGB vs-a-vis CIA. Two major intelligence organisations worked against each other spent billions of dollars on acquiring information from each other's satellites, at the same time they also used the smaller agencies for their purposes as a tool.

Russia used to get help with intelligence sharing from India, China, Iraq, Syria, Libya, Cuba, Central Asian countries, Eastern European countries and North African countries, while the United State of America used Iran, Pakistan, South Korea, Japan, Egypt, Israel, Saudi Arabia, Jordan, and most of the European states. In Afghanistan, the need for having an effective internal intelligence service was first established by the late President Mohammed Dawood Khan during his premiership to have an eye on military and new political movements from right and left (Muslim fundamentalist Nuhzat-e-Islami influenced by the Egyptian Brotherhood) and (Wesh Zelmain, Herkat Roshanfikran Afghan, Khalq and Purchum leftist Parties influenced by Russia).

When President Dawood decided to establish the secret agency (Estekhbarat-e-Seari-e-Dawlati, (Secret Intelligence Services of Afghanistan), he asked the Governor General of the Eastern zones (Nangerhar, Laghman, Kunner and Nuristan) to outline proposals, where my late grandfather Sayed Ibrar Pacha was a district governor, and had political affiliations with the President for a long time to consult him regarding this decision, he had made to restructure the semi intelligence working at the time known as (Riasat-e-zabt-e-Hawalat-e-Sadarat) into a proper functioning intelligence department woven into government structure. Prime Minister Dawood not only sought his view but requested him to accept the office of first Directorship of the agency. Dawood Khan was after all a person to be clean, honest, patriotic, and faithful and a strict administrator in order to be able to carry out such a huge responsibility.

My grandfather not only refused to accept the offer but he was offended by this request as coming from a spiritual family who had followers of its own would damage his reputation if he became a spy chief. For him it was very difficult to convince the people regarding the importance of this job as the literacy level was so low at that time, and the word "ESTEKHBARAT" (Intelligence) was taken face wise and understood as "Spy" and informer. However, he was well aware of the fact that even prophet Mohammed (PBUH) used intelligence for making war strategies and decisions on the basis of information from insiders and informers from the enemy comps.

The President established the agency under a new name and management with broader objective roles. It was very active and had a centralised agency with one aim: that national security must be free of all ethnic, religious or regional affiliations, the agency was named as Estekhbarat-e-Seari-e-Dawlati or "State Secret Intelligence", worked until the fall of his government in 1978. Since 1980s, after the Soviet intervention, Afghan governments established four intelligence agencies (KAM, AGSA, WAD, and KHAD) to ensure the stability of the country. The KHAD was established in 1980, and transformed into a Ministry, Wazarat-e-Amniat-e-Daulat "Ministry of State Security" (WAD), in 1986. President Noor Muhammad Tarakai was in power for a limited time, while Hafizullah Amin divided both the communist party and intelligence agencies into two factions (Khalq and Parcham). The AGSA (Safeguarding Agency of Afghan Interests), which was established by Mr. Tarakai, was dissolved due to his differences with Hafizullah Amin. In 1979, President Amin established another secret agency, KAM (Workers intelligence service).

Furthermore, the same thing happened once again as history repeated itself, when in 1992 after the collapse of Dr Najibullah government, Mujahedeen took over, before Najibullah went to the UN compound in Kabul and sought political asylum along with his brother, and some other Watan party colleagues he asked the Prime minister and Chairman Senate to make a peaceful transfer of power to the leadership of the Mujahedeen, according to the UN deal by Benin Savon, and Geneva Agreement signed by major parties to the conflict (USA and Russia as the guarantors and Pakistan and Afghanistan as two conflicting sides).

In Peshawar, an Interim Government was already established. A new power sharing agreement was signed between the Mujahedeen leadership known as the Peshawar Agreement, according to which Professor Mujaddidi would take power from the Kabul regime, and become first president of the Mujahedeen government for two months, after two months, power should be transferred to Professor Burhanuddin Rabbani. In the same, it was also decided that prior to the entry of a transitional Government into Kabul, an eight members' security delegation had to enter Kabul to take over the security charges, this team was called "Commission for security of Kabul", its eight members were respectfully representing their political party, while Ahmed Shah Masood and my father were named as heads of the commission. Lt. General S.M Shafi Fatimi, Deputy Chairman of the Military Department of NLFA was named as Secretary General of the Commission who was the representing President Mujaddidi.

Within their first meeting, Jihadi leadership high council plus the Kabul security commission's joint member session worked on cabinet, and its nominees. All parties introduced their nominees to the designated Ministry, my father; Lt. General S M Shafi was named as the head of NDS (National Directorate for Security). However, at this meeting, not only did he refuse to accept the profile, he asked the President to undermine this department as it had been a branch of KGB, being involved in bloodshed. He proposed that the old Secret Intelligence agency of Dawood era needed to be reinstated.

President Mujaddidi appointed General Yahya Nowruz, a prominent military figure as head of NDS. Soon after he started his work, he was cornered by General Qaseem Fahim who had strong links to the NDS. Thereafter, Gen Yahya Nowruz went back to his family in the USA until he passed away there. From his first day, Mr. Fahim made all his decisions outside ,and against the cabinet, he appointed his own people including ex-communists from the Purchum party using the organisation for political victimization of all other jihadi parties, especially Pashtuns and Hizb-e-Islami of Afghanistan led by Gulbuddin Hekmatyar. Most of the Afghan Intelligence personnel and police commanders in 34 provinces were ex-communist and skilled KGB spies, who later on, sought asylum in USA and other European countries in early 90s.

Now, they have returned to serve the old enemy against the previous masters, and at the same time, they sought to take their revenge from the Mujahedeen who defeated their government by destroying the red Empire. The US intervention of provided them with the chance to kill the Afghan and Arab Mujahedeen and all those fundamentalists from the Muslim world who had strong anti-American feelings. In order to do these, the US choose one of its old well trained spies inside the Muslim movement with strong links to the Egyptian Muslim brotherhood, Prof Abdul Rab Rasoul Sayyaf to fulfil its requirement?

Ultimately, America played into the hands of a small group of people who do not represent any ethnic, religious or linguistics sect (Tajik, Pashtuns, Uzbeks, Turkmans, Hazera's, Shiites or Sunnis). Anyhow, sue to these mistakes, the US military commanders admitted to having very little knowledge of Afghan culture and Taliban insurgents. They showed a predilection for military-led approaches to problems, including those that were essentially political. Another US commander, General Eikenberry, criticized the counterinsurgency strategy promoted by General Petraeus. The general rejected the COIN strategy as applied in Afghanistan in his article published in Foreign Affairs".

The way Panjshir played into the hand of the Americans against their own countrymen can be compared with the Israeli role in the Middle east, even Tajik's from Kabul city call them "Afghani Israelis" a tiny group has taken over major organs of the government (Defence, Interior and NDS). NDS has been used as tool of power against all Afghans by the Panjshiri mafia since 1992. The stories of the failure of Afghan intelligence agencies and their political and religious affiliations and loyalties have badly affected military strategies and counter insurgency measures of NATO and US intelligence circles; secret political and military reports are feared to have gone into the hands of war criminals, regional states and the Taliban insurgents. As per the nature of their controversial work, Afghan agents belong to various ethnic and political groups; therefore, they are bound to report to their masters. Like the Afghan police and army, intelligence network has also been divided between states, warlords, NGOs and foreign intelligence agencies"

The NDS and its predecessor in the last four decades had been through three phases, phase one starts from 1978 up till 1992 Afghan/Russia era KHAD used to work as branch of KGB and its intelligences were all trained by Soviet Union (KGB) even though it was a puppet branch it was still effective, organised and disciplined it was fighting inside and outside the Afghan border with (ISI and CIA) as they had one lord (Russia) and one aim to defend the Kabul regime. When General Ghulam Faruq Yaqubi, the last director of KHAD prior to the entry of Mujahedeen on the day of fall of Kabul, committed suicide, my father was second man in command of the Commission for Security of Kabul entered the NDS headquarter where General Ghulam Faruq Yaqubis' body was lying on ground.

My father opened the cupboards behind his desk were full with foreign currencies but nobody had ever touched that money, while in present modern democratic government, when Amrullah Saleh was removed from his post, he took away $6m USD secret fund with him. In 2001, despite the presence of US and its allies, 48 states, the NDS remained under Panjshiri faction. The NDS in the real sense is not an intelligence agency, it is an open secret "INDULGENCE AGENCY" where in a big bowl of stew all major shareholders are trying to dip in and snatch as big a bounty as they can; USA, Russia, Britain, France, Germany, Canada, Australia, Saudi Arabia, Iran and Pakistan are all stake holders in this pot of stew known as NDS.

During the last 16 years; five people were appointed as heads of NDS; Mr. Amarullah Saleh, Mr. Rahmatullah Nabil, Mr. Assadullah Khalid, Mr. Nabil second Term, and finally the present head Mr. Masoom Stanikzai, all are unfit and unprofessional, incompetent and working for foreign agencies. Mr. Rahmatullah Nabil is an Engineer by profession with close association with ISI-CIA, Mr. Masoom Stanikzai Military Civil Engineer with close link with British intelligence, Mr. Amarullah Saleh has been a former CIA and RAW insider in Panjshir, and Mr. Assadullah Khalid chief of Drug mafia and smuggler who worked with three different foreign intelligence agencies. All senior officers in the directorate are trying to satisfy their own lords to whom they are answerable they do not care about anyone else. The rest they use their profile for personal gain and making money.

The book in your hand is on Afghan intelligence (NDS) is the best source to know about NDS and other major local, regional and international secret agencies. The author (Musa Khan Jalalzai) is an established writer on the field and related subjects (Politics, Foreign policy, Terrorism, insurgency, policing, Narcotics, Drug trafficking, Human smuggling, Jihad, Nuclear arsenals, Cyber war and attacks) This book could provide a good guideline to those who really wants to make a difference in rebuilding the Afghan secret agency to take it out of this nightmare and make a huge difference. This book should be a handbook for Afghan NDS members, Police officers, professor, Military generals, intellectuals and senior government officers.

Sayed Bilal Ahmed Fatimi
M.A., International Relations and International Law
LLM/MA International Law
Diploma in Journalism IRC
Presidential Candidate 2010 and
Candidate for Afghan Parliamentary Election, January 2017, London

Patients were charred in their beds, doctors and other staff members were roasted. Medics were decapitated in the blast. Some patients and doctors tried to escape but they were gunned down by US aircraft. Doctors without Borders condemned the US war crimes in Kunduz Hospital. The MSF Chief, Dr. Joanne Liu, said: "No one calls a rape a complex gynecological emergency. A rape is rape, just as genocide is genocide." Sometimes, intelligence failure results in an ugly picture of war crime. The US army killed 42 people including 14 innocent patients and doctors in Kunduz hospital, and then argued that the $5 billion intelligence computer system had failed. This was undoubtedly an ignominious joke on the citizens of an occupied country, where the US is free to kill, torture, and kidnap civilians with impunity. A Persian proverb beautifully illustrates this inhuman act in few words: "Don't trust those who don't trust God, and if you don't recognize God, at least know Him by His power."

In 15 years of US war in Afghanistan, the CIA, Pentagon and the US army have slaughtered thousands of Afghan citizens in their unjust war against a weak and a poor country where 95 percent people have no idea what 9/11 means. They committed countless atrocities, bombed wedding parties killing over 150 in three separate attacks. A 2007 aerial bombing by NATO on a Helmand Province neighborhood left at least 50 civilians dead. In 2010, a group of 11 American soldiers in Kandahar who called themselves the "Kill Team" were caught murdering at least three civilians. In 2012, the U.S. military came under fire for a viral video showing Marines urinating on Afghan corpses. On many occasions, CIA and Pentagon men raped, tortured and cruelly treated detainees during interrogations in Afghanistan between 2003 and 2014.

The post-Cold War era has seen an appalling distortion in the definition of national security. In the Cold War, and the present new cold war, "intelligence failure" cause massive and repeated destruction. Poor understanding of intelligence mechanism and capabilities, coordination between agencies, and poor dissemination methods have also prompted failure. Terrorists are intelligent people. They operate like intelligence agencies in war and peace times; they spy on their targets, and collect intelligence information about the enemy's weak points.

Today's intelligence war presents an entirely different picture from the Cold-War era. The Cold War secret intelligence strategies and policies were aimed to protect sources and keep adversaries from gaining access to military secrets. For this purpose, the compartmentalized acquisition by secret agencies, information analysis, dissemination of information, and a professional and technical approach that worked intelligently well as long as policymakers knew who the enemy was what information to look for and who needed to have it.

During the Cold War, competition among agencies about intelligence information gathering was deeply complicated as every agency used different tactics of collection and dissemination. Today, the most important challenge faced by secret agencies is the issue of effectiveness. During the last four decades of civil war, we experienced numerous incidents of intelligence failure in Afghanistan, in which the lack of professional skills, staff and authentic source of information, and reliance on secret surveillance were major causes. The modern intelligence warfare among scores of foreign intelligence in Afghanistan presented a new picture; in which every agency learn from the operational capabilities, failures, gains and professional skills of its rival power. This complex business of secret war created numerous difficulties for the United States and its allies in Afghanistan.

Most intelligence studies ignore important aspects of the role played by intelligence in countering terrorism, but in modern war, intelligence is the most important weapon of state. In the information age, intelligence has taken on even greater importance. But in the popular media, the principles, role, and purpose of intelligence are very often misrepresented at best. Intelligence processing can include technical issues such as transcribing and translating intercepted telephone conversations, and verifying the reliability of information.

Intelligence is crucial to the development of understanding— it requires practitioners and experts to operate in a complex environment. The Taliban intelligence war in Kunduz and elsewhere in Afghanistan received mixed responses in military and political circles, where terrorist groups used cell phones to organize and coordinate surprise attacks against the government forces. The way Taliban and the ISIS advanced in small towns and cities was a new tactic of modern war, in which mobile phone technology played an important role in coordinating all forces on various fronts.

The rise and fall of Afghan intelligence agencies, and the way they operated during the last three decades, left reams of bloodstained and heartbreaking stories in newspapers, journals and books. The Afghan agency (KHAD) killed thousands in its secret prisons, in broad daylight, and in its torture cells, the NDS kills, tortures and forcefully disappears numerous innocent Afghan men, women and children alike. International human rights organizations and Afghanistan's Independent Human Rights Commission in their research papers deeply criticized the National Directorate of Security (NDS) for its brutal ways of retrieving information from detainees. These illegal tactics alienated the citizens from the state, and forced young people to take up arms against the government and its international partners.

The NDS demonstrated a lack of professionalism and failed to counter the Taliban and ISIS's geographical expansion. Chiefs of the intelligence agencies have been unlawfully critical of Afghan Presidents, parliamentarians and neighboring states in their print and electronic media statements, since 2001. They criticized former President Hamid Karzai's approach towards Pakistan, criticized President Ashraf Ghani's visit to Islamabad, and criticized NATO and Pakistan for failing to stabilize the teetering state. The chief of National Directorate of Security (NDS), Mr. Rahmatullah Nabil hammered Prime Minister Nawaz Sharif for his remarks about Afghanistan. His precursor, Mr. Amrullah Saleh, acted like an ethnic politician.

This controversial and unprofessional conduct by the Afghan intelligence agencies was irksome for the government of Afghanistan and international community. Despite scads of tips, the NDS failed to prevent an attack on Kabul. Conflicts between Pashtuns and the Panjshiri Tajik-dominated officer corps of the NDS have been cited as among the main reasons that information about the attack did not reach the right people at the right time in Kabul. The spy agency was severely criticized by parliamentarians after a brazen prison break in Kandahar and the fall of Kunduz to Taliban insurgents.

In fact, during the last 15 years, the US and its NATO allies failed to substantially improve governance and intelligence sharing systems or recruit the NDS officers. A strong centralized intelligence infrastructure remained a dream. The Americans took no interest in establishing a strong intelligence system in Kabul, and at the provincial level, the intelligence networks no longer exist. The ability of the Afghan state to establish its rule in rural areas has been completely undermined. For an ordinary Afghan, insecurity of all types destabilizes any attempt to rebuild a life. Corruption is rife in the justice system, and Afghans are completely fed up.

A central problem with intelligence gathering in Afghanistan has been the great emphasis placed on detailed information on insurgents. This information gathering takes place at the expense of more general information concerning the environment, in which they operate.

NATO still needs to identify various interoperability issues and come up with solutions. One issue that has yet to be resolved fully is the sharing of tactical intelligence in coalition operations. The nuances of ethnic and tribal traditions that have developed over centuries would be difficult to grasp in the first few years.

Without understanding the stakeholders and their concerns, intelligence gathering may remain ineffective. American commander, Major General Flynn argued that intelligence in Afghanistan should be demarcated by territorial lines rather than functional lines. Coalition partners were indeed given different districts and provinces to operate in; however the intelligence was not to stop at these demarcations as the insurgency does not respect those borders. The Afghan National Security Forces need a robust intelligence collection and targeting capability if they want to defeat the Taliban insurgency. They need more advanced voice intercept capabilities and cross communication between the National Directorate of Security (NDS) and security forces in the field. Distrust between the government and intelligence chiefs is a major obstacle. The agency chiefs consecutively issued statements, in which they opposed Pakistan's role in the peace process and branded the country as an enemy of the Afghans. The NDS admitted to a huge communication gap between different security wings of the Afghan government. International partners of the Afghan intelligence have also failed to understand the cultural way intelligence operates in the country. The CIA, Pentagon, Menwith Hill, MI6 and GCHQ have not made efficient use of technical means of intelligence like GEOINT, SIGINT, and MASINT, while the HUMINT has been missing throughout the entire war.

Their approach has been electronic throughout the decade. The lack of HUMINT in operations against Taliban terrorist groups' forces analysts to ascertain what is going on by staring at pictures, frantically searching through communications and scanning through newspapers. Professional intelligence assessment by the CIA, MI6 and NATO agencies didn't help answer the questions on crucial points regarding the course of the Afghan war, including the success of a counterinsurgency campaign, the unwillingness of Pakistan to degrade and disrupt Taliban efforts to launch military or terrorist attacks, and the uncertainty of stabilizing governments in Afghanistan.

In January 2010, Major General Mike Flynn, a US commander in Afghanistan at the time, prepared an intelligence report that revealed some of the worst intelligence failures of the CIA and Pentagon. General Flynn complained that intelligence was working hard but it was doing the wrong job. Later on, he suggested the separation of counterinsurgency strategy (COIN) from intelligence operations. In "Fixing Intel," General Flynn sought to drive home the concept that US intelligence needs to collect information about the population of Afghanistan. The US military commanders admitted to having very little knowledge of Afghan culture and Taliban insurgents. They showed a predilection for military-led approaches to problems, including those that were essentially political. Another US commander, General Eikenberry, criticized the counterinsurgency strategy promoted by General Petraeus. The general rejected the COIN strategy as applied in Afghanistan in his article published in Foreign Affairs.

All players in the battlefield used Afghan intelligence for their own purposes while the recruitment of its members along ethnic lines was worrisome. Experts argued this unethical treatment the main cause of the failure of the Afghan, US and NATO forces in rooting out insurgency and terrorism in Afghanistan. In a CNN report, President Karzai was criticized for appointing Mr. Assadullah Khalid as an intelligence chief: "The man tapped as Afghanistan's next intelligence chief faces allegations of drug trafficking and torture." In September 2012, Human Rights Watch reported the appointment of Mr. Assadullah Khalid, noting that KHAD already had a long and well-documented history of torture of detainees.

Due to the politicization of Afghanistan's civilian and military intelligence agencies, Afghan security forces were undergoing a serious security crisis. The ANA was lacking intelligence collection capabilities. NATO and the US lost thousands of troops, and spent half a trillion dollars to build a strong army, but now they seem unwilling to address the exponentially growing corruption culture within the Afghan armed forces. Civilian causalities rose to a record level as the Taliban retrieved sophisticated weapons from Russia. Desertion and retention became a persistent challenge for ANA commanders as thousands of soldiers and officers joined either Taliban or the ISIS terrorist groups. Afghan Defense Ministry was losing as many as 5,000 soldiers and officers every month in cases of desertion and casualties in 2015 and 2016.

In February, the ANA arrested and disarmed 30 cops with alleged Taliban ties, including the police chief of Helmand's Sangin district. Drug trafficking was another serious challenge where, according to the Russian Narcotics Agency report, almost a third of the ANA officers turned to drug trafficking. Army generals and officers were deeply involved in drug trafficking and kidnapping for ransom. The question of merited appointment also remained unsolved as the Military Headquarters and the Intelligence agencies done nothing to oversight selection process to ensure merited promotions.

Those who fought against insurgents during the last 15 years were removed from their posts, and those who enjoyed a comfortable life in Kabul were promoted to the rank of general. The ambassador of the European Union to Afghanistan expressed his dismay that the number of Afghan army generals exceeded several times than those in Britain, Italy, Germany and France. On 11 October 2016, President Ashraf Ghani sternly criticized appointments of unprofessional officers and soldiers within the ranks of the Afghan armed forces. On 15 October 2016, a number of MPs in the lower house of parliament criticized intelligence agencies and warned that the lack of war strategy resulted in the exchange of districts between ANA commanders and Taliban insurgents.

The matrix of the Islamic State was expanding towards the northern parts of the country. Terrorist groups were pledging allegiance to the ISIS struggle to establish their units in the Jalalabad province. In an exclusive interview with Pajhwok Afghan News Agency, NATO spokesman Brigadier General Charlie Cleveland confirmed the existence of more than 1,000 Daesh fighters in the Jalalabad province. On 19 April 2016, Russian diplomat, Zamir Kabulov warned that more than 10,000 trained terrorists of the Islamic State were preparing to enter Central Asia. Moreover, Abdul Rashid Dostum expressed the same concern and warned that some internal (government) and foreign circles want to transport more than 7,500 Daesh fighters (Chechen, Uzbeks, Tajiks, Iraqi, Syrians, Lebanese, and Libyans) to parts of Northern provinces. Who is financing and sponsoring this terrorist organization, and who support it? This fact was unveiled by Wiki leaks founder, Mr. Julian Assange in his interview with a UK based Australian journalist, Mr. John Pilger. Mr. Assange uncovered important facts about the wealthy officials from Saudi Arabia and Qatar donating money to the Hillary Clinton's Foundation and Islamic State (ISIS) respectively. In 17 August 2014, Mr. Assange made public an email in which Secretary of State; Hillary Clinton urged the then advisor to US President Barak Obama, Mr. John Podesta, to pressure Qatar and Saudi Arabia for funding Islamic State (ISIS). These revelations sparked wide-ranging debates in print and electronic media across the globe.

In Afghanistan, close cooperation between Daesh and some disgruntled Taliban leaders added to the pain of the Unity Government. The Khorasan terrorist group, which emerged with a strong military power in 2015, was in control of important districts in Jalalabad province, where it set to fire 60 houses of poor residents on 14 January 2017. The group's military tactics included beheading, public prosecution, kidnapping, and torture, looting and raping, and also forcing families from their homes. During 2015, it became clear that ISK was slowly encroaching on the Pakistani "jihad arena", partly because leading members of various Pakistani militant movements announced their allegiance to ISIS. In Afghanistan, some of the ANA commanders had established close contacts with the ISIS networks.

In October 2016, a number of Afghan parliamentarians from the Kunduz province accused the national unity government and its armed forces for supporting terrorist organizations like ISIS and Taliban. They alleged that military commanders were providing arms, financial assistance and sanctuaries to terrorists, and transport their suicide bombers to their destinations. These were some of the most disturbing accusations in the history of Afghanistan at the floor of parliament. The MPs also accused Afghan National Army (ANA) commanders for handing over dozens of check posts along with sophisticated arms to the Taliban. "All Afghan officials in the Kunduz province, including the ANA, police and local government officials in cooperation with the people from central government, handed the city to the Taliban," said Miss Fatima Aziz.

Afghan opposition leaders perceived the persisting disagreement between the two heads of state, and poor leadership as the reason that the Kunduz city fell to the Taliban. Moreover, a prominent military analyst, Javed Kohistani, hammered the ANA for selling weapons to the Taliban. "We have evidence that prove there are people inside the security forces that sell weapons and checkpoints to the Taliban and let their fellow colleagues being arrested by insurgents. There is the type of betrayal that exists among the security forces, especially the local police," said Mr. Kohistani.

This way of kleptocratic governance does not benefit the poor and insecure people of Afghanistan, a country where public aspirations are not respected and national interests are not considered the top priority. Both leaders were busy in sorting out their political issues but failed to settle the key issues like appointments of governors and military commanders. The desertion of soldiers to the Taliban and ISIS became a complicated crisis. More than 44 ANA officers disappeared in the United States, and 60 police officers were sold to the Taliban in the Badghis province and 70 in the Helmand province.

The frustrated and immature statements of the Afghan and Indian leaders in the Heart of Asia Conference in New Delhi raised important questions about the agenda behind the intentions of both the states in introducing a new concept of countering terrorism vis-a-vis neighboring states in South Asia. Afghan President opened the Heart of Asia Conference with inflammatory and derogatory remarks against Pakistan and snubbed the $500 million development aid from the country, saying that amount can be spent on controlling extremism and radicalization in Pakistan.

"I engaged Pakistan, I went to GHQ, met the military leadership, because each country has their own distinct place for institutions. My message was that there was a window. It could be broadened to a door or a corridor, or it could shut. We did everything to ensure peace with Pakistan. 2015 and 2016 have been extremely difficult years and the violence that has been inflicted on our people needs to be registered. To be quiet when people are dying is not acceptable. I am an elected political leader; I need to reflect my people's sentiment. Because the question of terrorism is not just a threat to us but to Pakistan and the Asian region, and hence the need for a public statement", President Ghani said.

Moreover, Mr. Ghani's special representative for reforms and good governance, Mr. Ahmad Zia Massoud criticized the policies of the Unity Government on nepotism, drug trafficking, and so called nationalism. Mr. Massoud said corruption in three branches of the government prevented good governance from being institutionalized in the country. Mr. Ghani's strong tone in Warsaw and Amritsar aroused the anger of Pakistani political analysts. However, intelligence war between Pakistan, India and Afghanistan intensified. In 2016, Pakistani intelligence prepared dossiers on clandestine activities of Afghan intelligence agencies on Pakistani soil and its nexus with Indian intelligence, RAW. In May 2015, ISI and NDS signed a Memorandum of Understanding (MoU) which was not implemented in letter and spirit by Afghan Intelligence agency. Former NDS head Rahmatullah Nabil, strongly opposed to the proposed agreement with the ISI.

In May 2016, Pakistani intelligence arrested six trained agents of Afghanistan's intelligence agency NDS who were involved in targeted killings, bomb blasts and the killing of 40 people in Pakistan. The notorious RAW-NDS nexus was first busted with the arrest of the Indian RAW agent Kul Boshan Yadev who confessed to be the serving Indian Naval Officer and was deputed to create unrest in Baluchistan. According to sources, RAW agent confessed during interrogation that he had been hosted by National Directorate of Security (NDS) of Afghanistan at many occasions. In August 2016, Watson Institute assessment of war fatalities shows the number of killed and injured civilians, foreign and Afghan forces across the country.

The New York Times offers the following estimates.

Afghan Civilians 2001-2015, killed 29,818, wounded 37,412. From January to June 2016, 1,601 civilians killed and 3,565 injured. Moreover, 30,470 police and military personnel killed and 17,000 injured. The same period shows all but 42,000 Taliban killed and 19,000 injured". However, during the last 15 years, more than 2,371 US soldiers and a Major General killed and 20,179 injured. The same period shows more than 2, 800 US allied forces and contractors killed and 20,000 injured. All but 111,442 Afghans American, and allied forces and contractors killed during the last 15 years war on terrorism in Afghanistan, and 116,603 wounded. Moreover, on 17 April 2016, New York Times also reported the killing of more than 2,000 civilians and 80,000 displaced in 2016 alone.

According to a UN report, the exponentially growing number of conflict-induced internally displaced people in Afghanistan was sensed deeply irksome. More than 2,900,000 Afghan civilians from all provinces were displaced during the last 15 years. There is no end in sight to the miseries of general masses who have suffered a lot from the over four decades of invasions and civil wars. The ISIS killed 74 children and 86 women among 3,000 civilians in just one year, and executed a total 3,027 people in 9 months.

On 22 November 2016, ToloNews TV reported the ISIS suicide attack on a Kabul mosque, in which 11 people killed and 50 injured.

The ISIS carried out two attacks during the Shiite ceremony of Ashura in 11 October 2016 in Kabul, and in 12 October in the northern province of Balkh, that altogether killed at least 32 people. The group also claimed responsibility for the attack, took place in July 23, against a demonstration by mainly Hazara Shiites in Kabul, killing at least 85 and injuring 413 people. On 14 January 2017, Daily Outlook Afghanistan reported Human Rights Watch (HRW) criticized the achievement of the Afghanistan government in improving human rights in 2016. The report revealed the death of more than 8,000 civilians in 2016. According to the report, thousands of families left their homes due to insecurity.

Before presenting the rest of my research and conclusions, I would like to thank prominent Afghan analysts and academics Mr. Sayed Bilal Ahmad Fatimi, and Muhammad Hafiz Sikandari for providing me with books and articles on Afghan intelligence. I also want to thank my editors Andrea Secara and Martin DeMers and their colleagues at Algora Publishing for their work on this book.

Musa Khan Jalalzai
London, January 2017

CHAPTER 1. AFGHAN INTELLIGENCE, INTERNAL POLITICS, AND WAR ON TERROR

In modern terms, intelligence involves a real struggle with human opponents, carried on to gain some advantages over them. However, the argument over the definition of intelligence resembles perhaps nothing so much as a trademark dispute. In essence, there is deep confusion over the basic job of an intelligence agency during war and peace times, but one thing is clear that, without high quality intelligence information, policy makers cannot lead stakeholders on right direction. Some define it as the ability to learn about, learn from, understand and interact, but Michael Herman (2011) argues that intelligence is a classified knowledge that support its own state's information security by advising on and setting standard of defensive, protective security measures.

In his well-written book, Herman argues that intelligence supply assessments of intelligence threat; engages in counter espionage; and seeks evidence of hostile countries' intelligence successes through counterintelligence penetrations of their organizations. In the case of Afghan intelligence agencies, we observed that they never adopted these and other professional measures to lead the government in positive directions. When intelligence planning and operation fails, it means something is not working properly in the machine. If the machine is not working properly, terrorists gain control on large portion of state territory. Intelligence failure often occurs due to preventable conditions, such as the way intelligence is understood, the way it is gathered, the way it is processed, lack of coordination and cooperation, and flawed distribution of intelligence among intelligence agencies. To counter intelligence and terrorist networks, good communication was needed between the three levels of intelligence: strategic, operational and tactical in Afghanistan.

Intelligence failure can be broadly defined as a misunderstanding of the prevailing situation or developing law-and-order scenario. To fix the intelligence machine of NDS, government needed to introduce a reforms package, fit intelligence to the fight, and fit it to the objectives of national security.[1] During the last 15 years war on terrorism, no intelligence reforms have been introduced in Afghanistan to make the NDS competent and professional. The National Directorate of Security was founded as the primary domestic and foreign intelligence agency of the Islamic Republic of Afghanistan in 2002, and it is considered the successor to KHAD, which was established by the communist administration in 1980s.

In Afghanistan, intelligence information is mostly retrieved from newspapers, internet, military and law enforcement agencies, and civilian informers. In view of their inability to provide an accurate information, in October 2013, British intelligence, MI6, called for immediate reinforcements in Afghanistan amidst fears that the country would become an "intelligence vacuum" where terrorists would pose an increased threat to Britain.

As we all know, by virtue of the incoherent and inconsistent intelligence approach of the US and Afghanistan government, the collection of accurate military and civilian intelligence from the majority of districts in eastern and western Afghanistan, and the tribal regions of Pakistan has been in deep crisis during the last three decades. When we study the role of NATO intelligence agencies, the CIA, Russian and Chinese intelligence, Defense Clandestine Intelligence and the Pentagon, we come across several stories of intelligence failures in the country, as they have never been able to bring stability to the country or counter the Inter-Services Intelligence (ISI) effectively.

For US and NATO intelligence agencies, the information needed by their military commanders to conduct a population-centric counter-insurgency operation in Afghanistan was very important, but they could not retrieve it from most of the remote districts. When intelligence is ignored or twisted to produce a desired result, it is truly a failure. Since the war in Afghanistan, the failure of US intelligence created many problems.[2]

The US and its allies' approach to the stabilization process and cooperation on the civilian and military levels with Afghan intelligence agencies, and the ISI in Baluchistan province, the stabilization process of tribal areas and Waziristan has never been satisfactory. They failed to gather information about insurgent cells in remote mountainous areas, where insurgents recruit their soldiers to carry out attack against the coalition forces. Now, as the NDS had divided on ethnic and sectarian bases, the balance of power has shifted in

---

1 *Intelligence in an Insecure World*, Peter Gill and Mark Phythian, Polity Press, USA, 2006
2 Afghanistan: Fitting intelligence to the fight, *Daily Times*, 09 March 2014

favors of Islamic State (ISIS) and Taliban. The US and NATO soldiers have lost confidence, and became hunted than hunters. The roles of the CIA and Afghan intelligence, and their strategies have been deeply contradictory, particularly since the re-emergence of Taliban networks and their attacks across the Durand Line. They failed to professionalize intelligence network and to provide military and strategic guidance to NATO commanders.

For a professional intelligence network, relevance in counter-insurgency operations is needed to supply wide-ranging military information from the war zone to commanders and policymakers. That information, along with much else including realistic presentations setting out the entire range of possible outcomes, the time needed to achieve objectives and the intractable issues tied to information collection, was an urgent need.[3]

In January 2010, a US commander in Afghanistan, Major General Mike Flynn, spotlighted some important points in his intelligence report. He suggested the separation of counterinsurgency strategy (COIN) from intelligence operations. In "Fixing Intel," General Flynn sought to drive home the concept that US intelligence needed to collect information about the population of Afghanistan on cultural bases as military commanders admitted to having very little knowledge of Afghan intelligence gathering culture and Taliban insurgents.

The constitution of Afghanistan (2004) outlines the function of the state and good governance, focusing on the role of intelligence and law enforcement agencies. In 2004, with some amendments, the Afghan Constitution again stressed the need for a centralized state. Article 137 of the Constitution defines the power distribution process: "The Government, in preserving the principles of centralism, shall transfer necessary powers, in accordance with the law, to local administrations in order to accelerate and improve economic, social ass well cultural matters, and foster people's participation in developing national life."[4]

The foreword of the Afghan Constitution suggests: "The creation of civil society free of oppression, atrocity, discrimination and violence and based on the rule of law, social justice...." Chapter 2 of the constitution bars "any kind of discrimination between, and privilege among, the citizens of Afghanistan." In Articles 1, 2, 3, 4, 6, 10, 17, 22, 33, 35, 50, 53, and 75, provisions regarding the issue of governance clearly set out that: "The state of Afghanistan is obliged to create a prosperous and progressive society based on social justice, protection of human dignity, protection of human rights, realization of democracy, and to ensure national unity, and equality among all

---

3 For a professional intelligence network to be relevant in counter-insurgency operations, it needs to supply wide-ranging military information from the war zone to commanders and policymakers. *The Crisis of Britain's Surveillance State*, Musa Khan Jalalzai, Algora Publishing, 2014
4 *The constitution of Afghanistan*, 2004, article 137

ethnic groups and tribes, and provide for balanced development in all areas of the country."

All these instructions and articles of the Constitution can be seen only on paper; in practice, the state and government have not been able to deliver accordingly. If we look at the rule of law in Afghanistan, warlordism, male prostitution, female prostitution, AIDS, Bachabazi, brothels, trafficking in women and children, kidnapping for ransom, drug and arm trafficking, drug addiction, religious conversion and violation of human rights, and all sorts of violation are in full swing.

The Bonn Agreement (2002) was a basic step towards the state building process in Afghanistan, which stressed the need of establishing an Interim Government, followed by the emergency meeting of Grand Assembly in 2002. Under the first Interim President, a constitutional drafting committee was established and the Constitution was restored with some amendments. The justice system was upgraded. Another development was the creation of Law and Order Trust Fund (LOTF) in 2002. In July 2003, reforms in the Interior Ministry were introduced, and in 2004, the donors' conference in Germany reviewed the reform progress in Afghanistan. Due to the exponential growth of Taliban insurgent networks in the country, in 2005, the US government decided to train Afghan police officers on a priority basis.[5]

In 2006, 2007, and 2009, the process of police reforms continued. In 2010, the Afghan Interior Ministry revealed that a balanced force was established to maintain law and order and support the good governance program. Between 2001 and 2011, foreign partners of Afghanistan spent more than $15 billion on security sector including the police department, but could not succeed in finding a satisfactory solution to the disease of corruption within the force. In 2013 and 2014, Afghan police numbered more than 150,000 personnel and received greater attention from international community, but illiteracy and corruption remained a basic challenge. In 2015, the emergence of huge corruption cases in Defense and Interior Ministries showed that many things were going on wrong direction. The issue of intelligence failure was widely discussed in print and electronic media in and outside the country while the NDS remained weak and under resourced.[6]

---

5 Afghanistan's Security: Political Process, State-Building and Narcotics, Bulent Aras and Sule Toktas, *Middle East Policy Council, Journal Essay, summer 2008, Volume XV, Number 2*

6 Between 2001 and 2011, foreign partners of Afghanistan spent more than $15 billion on security sector including the police department, but could not succeeded in finding a satisfactory solution to the disease of corruption within the force. In 2013 and 2014, Afghan police numbered more than 150,000 personnel, and received greater attention from international community, but illiteracy and corruption remained the basic challenge for their strength. In 2015, the emergence of huge corruption cases in Defense and Interior Ministries was not a new thing. Antonio Giustozzi and Mohammad Isaqzadeh, Afghanistan's Paramilitary Policing in Context, *Afghanistan Analysis Network*

Literature about the tactics, mechanism and fundamental structure of the Afghan intelligence agencies (KHAD and NDS) is not available in libraries or book shops. Researchers face challenges in finding information, reports and articles about the cultural, political and legal dynamics of intelligence operations in the country. The KHAD was established by KGB in the 1980s, and NDS was established by the CIA in 2000s. These two agencies were operating at odds with each other. Their ways of intelligence operation, their culture of information collection and process were quite different from each other.

The NDS is working for American interests, and KHAD was serving the interests of former Soviet Union. The KHAD and NDS tortured, killed and humiliated Afghans and destroyed their houses. From 2002 to 2016, Afghan governments tested three "corrupt secret weapons": (Mr. Amrullah Saleh, Mr. Assadullah Khalid, and Mr. Rahmatullah Nabil), who used their ethnic cards and filled the basket of NDS with hydras and violent snakes. In their turn, they appointed illiterate, corrupt and unprofessional men and women who never been in intelligence school or college, and never been admitted to any intelligence training centre or institute in order to learn how an intelligence agency operates.

Mr. Amrullah Saleh, an ethnic Panjshiri Tajik, is an illiterate man who concocted stories against Pashtuns, and cooked mixed words on their backs. Mr. Assadullah Khalid was an illiterate Pashtun war criminal, who sexually abused Afghan children, men and women in Kandahar and Ghanzni provinces, where he ruled with impunity. An engineer by profession Mr. Rahmatullah Nabil worked in an NGO. The three were deeply involved in an illegal intelligence operation, trained teenagers and used them in suicide attacks in Pakistan. They misused secret funds, purchased houses, and supported mafia groups, drug trafficking and abused female prisoners. They never tried to bring the NDS up to speed, because they all were totally unfit for the position.

Due to their personal interests, the NDS remained weak and unprofessional; it could not interpret threats within its traditional form. The ability of an agency to make comprehensive intelligence estimates for policymakers depends largely on its assessment and analytical capabilities, but the NDS hardly contributed. They were confused between traditional principles of counterinsurgency operations and conventional warfare. Their parameters of intelligence information gathering were confined to specific provinces.

The case of Afghanistan additionally raises the question of intelligence agencies gearing assessments to what their customers need or want to hear positive messages. The changing nature of dominant security threats during the last 15 years war on terrorism in Afghanistan and Pakistan, and the lack of intelligence cooperation between the two states caused misunderstanding, the blame game and severe fatalities in the region. Every month and every week, terrorists targeted either the Pakistani security forces or Afghan civilians, but they never thought to develop a joint strategy to tackle the menace of sectarian terrorists across the Durand Line. The same unprofessional political tactics and strategies were adopted by Afghan rulers after the Soviet Invasion.

Mr. Noor Muhammad Taraki became President. Two Politburo secretaries, Babrak Karmal (of the Parcham faction) and Hafizullah Amin became Deputy Prime Ministers. President Noor Muhammad Taraki appointed General Abdul Qadir as Minister of Defense and Ahmad Noor as Minister of Interior. In July 1978, a new intelligence agency known as AGSA was established under the leadership of Assadullah Sarwari.

Former Intelligence Chief Assadullah Sarwari, one of a handful of convicted Afghan war criminals, was released from prison in Kabul in 2016. He was responsible for the torture and arbitrary execution of thousands of detainees. An Afghan court convicted a former intelligence chief and sentenced him to death for killing hundreds of people during an especially bloody period of communist rule, in the country's first war crimes trial following more than two decades of conflict. The intelligence agency, AGSA launched mass purges of those it considered its enemies, with mass arrests, summary executions and disappearances.

Mr. Asadullah Sarwari, who has been in prison since 1992 for war crimes, sat in silence as the verdict was read. In 1992, after the collapse of the Communist regime, Sarwari was arrested and remained in prison for more than 13 years. On December 25, 2005, he was charged with the involvement in the arbitrary arrest, torture and mass killing of hundreds of opponents during his tenure as head of Afghan intelligence for a period of one year. On February 25, 2006, he was sentenced to death.

In 1979, amidst a deteriorating security situation in Afghanistan, the US ambassador Adolph Dubs was kidnapped and killed in Kabul. According to the *New York Times* report (2001), the Afghan army attacked the kidnappers when all attempts at negotiation failed. Afterwards the United States formally expressed to the Soviet Union its disapproval of the assault by the security forces, putting more stress on US–Soviet relations.[7]

After Hafeezullah Amin became president in September 1979, he renamed AGSA as KAM (Workers Intelligence Agency) and appointed first Aziz Ahmad Akbari and then Dr. Assadullah Amin as its heads. However, Mr. Amin ran the agency through his relatives and close associates and his agency received direct support from Eastern German intelligence and the KGB. When Babrak Karmal became President, more than 2,000 prisoners were released from Pul-i Charkhi jail. However, Russian KGB established a new intelligence

---

7 The Origins of the Soviet-Afghan War, Revelations from the Soviet Archives, *alternative insight*, 01 November 2001

agency (The State Information Services, or Khidamat-i Ittila'at-i Dawlati or KHAD.)

The KGB operated and planned within two units, the Residency and the Representatives. The basic objectives were to help Afghan forces in covert operations. From the winter of 1978/79 onward, KGB special units started operating inside Afghanistan, targeting the growing Islamist opposition. The operational capabilities of KHAD were extended to 19 provinces of Afghanistan, and more than 20,000 secret agents were recruited. The bulk of the work of the security organs had been the armed struggle against the insurgents.

There were 9,500 informers in the agent network. Special groups was set up comprised on 8,240 members of the military, 1,392 members of Sarandoy, 540 members of KHAD and over 1,700 party activists. The KGB tried to build a competent force, and by 1983, the KGB force numbered to 27, 715. The plan for Afghan border control and its force was comprised of 207 topographical reconnaissance batteries and 145 mortar batteries, but ultimately 1,732 officers 1,300 were members of the PDPA and over a hundred had been trained in the USSR. In May 1982, in the Afghan Interior Ministry, an intelligence unit under the name of FEDA was established. The FEDA further established 14 intelligence departments within the Directorate No-10, and within the KHAD's provincial offices. The FEDA was established to organize and develop intelligence work against Pakistan.

According to the UN Special Rapporteur on Human Rights in Afghanistan, torture took place in "the Ministry of the Interior, the Kabul prisons and all the KHAD detention centers." Among the latter, he specifically mentioned the "headquarters of KHAD, eight detention centers at Kabul controlled by the KHAD; [and] some 200 houses in the region of Kabul used as detention centers and controlled by the KHAD."[8]

War criminals should not remain unpunished. This conflict therefore still has the attention of international community. Previously, two former Afghan generals living in the Netherlands were convicted of acts of torture for which they had been responsible during their time with the Afghan security service KHAD. Another investigation into Afghan war crimes and enforced disappearance was closed prematurely in 2013, because the suspect living in the Netherlands died. It did, however, yield answers about the fate of thousands who had been arrested and killed by the former regime.

In the past, Afghan intelligence agencies adopted numerous strategies to counter insurgency but failed to defeat the Mujahedeen. In 1980s, after the Soviet intervention, Afghan governments established four intelligence agencies (KAM, AGSA, WAD, and KHAD) to ensure the stability of the country. The Council of EU (2001) reviewed Afghan intelligence KHAD in historical perspective in its research report, which gives us some fresh information about

8 *Kabul Times*, 01 January 1980

the function of secret services: "Some others understand that KHAD was established in 1980 and transformed into a Ministry (WAD), Wazarat-e-Amniat-e-Daulat in 1986. President Noor Muhammad Tarakai was in power for a limited time, while Hafizullah Amin divided both the communist party and intelligence agencies into two factions (Khalq and Parcham). However, the AGSA (Safeguarding Agency of Afghan Interests), which was established by Mr. Tarakai was dissolved due to his differences with Hafizullah Amin. In 1979, President Amin established another secret agency KAM (Workers Intelligence Service)".[9]

Russian intelligence agencies were directly involved in the regime change process in Afghanistan. The way they were changing regimes was cruel. Mr. Trakai was killed, Hafizullah Amin was killed and Mr. Karmal and Mr. Najibullah were left marooned, at the mercy of Mujahedeen and Taliban. Researcher Egor Eviskov in his paper spotlighted the internal political dynamics of Afghan communist regimes:

> Despite KGB attempts to maintain unity of PDPA personal, ethnic and ideological rivalries among Afghan Communists escalated. In September of 1979, new Afghan Prime Minister Amin seized power from President Taraki, and then secretly murdered him. Amin, who was an even more ideologically dogmatic Marxist than Taraki, initiated radical modernization reforms that were rapidly alienating conservative rural majority of Afghanistan. In order to create conditions for Soviet intervention, intelligence services initiated the December 1979 removal of Afghan Communist leader—Hafizullah Amin from power and replacing him with their protégé Babrak Karmal. In 1986, in an attempt to create conditions that would allow an eventual Soviet pullout, the KGB orchestrated another regime change by replacing Babrak Karmal with even more closely controlled by KGB leader Mohammad Najibullah.[10]

The successor to AGSA and KAM was KHAD, which was nominally part of the Afghan state, but it was firmly under the control of the Soviet KGB until 1989. In January 1986, its status was upgraded and it was thereafter officially known as the WAD (Ministry of State Security). This was an agency specifically, created for the suppression of the Democratic Republic's internal opponents. Mr. Egore spotlighted some other changes in the intelligence infrastructure of the Afghan communist regimes:

> The KGB and the GRU came up with a number of ways to combat the mujahedeen on operational, political, and tactical levels, including campaigns of disinformation, Special Forces operations that involved

9 The Council of EU, *Review of Afghan intelligence* KHAD, 2001
10 "Soviet Intelligence in Afghanistan: The Only Efficient Tool of the Politburo," Egor Evsikov, *Baltic Security and Defense Review Volume 11*, 2009

infiltration, sabotage, terrorism, recruitment of local support, and even of operations outside Afghan borders, striking at Pakistan and other mujahedeen backers. For this purpose, in 1980 they assisted with the creation of an Afghan intelligence service closely modeled after the KGB, called the Department of State Information Services (riasat-i khidmat-i ettela'at-i doulati), more commonly known as KHAD (after 1986 it was renamed the Ministry of State Security, or WAD (vizarat-i amniyat-i-daulati)). Officially, it was a department within the prime minister's office, but in reality it functioned as a powerful independent ministry (Halliday and Tanin, 1998). KHAD agents were trained in the KGB school at Balashikha, Uzbekistan, as well as in other KGB training facilities. After 1979, KHAD played a major role in consolidating the Afghan state and overall constructions of the PDPA institutions, a much more important role than is normally undertaken by a security organization. The KHAD became a major player within the politics of Afghanistan.[11]

The KHAD was responsible for the security of the state; therefore, it was working on uniting all tribes and ethnic minorities in collaboration of the Ministry of Nationalities and Tribal Affairs. The agency also funded religious leaders and established a separate directorate named Directorate of Religious Affairs (DRA). The political role of KHAD was of great importance. Former Afghan President Dr. Najibullah was the head of political directorate to convince all political factions that the Soviet war in Afghanistan was a just war. In 1985, Dr. Najibullah became secretary of the People Democratic Party of Afghanistan (PDPA). President Najibullah had trained KHAD's agents and adorned its military unites with modern technology, but unfortunately, the agencies failed to save President Najibullah or defeat the Dostum criminal militia.

In fact, governments in Afghanistan paid little attention to the basic function of intelligence during the last four decades. Various intelligence agencies were established with the technical support of KGB and GRU, to make effective the war against Mujahedeen, but couldn't manage their way of operation. From 1980 to 1992, these secret agencies played vital role in countering insurgency in Afghanistan, but after the fall of Najibullah government in 1992, the whole infrastructure of the state collapsed, and Afghanistan lost its state, and intelligence agencies.[12]

After the US invasion of Afghanistan, in 2001, the National Directorate of Security (NDS) was established by the CIA. This new agency was the successor to KHAD and called "Department of Security" or National Security or State Security. It functions in accordance with the government policies. It is both offensive and

---

11 Ibid.
12 *The Secret War in Afghanistan: The Soviet Union, China and Anglo-American Intelligence in the Afghan War*, Panagiotis Dimitrakis, I.B Tauris, 2013

defensive. When the Taliban were defeated in 2001, the reform of the security sector was one of the key issues, and the USA was directly responsible for the reorganization of the army and NDS and later for the police as well.

Writing on Afghan intelligence is not an easy task as there is limited amount of information available to the writers and researchers in libraries and market. During President Karzai's years, no intelligence reforms were introduced and no reinvention program was undertaken to improve the performance of the NDS operatives. Afghan intelligence agencies relied on human intelligence due to the lack of equipment and funds. They were collecting information about the insurgent from remote districts through farmers, which was of low quality and unauthentic. There were numerous factors that hindered the achievement of NDS. For instance, the NDS members had no access to face book, email, YouTube and other social media sources.

The main source of Afghan intelligence collection boils down to interaction with tribal elders and villagers through local commanders. Sometimes, due to its ineffective intelligence work, NDS faced criticism from parliamentarians and media, but it never reacted in a positive direction. The NDS did not share all information with the police department and Defense Ministry, and failed to provide reliable information to policy makers. The other major weakness of the agency is the lack of modern way of intelligence analysis.

The National Directorate of Security (NDS) is presently fighting against terrorists, provides information to the army and police, and working closely with the intelligence agencies of international coalition in Afghanistan. The agency is using special troops against terrorist network directly, depending on the situation. The strength of NDS is based on limited funds provided by the US and NATO member states. The nature of enemy in the region demands covert operations of unconventional special operations in response to the enemy activities. Today countries are using intelligence elements extensively and special operations are needed to deny their access to the homeland.

The NDS operations in 2016 failed to restore the confidence of the Afghan government and international community. Taliban captured the Kunduz province and is still dancing in the streets and markets, but NDS was unable to provide true information about their hideout to the Afghan army. The Islamic State (ISIS) kidnapped 31 people from Hazara minority community in 2015, and demanded ransom, but NDS failed to arrest the kidnappers. Internal politics and the involvement of foreign intelligence caused confusion when the national security advisor, Muhammad Hanif Atmar forced the intelligence chief Rahmatullah Nabil to resign.[13]

---

13 *Daily times*, ToloNews 2015

The personality of Afghan NSA, Mr. Hanif Atmar (former Interior Minister and National Security Advisor) is suspicious as he is being criticized from different aspects including his collaboration with the terrorist group (ISIS) and Taliban in Afghanistan. These allegations may be true or false, I do not want to discuss all details in this chapter, but one thing is clear that his political journey has been controversial and complicated. The abrupt emergence of his personality on the political scene of Afghanistan after the US intervention in 2001, and his evolving allegiance to different stakeholders in the country, is an interesting story. He is a powerful man, even more powerful than the President, and he can be spotlighted through different glasses as a controversial, suspicious and kingmaker.

Due to the lack of reforms, the NDS became out of control. Its agents killed many suspects during investigation. Distrust between the government and intelligence was exacerbated when NDS officials refused to listen to the President office. President Karzai changed three NDS chiefs due to their sarcastic behavior, but no change occurred in their mind. In fact, NDS was divided between the Presidential office, foreign stakeholders, sectarian groups, and the Northern Alliance. It was mandatory on the agency to provide an intelligence report to every stakeholder every week and every month.

The main question conventional wisdom asks is; why does Afghan intelligence still remain incompetent and crippled, notwithstanding the current development in several emerging intelligence field in neighboring states? Intelligence failures in several districts of the country occur when an attack happens without warning. A majority of the Afghan intelligence agencies are entirely unschooled, while their appointments have been made on political, religious, and ethnic bases. They happen to be more like politicians and less like secret agents. Therefore, they arrested, tortured and targeted their opponents on these bases.[14]

On 23 April 2012, *The Christian Science Monitor* pinpointed some weaknesses of Afghan intelligence in its report: "In the NDS or the military it should be really difficult to get a promotion; you should not get it overnight. You must work hard. But in the NDS someone will join today and tomorrow he will be a major. They just make fake papers and everything. Even if the guy is illiterate, he will become a major in the NDS."

In spite, all these stories of the failures of Afghan intelligence, former President Hamed Karzai never tried to introduce reforms or fix the broken window. Mr. Karzai sidelined Amrullah Saleh for his failure to counter Taliban attacks, while Mr. Nabil also failed to demonstrate professionally. They had different political loyalties. In 2012, when Mr. Nabil was reinstated, there were suicide attacks across the country. The Unity Government also condoned the NDS

14 "Reforming Afghan intelligence agencies," Musa Khan Jalalzai, *Daily Times*, 23 December 2014

and deposed Mr. Nabil due to his personal differences with the National Security Advisor, Mr. Hanif Atmar. Mr. Atmar verbally abused him and threatened him of dire consequences.[15]

When the NDS failed to counter foreign intelligence networks, and MPs bashed Mr. Hanif Atmar for his collaboration with the Islamic State (ISIS) terrorist network in Jalalabad and Paktika provinces, the issue of intelligence sharing between the government and parliamentarian came to the fore. President Ghani supported his advisor while Parliamentarians supported Deputy Speaker of the lower house of parliament, Mr. Zahir Qadeer, who later on, exposed secret relationship between the ISIS and National Security Advisor, Mr. Hanif Atmar.[16]

Mr. Zaheer Qadeer argued that some elements in the National Security Council including the National Security Advisor, Muhammad Hanif Atmar were supporting the ISIS. The Wolsi Jirga (Lower House of Parliament) decided to send a fact-finding team to Jalalabad, Kunar and Laghman to prove the allegations. On 02 December 2015, Mr. Zahir Qadeer showed a CD on the floor of parliament, and said some political pressures had prevented him from airing the CD. The government rejected the allegations, but Mr. Zahir Qadeer claimed that he is in possession of documents that show that the government had provided ID cards for free movement to a number of people belonging to Pakistan's militant groups.[17]

The NDS became the center of debates in national and international forums, when chiefs of the agency started acting like politicians—criticizing the President, neighboring states and the parliament. This kind of behavior raised many questions that whether NDS is an intelligence agency or political party. From 2002 to 2011, the NDS Chief Mr. Amrullah Saleh criticized regional states on one hand, and ethnicized the agency on the other. He appeared on television screen times and again and demonstrated differently.

The torture story of Mr. Kamal Achakzai (Haji Gulalai) still reverberates in the ears of those Afghans who were severely torture in the NDS secret prisons. Mr. Kamal Achakzai joined the NDS in the early 2000s. According to a secret memo circulated among western diplomats in Afghanistan in 2007, Mr. Kamal was responsible for the systemic abuse of NDS prisoners. His methods include beating them, suspending them from ceilings, fastening them in handcuffs for long period of time and depriving them of sleep.[18]

Mr. Nabil also acted like a politician-criticizing neighboring states for their interference in the internal affairs of his country. In March

---

15 *Daily Times*, 23 December 2014
16 *Pajhwok Afghan News*, 27 December 2015
17 On 02 December 2015, Mr. Zahir Qadeer showed a CD on the floor of parliament, and said some political pressures had prevented him from airing the CD. *Daily Outlook Afghanistan and ToloNews*
18 "The Politics of Intelligence in Afghanistan," *Daily Times*, 06 January 2015

2013, the NDS chief, Mr. Nabil warned Afghans to unite against the ISI plots, and criticized the policies of the Unity Government on the floor of the parliament. However, in 25 March 2016, Mr. Nabil again warned about the ISI plots against the people of the North. ToloNews reported the former chief of NDS warning that Afghan must united against the ISI plots in Afghanistan. He also shared his statement on Face book, in which he advised Afghans to unite because the ISI supports terrorists in Afghanistan. In his statement, Mr. Nabil claimed that NDS had confiscated some documents showing that ISI had ordered spies to divide Afghans on ethnic bases.[19]

These and other statements painted an ugly picture of the agency in international media. With the establishment of the Unity Government in 2014, relations between the government and intelligence agencies remained in strain. The blame game between the NDS Chief, Mr. Nabil and President Ghani created misunderstanding when Mr. Nabil accused President Ghani for his propensity towards ISI and Pakistan army. The war of words intensified between different political camps, while Pakistani intelligence talked to the NDS authorities on the intelligence sharing and cooperation, which further caused many controversies. The purpose of this meeting was to persuade the National Directorate of Security (NDS) to help in the arrest of terrorists involved in the Bacha Khan University attacks, but the stance of the NDS was not clear, because the Afghan agency was helpless to arrest a single terrorist leader or war criminal that channeled weapons and funds to terrorist organization in Afghanistan, how can it arrest the terrorists wanted by Pakistan? The question is; how can NDS whose chief resigned in protest with President Ghani who approached Pakistan for a joint fight against the Taliban, share information with ISI? The answer is deeply complicated as the agency has various political and sectarian groups within its infrastructure that have embroiled it in a crisis of incompetence, corruption and multifaceted loyalties.[20]

It is a well known fact that the US, NATO and Afghan intelligence agencies do not always get things right, and their analysis leads policy makers and military commanders to wrong conclusions. Their poor data, inaccurate intelligence information about the ISIS and Taliban activities, their sources of low quality information and their misinterpretations and flawed strategies often caused civilian casualties and infrastructure damage. They showed a predilection for military-led approaches to problems, including those that were essentially political. Research scholar Matt Waldman also described

---

19 On 25 March 2016, Mr. Nabil again warned about the ISI plots against the people of the North. *ToloNews* reported the former chief of NDS warning that Afghan must united against the ISI plots in Afghanistan. He also shared his statement on Face book, in which he advised Afghans to unite because the ISI supports terrorists in Afghanistan. *ToloNews*, 25 March 2016.

20 "Intelligence Sharing," Musa Khan Jalalzai, *Daily Times*, 09 February 2016

the flawed policies of the US and its allies in a recent article: "In the eyes of US officials and informed observers, high level US policy-making on Afghanistan was severely impaired by fundamental, structural flaws, many of which are interrelated and reinforcing." Another US commander, General Eikenberry, criticized the counterinsurgency strategy promoted by General Petraeus.

The general rejected the COIN strategy as applied in Afghanistan, in his article published in Foreign Affairs. Two months after the publication of this article, a new intelligence report from the US highlighted the failure of intelligence in Afghanistan. The US National Intelligence Estimate (NIE) warned that the country would quickly fall into chaos if President Hamid Karzai refused to sign a security deal with the US. The NIE, which includes input from 16 intelligence agencies in the US, predicted that the Taliban would become more influential as US forces draw down at the end of 2014. Moreover, in response to these allegations, Afghan President Hamid Karzai expressed concern that his country was the victim of a war that only served the interests of the US and its western allies.

"Afghans died in a war that is not ours," President Karzai said in an interview with *The Washington Post*. President Karzai said he was in trouble for war casualties, including those in US military operations, and felt betrayed by what he described as insufficient US focus on going after Taliban sanctuaries inside Pakistan. The US and its allies should know that Chinese and Russian agencies seek influence in the country as a means of securing their borders. In reality, the presence of US forces in Afghanistan provided China with a sense of stability. Beijing understands that now the US is focusing on terrorist networks in the country, and it is in China's interest to engage NATO and US forces there. China is seeking the ISI's help in stabilizing Afghanistan. China knows that the ISI has influence in Kabul but wants to deal with Afghan security as a separate issue altogether.

Chapter 2. Making Intelligence Relevant and Fitting It to the Fight

In the contemporary international system, states are the fundamental customer of classified and processed intelligence information for security, law enforcement and policymaking. However, Islamic State (ISIS) and the Taliban also perceive a need to collect and process advanced information to protect their networks against the theft of their strategic, Defense and political secrets. As intelligence is more than an organized collection of targeted information, processing can include technical issues such as transcribing and translating intercepted telephone conversations, and verifying the reliability of information. In modern philosophy, intelligence involves a real struggle with human opponents, carried on to gain some advantage over them. In essence, the debate among intelligence experts has caused deep confusion over the basic job of an intelligence agency during war and peace times.[21]

The above-cited way of intelligence information collection, process and analysis elucidated by experts is quite different from the way Afghan intelligence operated in yesteryears. During the last 15 years, we have heard or seen no successful story from the National Directorate of Security (NDS) as the agency adopted a political culture, and its leadership acted like politicians. The fall of Kunduz in 2016, consecutive terror attacks in Kabul, and the exponentially growing network of (ISIS) in Afghanistan, raised important questions about the credibility and competency of the Afghan intelligence agencies. Before the Taliban attacked Kunduz, the NDS operatives safely left the city without informing central government in Kabul.

Large-scale desertion of the Afghan army soldiers, intelligence units and the police also enabled the Taliban to enter the city unopposed. After their capture of the city, they looted houses, banks, weapons, and tanks. The President's appointed investigative team in its 30-page summary report also noted that there was no coordination among the police, intelligence and Afghan army commanders.

The state and system of government was ultimately hijacked by these agencies. The secret war between Russian, Chinese and US strategic clandestine intelligence in northern Afghanistan raised serious question about the intensifying Great Game in the country, which might possibly prompt a destructive nuclear war in Central Asia. The exponentially growing web of foreign espionage in the region and the recruitment of Afghans agents for it caused fear and anxiety. Dr Abdullah raised concern about the existence of foreign spies within the state institutions. "Double agents are more dangerous than insurgents," he said. The fall of Kunduz, Pakistan's re-engagement in the peace process and policy differences between Hanif Atmar and Intelligence Chief Rahmatullah Nabil forced him to resign.

Mr. Nabil was an incompetent intelligence chief who knew nothing about the way intelligence operates. He was acting like a politician, engineering events, concocting stories and cooking words on the back of Pakistan's military and intelligence establishment. His precursors were also acting like street children who made the agency ethnicized, sectarianized and regionalized. The appointment of Major General Masoud Andarabi as the chief of the NDS did not help peace and stability.

Distrust between the government and intelligence chiefs affected friendly relations between Afghanistan and its neighbors. They bluntly issued statements on television channels and criticized Presidents of both Pakistan and Afghanistan. They opposed Pakistan's role in the peace process and branded the country as an enemy of the Afghans. Afghan leadership needed to depoliticize the agency and expel illiterate elements from the agency, appointed on ethnic and sectarian lines, but the mujahedeen and Taliban supporters within the intelligence agency are making things worse as well. The roots of the NDS should have been re-established in the south and east, and the influence of drug smugglers and war criminals needs to be undermined. The NDS' leaders are making money, purchasing properties and plundering secret funds. The government never dared to investigate the corruption and smuggling business of its intelligence mafia.

On December 13, 2014, the NATO and International Security Assistance Force (ISAF) mission in Afghanistan came to an end with the transfer of security responsibilities to the Afghan National Security Forces (ANSF). This was, no doubt good news, but they retreated with great failure and could not succeed in establishing the writ of the government in all provinces of the country. The challenges of building a strong army for the country remained a dream, because the power of the central government depends on negotiations with the Taliban, Islamic State (ISIS) and, regional criminal private militias. In the

US-led war on terrorism in Afghanistan and, the ongoing civil wars in the Middle East and Pakistan, professionalization of intelligence was the only way to assess the strength and lethality of terrorists and insurgent groups, but due to the inattention of all stake holders, thing gone worse. However, the Afghan government never focused on reforming the National Directorate of Security (NDS), or makes it fit to the fight against Taliban and the Islamic State.[22]

The withdrawal of US and NATO intelligence staff from Afghanistan and the desertion of NDS professional officers to join the Taliban and private militias, left a, intelligence vacuum that facilitated ISIS and the Taliban in their fight against the Unity Government. Regrettably, one of the major problems of Afghan intelligence was that the relationship between the local population and policy makers broke down. During the ISIS and Taliban attacks on Kunduz province, the NDS's local officials did not accurately estimate the Afghan army's strength and resources. The NDS misled the army commander to take pre-emptive action and disrupt the terrorists' supply line.[23] The NDS did not share all information with the police department and failed to provide information to policy makers, Afghan army commanders, or other stakeholders about the ISIS and Taliban activities. The second major challenge has been the lack of experience and education in its ranks. They have no knowledge of modern intelligence systems or their role in conflict management across the world. The third challenge was adapting intelligence to local needs. The NDS supported and provided intelligence information to leaders, commanders, ethnic and sectarian stakeholders, and private criminal militias.

The Afghan Military Intelligence (AMI) was also facing numerous difficulties in collecting information about the war strategies of ISIS and Taliban commanders from remote districts. The agency lacks trained officers to reach remote districts or even those outside the provincial headquarters to interact with the local population; farmers, maliks and village elders. If the AMI and NDS agents in war zones decide to collect analyze, and process correct intelligence information at any cost, their efforts can allow policy makers and army commanders to discern friend from foe, and thus apply professional measures with precision and minimal collective damage.[24]

A major portion of intelligence information collection and analysis for countering insurgency in Afghanistan is labor intensive and, relies on the local commanders being able to interact with farmers, Maliks, educated people and religious clerics regularly. The agencies do not rely on modern methods and cannot differentiate between Pakistani and Afghan Pashtuns, or between Afghan Tajiks, Turks and their Central Asian friends. The NDS has often been repudiated

---

22 Intelligence Sharing, *Daily Times*, 09 February 2016
23 Ibid
24 Ibid

by parliamentarians, press analysts and ordinary Afghans for its unprofessional modes of operation, torture and death in custody.

Afghan intelligence agencies also rely on human intelligence because they still lack the availability of modern intelligence collection technologies. The NDS and RAMA (Riasat-e-Amniate-e-Milli Afghanistan) have a weak human intelligence network in the cities and most of their sources are unreliable. The information they receive is useless because they are unable to analyze or process low quality information retrieved from remote districts. There are numerous factors that hinder the performance of the agencies. For instance, many NDS agents cannot use Face-book, e-mail, YouTube, and Google for intelligence purposes.

After the US invasion in 2001, Afghan National Military Intelligence Center (ANMIC) was established to support senior military commanders in the battlefield, but the President and army chief were not satisfied with its performance in the past. The Directorate of Policing Intelligence (DPI), which provides intelligence information about the arrest and prosecution of criminals, National Information Management System (NIMS), Wolfhound Information System (WLS), National Target Exploitation Center (NTEC) and dozens more military and police intelligence organizations have so far failed to lead countrywide military operations in right direction.

On May 14, 2015, ToloNews reported the closure of 69 schools in Uruzgan province due to the deteriorating security situation. Some 14 civilians, including nine foreigners, were killed after Taliban gunmen stormed a guesthouse on the outskirts of Kabul.[25]

On May 16, the Pajhwok News Agency reported that ISIS had kidnapped 27 passengers in Sayed Karam district of the south-eastern Paktia province. The residents said gunmen took passengers with them in Badam Kanda. The Taliban forced passengers out of 30 vehicles and took them to an undisclosed location. All these fatalities occurred due to the inability of NDS and AIM to inform the authorities in time.[26]

Much of the debate over recent mistakes started from the belief that major reforms are necessary to prevent intelligence failure in future. The government needs to make major changes in NDS's structure because, after years of neglect, human intelligence in Afghanistan remains seriously deficient. Signal and imagery intelligence has also been inadequate during the last three decades. The Unity Government needs to initiate the process of de-radicalizing and de-politicizing the NDS, KHAD and policing agencies, and appoint professional management to tackle the Taliban and ISIS effectively. The Government cannot get away with simply expressing concern over the presence of ISIS in the country; professional measures need to be taken to tackle the issue on a long-term basis.

---

25 14 May 2015, *ToloNews*
26 16 May 2015, *the Pajhwok News Agency*

CHAPTER 3. THE PROFESSIONALIZATION OF INTELLIGENCE MECHANISM, INTELLIGENCE SHARING, AND INTELLIGENCE OPERATIONS IN AFGHANISTAN

The professionalization of an intelligence agency depends on its performance, strategies and civilian popularity. If we look at the professional mechanism of UK and US secret services, and their way of intelligence operation, we can judge their success and achievement from the fact that they have closely followed the process of accountability and oversight. Now the question is why Afghan intelligence agencies have remained incompetent and unprofessional and why they have failed to support policy makers by collecting true information from war zones? In fact, Afghan governments paid little attention to the importance of intelligence agencies during the last few decades; they neither established intelligence analysis and research centers, nor constituted an accountability and oversight body to check the activities of secret agencies.

The professionalization of intelligence mechanisms, or at least efforts leading in that direction, became increasingly necessary when the Tehreek-e-Taliban Pakistan (TTP), Afghan Taliban and ISIS extended their terrorist networks beyond their spheres of influence. Heightened, sustained vigilance and a coherent approach to professional intelligence mechanisms are considered central to countering their way of misgovernment. Worse can emerge; when thinking in terms of the professionalization of intelligence cooperation, its counter or antithesis, namely poor intelligence sharing, can increasingly become the dominant theme.

The need to make intelligence cooperation in Afghanistan more professional has received little attention; the majority of foreign intelligence agencies in the country do not sincerely cooperate with anyone. Afghan intelligence agencies operate inside Pakistan, while Pakistani intelligence agencies operate in Afghanistan, and Indian intelligence (RAW) making things worse by providing financial assistance to war criminals and terrorist organizations. Thus the concept of intelligence sharing remains a paper truth, not a ground reality. The activities of the Afghan National Directorate of Security (NDS), RAMA, ISI, RAW, CIA, MI6, MGB and other secret agencies in various parts of Afghanistan, particularly along the Durand Line, have long been the subject of conjecture and supposition. These agencies usually adhere to their national interests; they do not necessarily want to share their collected data with each other.

During the last 15 years war in Afghanistan, the NDS proved incompetent, mired in corruption, nepotism and ethnic politics. With the recent intensification of the Taliban insurgency, chain of suicide attacks against Afghan security forces and, government installations, the Unity Government needed to realize the importance of a professional intelligence agency, but the interference of war criminals in the NDS affairs caused more difficulties. On 15 December 2014, Afghan President Muhammad Ashraf Ghani Ahmadzai announced that his government wanted to introduce security sector reforms to undermine the culture of corruption, and political loyalties within the intelligence infrastructure of the country, but failed to address the involvement of Mujahedeen and Taliban within the NDS operational mechanism. The President was helpless and unaware of the things going on under the carpet.[27]

The *Christian Science Monitor* spotlighted some important facts in its recent report: "In a nation that is a patchwork of ethnic groups, many with their own languages; about 70 percent of those at NDS (National Directorate of Security) hail from Panjshir or have ties with the Northern Alliance." Correspondent Tom A. Peter noted some important facts about the NDS's professional credibility in his investigative report: "In the NDS or the military it should be really difficult to get a promotion; you should not get it overnight. You must work hard. But in the NDS someone will join today and tomorrow he will be a major. They just make fake papers and everything. Even if the guy is illiterate, he will become a major in the NDS."[28]

The NDS members had established secret links with different Taliban groups, drugs and arms smugglers, foreign intelligence networks. Mismanagement of secret funds also raised serious questions about the basic strategy of its leadership. They sold national secrets and membership cards (Khamaa Press, 2012) to the Iranians, Pakistanis and the Taliban, facilitated terrorist networks like ISIS,

---

27 *ToloNews*, 15 December 2014
28 Why Afghanistan's intelligence agency has a major blind spot, Afghanistan's intelligence service is dominated by men from one small province of the country. Has this hampered the Afghan government's ability to infiltrate the insurgency? By Tom A. Peter, Correspondent 23 *April, 2012, the Christian Science Monitor.*

and received huge amounts of money from underground drug and arms mafia groups.[29]

Former NDS Chief Rahmatullah Nabil exposed the illegal businesses of some parliamentarians who have been deeply involved in kidnapping, money laundering and drug trafficking. An MP from Kunar province, Wagma Safi, responded to the intelligence chief in harsh words: "You have not done anything to improve the insecurities of Dangan district in Kunar province. You are the spies and servants of foreigners," she said. Mr. Nabil failed to respond positively. He criticized the unity government for supporting terrorist groups to operate more freely.[30]

Notwithstanding all these impulsive acts of the agencies, former President Hamid Karzai never thought to audit the secret funds of KHAD and NDS, or establish a political or parliamentary oversight body to check their activities. When Mr. Amrullah Saleh failed to intercept the Kabul attack, he was removed and replaced by Mr Rahmatullah Nabil as the head of Afghan intelligence. Mr. Nabil also failed to demonstrate professionally. Finally, Mr. Karzai appointed his friend and a notorious war criminal, Mr. Assadullah Khaled, as a new chief of the NDS. Mr. Khaled faced allegations of drug trafficking, sexual abuse and torture of men and women as a powerful warlord in Kandahar and Ghazni provinces.[31]

On 26 December 2016, Journalist Sune Engel Rasmussen in his investigative report revealed important facts about the NDS funding of abusive militias across the country: "The Afghan national directorate of security (NDS) arms strongmen ostensibly to fight the Taliban and other militants. But some militia leaders use their new power to fight local turf wars, including against elected government officials, rather than insurgents. One such commander, Perim Qul, in the northern province of Takhar, has received about $85,000 (£70,000) to arm 500 men. However, he allegedly spends part of that money on a private prison where he beats and extorts local people. His men have even ambushed and killed a local politician".[32]

Not only has this abusive business, the agency also run the business of killing across the country. On 15 January 2017, Tolo News reported senior police official of United Arab Emirates (UAE) held responsible the Unity Government for the deadly bombing in Kandahar, in which 11 people including five UAE diplomats killed. The blast occurred inside the Kandahar governor's high-security guest house where the UAE diplomats, including Ambassador Juma Mohammed Abdullah

29 *Khamaa Press*, 2012

30 *ToloNews* 17 December 2014

31 President Karzai appointed Mr. Asadullah Khaled as a new chief of the NDS. Mr. Khaled faced allegations of drug trafficking, sexual violence and torture that stem from his work as a powerful warlord in Kandahar and Ghazni provinces. He was attacked by a suicide bomber. *Daily Outlook Afghanistan*, 07 December 2012

32 Afghanistan funds abusive militias as US military 'ignores' situation, Sune Engel Rasmussen. The Guardian, On 26 December 2016.

Al Kaabi, gathered for dinner. However, Chief of Dubai police, Lt Gen Dahi Khalfan Tamim disputed the claims by the NDS officials and said the NDS is responsible. "The Afghan security officials (NDS) are directly responsible for the incident to the UAE Ambassador and mission members, who died or were injured, because the explosives were planted inside the guesthouse where people can enter only through security clearance," General Tamim said on his official Twitter. "The attack is treason as the blast occurred inside the building. It would have been something else if the attack had been launched from the outside," he said.[33]

Every day we read controversial statements of Afghan intelligence chief's in newspapers and on television screens, in which they act like politicians instead of being professional managers. This kind of behavior by National Directorate of Security (NDS) chiefs shows that the agency seems to have been deeply politicized. From 2002 to 2011, former NDS Chief Mr. Amrullah Saleh ethnicized, regionalized and politicized the US-backed NDS ranks and files, and acted as an opposition party leader, criticized the role of states and personalities in his country. He shamelessly loved to appear on television time and again to show his regionalized activism and political affiliation, but the fact of the matter is that all professional intelligence chiefs of Pakistan, India and Iran act differently.[34]

They have never issued political statements and have never criticized neighboring states or politicians of their own states. Having exercised his jingoistic approach to the national security mechanism of his country, Mr. Saleh criticized every peace effort between the Taliban and Pakistan, between Taliban and Afghanistan and, according to some diplomatic sources; he used the NDS to target agencies and officials in favor of talks with the Taliban. He also terrorized Pashtun elders, politicians, and those who were critical of the US and NATO way of terrorizing the people of Afghanistan. He also facilitated terrorist activities of Indian intelligence (RAW) across Afghanistan.

These are harsh realities while Afghan intelligence agencies may still have not been able to provide reliable intelligence information to the government. The agency should have demonstrated professionalism to provide reliable information to policy makers, but its controversial approach raised many questions. To fight a successfully against Taliban, the NDS required a reasonably professional and honest approach that Afghans believe is worth of supporting. When the CIA established the NDS in the 2000s, the agency mostly recruited

---

33 Not only this, Senior police official of United Arab Emirates (UAE) held responsible the Unity Government for the deadly bombing in Kandahar, in which 11 people including five UAE diplomats killed, Tolo News reported on 15 January 2017.
34 *Daily Times*, 05 January 2015

illiterate, untrained and unprofessional Panjshiri Tajiks who never been in school or college.

To address these challenges, fundamental changes were needed in the basic infrastructure and improvement in way of information gathering, assessed and redistributed. Ethnic and sectarian factors should be addressed by introducing religious tolerance related reforms. Decriminalization, de-politicization, de-radicalization and sectarian affiliation needed to be addressed if the government wanted to reinvent a professional intelligence infrastructure in the country. There are dozens of intelligence networks operating across the country. The intelligence agencies of former Afghan mujahedeen leaders, recruited by the ISI during the 1980s and 1990s, are still in operation. Private intelligence companies, war criminals networks, Taliban intelligence, and the ISIS intelligence are making thing worse.

These agencies are more professional than the NDS. They provided intelligence to their parties and to the channels from which they receive funds. Mujahedeen leaders maintained both their intelligence wings, international affiliations and sent their workers for further training to some secret networks in and outside the country. Some established a clandestine relationship with the Taliban and, some with regional intelligence agencies. There were speculations that, in Afghanistan, the KGB, Federal Security Service (FSB) and Military Intelligence Directorate (GRU) have also returned to reinvent their previous contacts in Afghanistan.

If this chapter is added to the ongoing intelligence war in the country, the partition of the country cannot be ruled out as Afghanistan is already facing a precarious national unity crisis. Suicide terrorism, warlordism, regionalism, Talibanization, ethnic and sectarian violence is the biggest national security threats in the country. The cloud of civil war has intensified as several warlords and mujahedeen leaders have mobilized their private criminal militias in various provinces. The new wave of suicide terrorism, internal political turmoil and, poor state of the economy and corruption could pose a bigger threat to Afghanistan's long-term viability.

With the establishment of Unity Government, everyone breathed a sigh of relief, but very soon they faced irksome situation when the ISIS emerged with a strongest network across the country. The initial days of the two-heads' regime were pleasing but after three months, it became a headache and caused serious torment for politicians, parliamentarians and security forces. The present government represents two states in a weak and ethnically divided country, which has not yet agreed on several issues. In 2016, government was under deep pressure from war criminals, narco-smugglers, and arms traders, ethnic and sectarian leaders, whose share had been promised in the election days by the two heads of the state. The Taliban were in full control of Kunar, Nooristan, Helmand, Logar and Kandahar provinces, and the ISIS established hundreds networks in the South.

In northern parts of the country, government hardly controlled 50 percent of the territory.

In his 2011 speech, US Defense Secretary Chuck Hagel accused India of financing problematic groups against Pakistan and Afghanistan. Such statements further widened the gulf in trust between Kabul and Islamabad. Islamabad also complained that two of its neighbors, India and Iran, were secretly bidding to destabilize Pakistan using Afghan soil. India rejected these allegations and stated that these were nothing more than an attempt to pressure India to scale back its activities in Afghanistan. India understands that its presence in Afghanistan has promoted it to a regional power in global terms. In 1999, Pakistan enjoyed the same position, but now India has become a rising global power.

These allegations and the war of words halted the process of intelligence sharing among India, Iran, Pakistan and Afghanistan. International Security Assistance Force (ISAF) established different intelligence units, but most of its secret operations were carried out by individual states. The CIA did not share all information with its allies while German intelligence agencies had their own operational role in Kabul and northern Afghanistan. The ISI was still considered a professional organization but its changing loyalties have made it suspect in the eyes of most Pakistani citizens. The ever-changing shape of its alliance with the CIA raised deep and serious questions about its role in the war on terrorism. At present, the ISI has shrunk as its funding and regional role has been confined to specific areas, because Prime Minister Nawaz Sharif wants to restore the culture of civilian intelligence in his country.

Outside the Middle East, intelligence cooperation and sharing partners have been instrumental in the roundup of terror leaders in the subcontinent. With Pakistan's proximity to Afghanistan and its links with insurgent groups, its intelligence support has been critical in the war on Terror. As a full-fledged partner of the US, Pakistan provided an air corridor, logistics, and intelligence support, and facilitated CIA and Pentagon in extending their sphere of influence in the region. Mutual trust between the two states remained fundamental in their critical intelligence cooperation.[35]

This intelligence cooperation between the two states represented one of the most significant challenges in Afghanistan, but later on, US distanced Pakistan due to its propensities towards Russia and China. The exponentially growing terrorist networks of the TTP and Afghan Taliban in Pakistan and Afghanistan necessitate increased cooperation among the intelligence agencies of ISAF-NATO, the ISI, NDS and Iranian intelligence, but in reality, none was willing to share their intelligence with partners. The present new emphasis on intelligence sharing between the CIA and ISI created new challenges.

---

35 *The Prospect of Nuclear Jihad*, 2015

The CIA relationship with the ISI has arguably been one of the most complicated intelligence partnerships in South Asia.

Challenges persist in fostering closer cooperation on, though both states appear publicly committed to fostering closer relationship in the areas of counterterrorism, law enforcement and border control. After the Swat and Abbottabad operations in 2009, and in 2011 respectively, the CIA-ISI relationship raised serious questions. Suspicion grew, the two sides became near adversaries. The arrest of Raymond Davis in Lahore, and the US's unfriendly attitude towards Pakistan, further complicated relations between the two states. Meanwhile, intelligence sharing and cooperation between the two intelligence communities completely stopped. As far as Afghan intelligence is concerned, in fact, extending intelligence cooperation to the ISI was not in its control—external powers had the Afghan remote-control in their hands. The US intelligence officials once disclosed that their country's intelligence network was one of the largest in the world— the Agency had built more than 1,000 personnel including operatives and technical staff.[36]

Moreover, there were number of intelligence sub-units, like the Serious Organized Crime Committee (CCSC) and Military Counterterrorism Investigation Group with 3,000 soldiers from the Afghan army, working under the CIA across Afghanistan, but all these units, Blackwater, NDS, and other private intelligence companies, had different intelligence cultures, priorities and programms. Their relations with the main CIA were also in strain. Russian intelligence experts reiterated the exaggerated capabilities of the CIA in Afghanistan and said it does not give any wider role to the intelligence agencies of other NATO and ISAF member states. Disagreement between EU member states and the CIA also negatively affected the professionalization of intelligence cooperation. Fundamental divergences regarding the way terrorism was about to be tackled, and the US's unprofessional approach to the wars in Iraq and Afghanistan, estranged partners and hindered the advance of intelligence cooperation.

In Afghanistan, the CIA closely worked with Northern Alliance war criminals and drug smugglers. Therefore the roots of Afghan intelligence remained in northern Afghanistan. Pashtuns were marginalized and the Taliban who accepted the new administration were targeted. Intelligence was skewed to meet immediate operational needs, rather than directed to build up a multidimensional picture of key actors, context and dynamics. The ranking US commander in Afghanistan, Major General Michael Flynn, complained about the poor intelligence cooperation in Afghanistan. Military officers and civilians working with ISAF were non-cooperative and did not share a single word with each other. There was no common database, no common strategy and no common thinking among the ISAF allies.

36 *Daily Times*, 19 March 2014

The lack of digital networks available to all participating states raised serious questions about their partnership in the war on terror in Afghanistan.

In these circumstances, Russian intelligence was also caught between varieties of threats. President Putin's special representative admitted that his country was sharing intelligence information with Taliban commanders about the terrorist activities of Islamic State (ISIS) in Afghanistan. Mr. Zamir Kabulov told Interfax News Agency that Taliban's interests coincided with the fight against ISIS: "I have said before that we have communication channels with the Taliban to exchange information."

Russia Today television (RT) aired Mr. Zamir Kabulov's statement about the ISIS training camps. "ISIS is training militants from Russia in Afghanistan as part of its efforts to expand into Central Asia," Mr. Kabulov told a security conference in Moscow. He added that US and UK passport holders of Pakistani and Arab descent are training these terrorists inside Afghanistan. This statement prompted a violent reaction in Afghanistan where the reconciliation process with the Taliban was underway. Afghan parliament demanded a thorough investigation of his statement while the two Presidents remained silent. These revelations were a great shock for the US, NATO and British intelligence agencies operating in Afghanistan.[37]

In response to this statement, the ISIS threatened to attack Russia's territory: "We will make your wives concubines and make your children our slaves," the ISIS commanders warned. However, President Vladimir Putin vowed that Russia would destroy the ISIS infrastructure. Speaking at a meeting with senior commanders, he said that additional aircraft and air defense weapons were shifted to a Russian base in Syria. To sternly counter the terrorist group, Russia also adorned Kyrgyzstan's forces with modern weapons and deployed an additional force in Tajikistan and Uzbekistan. The Putin administration is trying to use the Taliban against the ISIS. In 2016, Russia warned about the growing ISIS strength in Afghanistan. Once ISIS fighters enter Central Asia, they will destabilize the region, a Russian police commander warned.

The recent rapprochement between Pakistan and Russia was considered by military experts to be a positive development but the changing attitude of the GHQ and Inter-Services Intelligence (ISI) sometimes disappoints China and Russia. According to the recent *Indian Defense Review*, five battalions of Northern Rifles were maintained in Gilgit and thence in Skardu during the Kargil conflict in 1999. Moscow and Beijing also ordered their intelligence agencies to closely monitor Afghanistan's borders with Central Asia. Russian intelligence also claimed that the ISIS had planned attacks in Central Asia. "Citizens from 100 countries are currently fighting in the ranks of the terrorist structure and the recruits constitute up to 40 percent

37 On October 8, 2015, Russia Today television (RT)

of their forces," Moscow intelligence Chief Alexander Bortnikov warned.[38]

Military alliance between Russia, Pakistan and China and their tacit support to some insurgent groups challenged the US and NATO presence in Afghanistan. When India signed strategic partnership agreement with the United States, Pakistan realized the changing nature of US behaviour and its resentment towards the country. Pakistan immediately realized to become an ally of Russia and China to defeat India inside Afghanistan. In 2015, Moscow agreed to sell four Mi-35M helicopters to Pakistan and welcomed Islamabad to join the Shanghai Cooperation Organization (SCO). This year already, Russian Army Commander-in-Chief Oleg Salyukov has announced the first-ever "mutual special drills in mountainous terrain," and Khawaja Asif, Defence Minister of Pakistan, visited Moscow to further discuss enhancing cooperation. The recent purchase of Russian helicopters and jets is indicative of Pakistan's attitude towards the United States. On 25 December 2016, Polina Tikhonova in her paper elucidated some facts of military partnership between Russia and Pakistan:

> Islamabad is trying to boost its close air support capabilities, and both Russia and China have agreed to help. In addition to the purchase of the Mi-35Ms from Moscow, Islamabad is also considering buying China's Z-10 helicopter gunship. Islamabad is also mulling over the purchase of the T-129 attack helicopter from Turkey. In addition to strengthening their military ties, Russia and Pakistan have also ramped up their relations in the diplomatic sphere.........The Russian-Pakistani partnership in the area of defense doesn't end with the purchase of the Mi-35Ms. Islamabad is also importing Russian-made Klimov RD-93 engines for its JF-17 multi-role fighters, which Pakistan co-produces and co-develops with China.

The abrupt jump of Russian and Chinese intelligence agencies (MSS, MGB) into the unending war in Afghanistan and the shifting priorities of Pakistan's ISI further complicated the task of Afghan intelligence (NDS), to effectively counter all these powerful players. Indian intelligence (RAW) was also trying to maintain its networks inside Afghanistan to help NDS in making its body relevant to the fight. However, China's longstanding concern that Afghanistan might turn into a safe haven for the Uighur Islamic Movement was now coupled with worries about the security of its economic corridor project. In a series of meetings with the Taliban leadership, China tried to persuade it to come forward for a permanent reconciliation with the Afghan government.[39]

With the exacerbation of the security situation in Afghanistan, Chinese and Russian intelligence agencies began translating their

---

38 Ibid.
39 Ibid.

efforts against the ISIS into a practical form and extended their networks to all districts of the country. China is engaged in counter-intelligence efforts through the MSS and has employed various tactics including cyber spying to obtain sensitive information about the activities of ISIS near its borders. Recent research reports documented the proxy war between the US and China due to the increasing Chinese influence in Afghanistan and Central Asia, together with the strengthening of the Russian economy and military, caused concern in the US. The establishment of a new military intelligence agency, the Defense Clandestine Service (DCS), by the US and its focus on global threats and emerging economic and military powers, means that Pentagon wants to contain and confine both China and Russia to specific regions, but the defeat of ISIS in Syria and Iraq, and the exponentially growing Chinese and Russian intelligence networks across Afghanistan and Pakistan made the US mission impossible. China and Russia established their own Taliban to counter the ISIS influence, and approached Haqqani network to make the war against Daesh effective.

The NDS, according to the Pentagon's report, worked closely with both the Pentagon and CIA, recruiting spies from Defense intelligence agencies and deploying them in most parts of South Asia to closely watch the military and economic movements of communist China in South and Southeast Asia. In the presence of all these foreign intelligence agencies and their designs, Afghan intelligence was unable to play its role professionally or keep the balance of mutual relationship intact. The NDS was too incompetent and corrupt to counter terrorism and foreign espionage effectively as Afghan army also warned that due to the lack of intelligence in the battlefield, the army has weakened.

During his five-year tenure, former intelligence chief, Mr Rahmatullah Nabil, held Pakistan responsible for the deteriorating security situation in Afghanistan, but the fact of the matter is; misidentification of targets and abuse of intelligence has been a weak aspect of the NDS mechanism in the past. There was a lack of compatibility between the unity government and the NDS management. The politicization of the NDS's intelligence infrastructure also caused its failure.

In February 2014, the killing of 21 Afghan soldiers in Kunar province triggered the anger of an Afghan National Army (ANA) general who never expected the Afghan military intelligence to fall prey to the divisions of ethnic rivalry. The NDS spied on ethnic Pashtun generals, officers, soldiers and their families, in and outside military barracks. In 2013, Afghan Defense Ministry once warned Pashtun officers and soldiers that they would lose their jobs if they did not shift their families from Pakistan to Afghanistan, because Defense Minister had received reports that Afghans living in Pakistan work for the ISI and other intelligence agencies.[40]

This warning further caused mistrust between Pashtun and non-Pashtun officers within the ANA. Pashtun military officers complained that NDS was spying on them within the army and police force, which caused alienation, frustration and suspicion. The killing of 21 officers was termed as an intelligence failure by the Defense Ministry of Afghanistan, which fired some military commanders including regional intelligence chiefs. Daily Outlook reported the biggest backlash of the Afghan media where former President Hamid Karzai's policies towards the Taliban were harshly criticized. Interestingly, the President did not attend the funeral of the soldiers but cancelled his visit to Sri Lanka. There were speculations within the Afghan Parliament and Defense Ministry that, because of their ethnicity, the president did not consider it necessary to attend the funeral of the murdered soldiers.

In the last four decades, ethnic rivalries between the central government and local ethnic groups have been reported in the Afghan press time and again. After the Soviet withdrawal and the fall of the Dr Najibullah's government, Afghan army and its intelligence infrastructure collapsed and a new realignment of ethnic and sectarian actors emerged with their criminal militias. They established their own ethnic intelligence units to gather information about their rivals' military activities. Their intelligence units were influenced by the intelligence agencies of neighboring states to further their national interests in Afghanistan.

The ISI was also trying to influence Afghan army and its intelligence wing because dozens of army officer's families were living in Pakistan. They had purchased properties there, built houses in posh area and established businesses in Punjab and Khyber Pakhtukhawa provinces. The fragmentation of millions of Pashtuns in Afghanistan and Pakistan has been a key factor in this crisis. Perceiving them as a formidable ethnic group, the ISI and Saudi intelligence agencies tried to keep them on their side, because Afghanistan has never been able to support Pashtuns in Pakistan.

In addition to ISI and Saudi intelligence designs, Iran pursued a policy of its own, shaped by its national security interests. Iran supports Taliban, and recruits their fighter on its soil. In reality, all Afghan neighbors were busy in provoking ethnic and sectarian groups to strengthen their position in the country. There were speculations that Pakistan wanted to maintain its influence in Afghanistan and also try to stabilize the country to secure its own territory but, unfortunately, Afghanistan has been in trouble due to its own complicated ethnic politics. The dismal incident in Kunar province was considered an intelligence failure. The Kunar province

40 *ToloNews*, February 2014

was mostly controlled by Taliban forces where Afghan intelligence had no access to collect intelligence information about the dissidents.

Speaking at the funeral ceremony, Defense Minister Bismillah Khan Muhammadi criticized the controversial role of the Taliban, ISI and his own country's military intelligence. Maulana Muhammadi regretted the failed and unprofessional strategies of his country's civil and military intelligence agencies, and the ethnic tendencies of his military commanders, who intentionally or unintentionally allowed Taliban fighters to safely enter the fort and kill soldiers, not officers.

We have often been told that corruption and illegal use of power, nepotism, regionalism, ethnicity and sectarianism within the ranks of the ANA divided the loyalties of ANA officers. Such accusations also harmed the reputation of ANA officers. There is no check and balance in the armed forces. The Kuner incident was an eye opener to put into practice the laws responsible for keeping a proper check and balance on the top tier of the police and national army.

There was also mistrust between the government and its intelligence agencies as the Taliban intensified their efforts to inflict more harm on the ANA and the police by taking them hostage in large numbers. The recent investigation of Afghan Defense Ministry proved that intelligence had failed to counter Taliban infiltration into the ranks of the armed forces. The main reason behind all these incidents was the ethnic role of Afghan intelligence agencies and their targeting of Pashtun military officers. Since 2001, non-Pashtuns continued to target Pashtun officers in state institutions, which caused alienation.

In 2002, army was dominated by mafia groups who use it against ethnic Pashtuns in the western and eastern parts of the country. Having broken the system that was in place, the US and NATO decided to leave Afghanistan to face Taliban elements, criminal warlords and private militias, which disrupt any efforts to pull the nation together. Former chief of ISI, General Asad Durrani once told me: "Yet the ANA arose under foreign tutelage and will remain dependent upon foreign support for the foreseeable future. Thus it can only be seen by the majority of Afghans as a legacy of the occupation and not a 'national' institution". The current state of the ANA, Taliban infiltration, intelligence failures, 'intelligence war' among various nations and alliances (NATO, US, UK, ISAF), green-on-blue attacks and the rise of war criminals heading private militias present the biggest challenge to the reorganization of state institutions in Afghanistan.

The three intelligence agencies (RAW, ISI, NDS) have been engaged in a murky, and illegal war against Afghan civilians since the US invasion in 2001. This war killed numerous Afghan women and children during the last 15 years. The ISI supports Haqqani network, NDS supports Pakistani Taliban, and RAW supports Baluch insurgent. The three are leading operations in opposite directions but their intelligence strategies are the same. They are fighting in Afghanistan for their national interests. However, collaboration between the Indian and Afghan intelligence agencies caused precarious security crisis in Baluchistan, where Pakistan army and ISI failed to counter their networks.

On 09 August 2016, Baluchistan's Home Minister issued a detailed statemnet about the terrorist attacks carried out by Indian Intelligence RAW and Afghan Intelligence NDS. Mr. Bugti explained about the handlers of Lashkar-e-Jhangvi in Afghanistan who hired the perpetrators and executed their actions through TTP. "TTP provided them with suicide bombers", he said. In November 2016, Chief Minister of Baluchistan province, Nawab Sanaullah Zehri said that Indian intelligence agency 'Research and Analysis Wing' (RAW) and Afghanistan's spy agency 'National Directorate of Security' (NDS) was providing funds to anti state-elements in Pakistan.

On 24 October 2016, in their analysis, Waqar K Kauravi and Umar Waqar reviewed the Indian intelligence role in the proxy war, and elucidated the strategic importance of Baluchistan province: "RAW's next big game coincided with US War on Terror in Afghanistan. She exploited the swaths of ungovernable areas of Afghanistan for setting bases with following objectives; support ruthless terrorist organizations like TTP, Lashkar e Jhangvi and Daish etc; penetrate the area west of River Indus including Baluchistan to support proxy war against Pakistan, support dissident leadership of BLA etc to sabotage life lines of Baluchistan, provide diplomatic support to dissident leaders and organize seminars and conferences in major capitals of the western world to highlight cause of liberation of Baluchistan".[41]

Afghan intelligence agencies has been adamant to blame Inter Services Intelligence (ISI) for its interference in the internal affairs of Afghanistan since 2001, but never thought to fix its own clefts. The ISI is expert of making alliances with war criminals, sectarian elements, Taliban and ethnic groups inside Afghanistan and Pakistan. In 1982, ISI and CIA were deeply involved in military operations against the Soviet occupation in Afghanistan.[42] From 1982–1997, ISI received money and arms from the United States. Former Indian intelligence chief, the late B. Raman once revealed in one of his research papers; that the CIA relied on the ISI to train fighters, distribute arms, and channel money to Mujahedeen leaders. The armed forces of Pakistan trained more than one hundred thousand Afghan mujahedeen between 1983 and 1997, and dispatched them to Afghanistan gradually.

Mr. B. Raman also claimed that the Central Intelligence Agency (CIA) promoted the smuggling of heroin into Afghanistan in order to turn the Soviet troops into heroin addicts and thus greatly reducing their fighting potential.[43] In 1986, according to brigadier Tarmizi's revelations (1985), the ISI successfully convinced Mansour Ahmed who was the Charge-de-Affairs of the Afghan Embassy in Islamabad to turn his back on the Soviet backed Afghan government. He and his family were secretly escorted out of their residence and were given safe passage on a London bound British Airways flight in exchange for classified information in regard to Afghan agents in Pakistan. In 1997, the ISI and Pakistan army controlled Afghanistan and ruled it for four years. According to an Afghan expert, more than 100,000 Pakistani extremists were shifted to Afghanistan in 1990s to expand the matrix of civil war to all parts of the country. In 1992, Afghan state, army, intelligence, and the police collapsed.[44]

From 1992 to 2001, Civil war ruined Afghanistan, while Taliban with the financial and military assistance of Pakistan established an Islamic government. In 2001, with the collapse of Taliban regime, the US invaded the country and established a democratic government under the leadership of President Hamid Karzai. The ISI recruited Afghan Taliban and used them in the fight against Afghan army and US forces inside Afghanistan. In her research paper, Indian analyst Chidanand Rajghatta spotlighted some important facts about

41 ISI vs RAW, Waqar K Kauravi and Umar Waqar, The Nation, 24 October 2016 http://nation.com.pk/columns/24-Oct-2016/isi-vs-raw
42 "Muslims Condemn Soviet Invasion of Afghanistan." *Pittsburgh Post-Gazette*, January 29, 1980
43 Ensalaco, Mark (2007). *Middle Eastern terrorism: from Black September to September 11.* University of Pennsylvania Press
44 Ray. Ashis *Times of India*, 7 March 2011

the 2009 ISI–funded attack on CIA center in Khost province of Afghanistan:

> Pak funded the 2009 attack on a CIA camp on its border with Afghanistan. Seven American agents and contractors and three others were killed in attack. The explosive disclosure comes in a declassified 2010 cable published by the national security archive that, despite being redacted in parts, asserts unequivocally that "some funding for Haqqani attacks are still provided by the Pakistan Inter-Services Intelligence directorate, including $200,000 for the December 30, 2009, attack on the CIA facility at Camp Chapman. The Camp Chapman attack was carried out by Khalil Abu-Mulal al-Balawi, a Jordanian doctor and double agent, whom the CIA was trying to use to infiltrate al-Qaida in Pakistan in its hunt for Osama bin Laden and Ayman al Zawahiri. Instead, he was turned around the Haqqani group, a terrorist proxy for Pakistan's intelligence agency.... The Act, stemming from what is known as the Kerry-Lugar Bill was introduced to Congress on September 24, 2009, and passed into law on October 15, 2010. The ISI–sponsored attack on Camp Chapman occurred on December 30, 2009. By February 6, 2010, the date on the explosive cable detailing the Pakistani role, Washington knew ISI had engineered the attack on the CIA forward post. During discussions at an unknown date between Haqqani, Salar, and an unidentified ISID officer or officers, Haqqani and Salar were provided $200,000 to enable the attack on Chapman... Haqqani then provided the money to Salar who then communicated the planning details to Mullawi (Sakh). Sakh then contacted Arghawan Afghan border commander of the Khost Provincial Force.[45]

These are harsh realities Chidanand Rajghatta described, but after this incident, ISI continued to counter Indian Intelligence networks inside Afghanistan. In 2015, former President Pervez Musharaf admitted in his interview with the Guardian newspaper that he had ordered ISI to constitute suicide attacks inside Afghanistan, kill men, women and children indiscriminately. After this controversial interview, the issue of signing intelligence sharing agreement between ISI and NDS raised many suspicions. Controversies involved the Afghan government's move to have the National Directorate for Security (NDS) sign a deal with Pakistan's intelligence agency, ISI, clearly indicated the sensitivities of mutual relations between Pakistan and Afghanistan, particularly in security and intelligence areas. Since its formation, the new unity government made it clear that it would pursue peace talks with the Taliban through building trusts with Pakistan.

---

45 *Times of India*, 14 April 2016

To achieve this goal, President Ashraf Ghani moved fast and took measures that were unthinkable during his predecessor Hamid Karzai regime. The approach of the new government towards friendship with Pakistan alarmed many in Kabul, who warned that it was not in Afghanistan's interests, and that Afghanistan cannot trust Pakistan. Regarding Pakistan's potential role in bringing peace in Afghanistan, it was widely believed that Pakistan's ultimate influence on Taliban leadership can persuade them to come to table of negotiations and end the conflict.[46]

The ISI and NDS signed a landmark Memorandum of Understanding (MoU) for intelligence cooperation. The details of the agreement involved identification of the common enemies for effective action. Towards that end, extremist and terrorist elements including Tehreek-i-Taliban Pakistan (TTP) and Mullah Fazlullah were also been identified in the pact. Moreover, the NDS provided a list of extremist outfits to the ISI, against which Afghanistan was seeking Pakistan's assistance.[47] The pact was expected to help strengthen ties between Islamabad and Kabul in addition to reinforcing their resolve on war on terror. India was in hot water now, Indian National Security Advisor Ajit Doval said on May 23 that the agreement was based on "faulty assumption" that India uses its influence on Afghan officials to malign Pakistan for every problem in Afghanistan. Many Afghan groups continued to distrust the ISI regarding its covert support for the Taliban.[48]

The intelligence sharing agreement between Pakistan and Afghanistan was fundamental to the establishment and preservation of security and stability in the region. During the last 15-year-long war on terrorism, Pakistan and Afghanistan signed several Memorandums of Understanding (MoUs) on intelligence sharing that helped both the states in many ways. The MoU signed between the two states in May 2015 was considered of vital importance because they have been fighting terrorism and insurgencies since the US intervention in Afghanistan. Since Pakistan's former Army chief General Raheel Sharif declared in Kabul that the enemy of Afghanistan is the enemy of Pakistan, the two states entered a new era of long-term friendship. But unfortunately, when Pakistan army started cheating the Unity Government, the dynamic of relationship changed. The GHQ and its generals followed the old track. The threat of the Taliban and Islamic State (ISIS) significantly changed the direction of intelligence sharing between the neighbors as well. Although the threat of the Taliban and ISIS is by no means new, the scope and global reach of their networks, both leading up to and following the terrorist attacks in New York,

---

46 The NDS-ISI Deal Controversy May 24, 2015, Abdul Ahad Bahrami, *Daily Outlook Afghanistan*
47 Ibid.
48 *The Guardian*, 19 May 2015

made intelligence sharing a top priority for the war on terrorism in Afghanistan.

Secret agencies commonly negotiate MoUs, setting out the modalities of intelligence exchange. However, in contrast to agreements, memorandums do not require approval by national assemblies and can be implemented by the intelligence agencies themselves. Since General Musharaf's revelation in February 2015 about the involvement of the Inter-Services Intelligence (ISI) in a suicide bombing in Afghanistan, a new perception about the role of ISI developed that as the agency killed Afghan children and is behind all misadventures and grievances of Afghanistan, no cooperation with Pakistan on countering terrorism was needed. If we look at the statements of certain Pakistani generals and religious clerics, and their resentment towards Afghanistan, the fear and reservations of the Afghan leadership can be justified.

Former Afghan President Hamid Karzai expressed deep concern over the signing of the MoU. The office of the former President issued a statement called on the government to cancel the memorandum. Chairman of Senate Mr. Fazal Hadi Muslimyar criticized ISI and termed Pakistan as an enemy of Afghanistan. In a bid for peace with the Taliban, President Ghani ordered the Chief of National Directorate of Security (NDS) to end propaganda campaign against ISI, while the NDS chief and advisor for national security exchanged harsh words in an official meeting.

Dr Abdullah also demanded an amendment in the MoU's text. He was informed about the contents of the Memorandum by former President Hamid Karzai. The signing of an intelligence sharing MoU between the ISI and NDS caused growing concern at all levels in the country. War criminal Abdul Rasool Sayyaf also criticized the MoU and said that the deal can only benefit Islamabad. Former chiefs of the NDS, Amrullah Saleh and war criminal Assadullah Khalid, asked the government to revoke the memorandum. The National Solidarity Party (NSP) also criticized Islamabad for interfering in Afghanistan through an intelligence agreement.[49]

Ethnic and political divisions within the NDS, and political confrontations caused the deterioration of the security situation in Afghanistan. In all parts of the country, fight against the ISIS was a big challenge for Afghan intelligence. Afghanistan wanted to settle all issues with Pakistan to tackle the threat of the Taliban and ISIS effectively but, unfortunately, Pakistan abruptly changed its position and continued to send hundreds of proxies into Afghanistan.[50]

On May 24, 2015, Khaama Press reported President Ashraf Ghani also changed his position on Pakistan. Afghan President warned

---

49 What Pakistan wanted was to get an assurance and put pressure on Afghanistan so that it will not allow its territory to be used for any security related work by India. *The Hindu*, 23 May 2015, Ajit Doval
50 *The Hindu*, 23 May 2015, Ajit Doval

that Pakistan was engaged in an undeclared war with Afghanistan. He made these remarks at the nomination ceremony of Muhammad Masoom Stanekzai as the new Defense Minister of Afghanistan: "The war has been imposed on us and Afghans are determined not to ever bow to the imposed war. We will respond to the imposed war with war." This was the first time Afghan President clearly given this message to Pakistan. In these circumstances, the trust deficit between the two states further exacerbated because Afghanistan did not want to eliminate India's political influence.[51]

In response to these remarks, Pakistan said that people of the country were well-wishers of the Afghan government and its people. "We are committed to the recent agreement on intelligence sharing to root out the menace of terrorism," the official said. He also remarked that good neighborly relations and commitment to our relations with Afghanistan was Pakistan's first priority. "We would keep ignoring such allegations just to help the new Afghan government regain its strength against terrorists," a Pakistani official said.[52]

Politicians and civil society criticized Pakistan for its double game against their country. Afghan MPs opposed the MoU in Wolesi Jirga (lower house of parliament), saying it provides no benefits to Afghanistan. After lawmakers sought a clarification from the National Security Council (NSC), the first deputy speaker of the Wolesi Jirga, Zahir Qadir, asked parliamentary panels to summon NSC officials to explain what was going on under the carpet. According to Tolo TVNews, MP Rahman Rahmani told the House: "During (Pakistan Prime Minister) Nawaz Sharif's trip to Kabul, three Pakistani intelligence officers also arrived and you signed a shameful intelligence sharing agreement. By signing this agreement you have made yourself blind and dumb." Deputy head of parliament's internal security commission, Mohammad Faisal Sami, said: "The government should have endorsed its defeat to Pakistan before signing this agreement and announce it publicly."[53]

Members of parliament sought copies of the text, which had not been made public, and warned that they would invalidate the agreement if their complaints were not addressed. The NDS chief Rahmatullah Nabeel, who reportedly opposed signing the deal, appeared before a closed door session of parliament, while national security advisor Mr. Hanif Atmar did not attend. Kandahar Police commander Mr. Abdul Raziq criticized the agreement in remarks saying that: "the actions of the national unity government will have negative impacts on the morale of security forces", he said.[54]

51 *Khaama Press* 24 May, 2015
52 Pak's ISI, Afghan spy agency NDS sign MoU on intelligence sharing. Rezaul H Laskar, *Hindustan Times*, New Delhi May 19, 2015
53 *ToloNew* 18 May 2015
54 *ToloNew* 18 May 2015

Another lawmaker Shukria Barakzai strongly criticized the MoU and demanded revoking of the agreement immediately. She said signing such agreement meant Afghanistan recognized the Durand Line as legal border between the two countries. Speaker Abdul Rauf Ibrihim said Afghanistan suffered the most due to Pakistan's hidden policies and middling in Afghan affairs. He said Pakistan was solely responsible for killing of innocent Afghans in bombing and other incidents of violence. "The agreement is not in the interest of Afghanistan. It will not end the ongoing wave of violence in Afghanistan," he noted.

The NSC in its statement said the signing of a memorandum of understanding between the National Directorate of Security (NDS) and Pakistan's Inter-Services Intelligence (ISI) on intelligence cooperation, its legal status, contents and the framing process had become a hot topic these days. Without going into details, the statement said as part of the discussions, some dubious sources had been providing misleading information to the NSC and the media. The NSC said it was concerned that the country's high interests were being used for personal gains and character assassination and that the NSC considered it mandatory to explain few words about the agreement in order to remove common fears.[55]

The memorandum includes a number of traditional points: intelligence data sharing, joint development and coordination of anti-terrorist operations on both sides of the Pakistani-Afghan border. The ISI showed commitments to train Afghan specialists, etc. At the same time the document contained a number of new provisions, such as joint investigation of cases in which perpetrators were known or suspected to have committed a terrorist act. This provision should be considered as know-how of the Pakistani intelligence agency, seeking not only to possess a complete and updated database, but to control and manage the armed opposition in neighboring countries. At the same time, Pakistan consistently emphasized the fact those they "... strictly adhere to the policy of non-interference in the affairs of Afghanistan."

On 15 January 2017, Pakistan Army Chief General Qamar Javed Bajwa once again proposed intelligence sharing between NDS and ISI, and suggested installing a "robust border management mechanism and intelligence cooperation" to restrict the movement of terrorists across the Durand Line. "Elements inimical to peace in the region are strengthened by blame game. All safe havens of terrorists have been eliminated from Pakistan," the army chief was quoted as saying, Bajwa said. Gen Bajwa reportedly empathized on the "tragic series of events" that unrolled on the "people of both the brotherly countries" over the last few years. "Pakistan has come a long way in its fight against terrorism of all hue and color," the statement read, adding that

---

55 India's National Security Advisor Criticizes NDS-ISI Agreement, 23 May 2015, Ratib Noori

"all safe havens [of militants] have been eliminated in the process", he said.

Researcher, Christian Fair warned that Afghanistan-Pakistan borderlands remained the theatre of international rivalries since 2001. Durand Line, writer Mr. Fair argued marks the boundary between Afghanistan and Pakistan is an illegitimate colonial construct. Pakistan's armed forces believe they have won. However, Pakistan stands to lose more than it gains for several reasons. During their heyday, the Taliban never delivered a resolution on the Durand Line, and encouraged Pashtun nationalism. Researcher Olli Ruohomaki in his recent article noted the fatalities of proxy war between Pakistan and India in Afghanistan, which causes a bigger challenge to peace and stability in the country: The long-standing conflict between India and Pakistan is played out in Afghanistan, where both engage in outright proxy wars. On the bilateral front, Islamabad's actions, particularly by its military intelligence organ ISI, and its support for the Afghan Taliban movement, are not exactly conducive to enhancing peace in Afghanistan. Afghans cross the border at will and insurgents seek refuge and sanctuary on both sides thereof.

Despite mutual accusations the ISI–NDS signed the Agreement in May 2015. Pakistan was as much as Afghanistan interested in eliminating armed outbreaks in the Af–Pak region. The army launched large-scale military operations in June 2014 to destroy foreign and local militants in North Waziristan, but killed thousands of its citizens there. Most of the extremists crossed the Hindu Kush to enter the Afghan territory which significantly strengthened anti-Kabul armed opposition. It continued to create a major threat to the social and economic reforms planned in the Pakistani province of Khyber Pakhtunkhwa. But it was in May 2015, the ISI–NDS agreement that caused another chill in relations between the two countries. President Ghani sent a letter to civilian and military leadership of Pakistan in which he put forward several demands:

1. An official declaration by the political leadership of Pakistan condemning the launching of the Talban offensive operation;

2. A directive by the military leadership that sanctuary will be denied to the Taliban and effective measures by the security forces and civil authorities that the directive is carried out

3. A directive to extend the counter-terror campaign to the Haqqani network and verification that those responsible for the recent terror campaign in Afghanistan are arrested.[56]

56Pakistan–Afghanistan: an Intelligence War in the Making? Natalya Zamaraeva, *"New Eastern Outlook"* http://journal-neo.org/2015/06/15/pakistan-afghanistan-an-intelligence-war-in-the-making/

CHAPTER 5. WAR OF INTERESTS AND THE BLAME-GAME

The changing nature of dominant security threats during the yesteryears war on terrorism in Afghanistan, and the lack of intelligence cooperation between the NDS and ISI caused misunderstanding, the blame game and severe fatalities in the region. Every month and every week, terrorists target either Pakistani security forces or Afghan civilians but they never thought to develop a joint strategy to tackle the menace of sectarian terrorists across the Durand Line. In 2015, intelligence memorandum signed between the Inter-Services Intelligence (ISI) and National Directorate of Security (NDS) enraged Afghan politicians and members of parliament. The President came under severe criticism from all segments of society that even called him a traitor but, later on, realized the important of intelligence sharing with Pakistan. As intelligence is more than just surveillance and information gathering, the two states can exchange data of their surveillance on people who pose precarious security threats to their national security.

Very often, theories explaining intelligence failures advanced by politicians and intelligence review committees are weak, ambiguous and fail to address one core hiccup of the intelligence community. At its core, intelligence differs from research information management and investigative interviews in that it includes three unique activities: interpreting threats, the use of actionable intelligence and intelligence-led secret operations. Afghanistan and Pakistan lack these professional skills and cannot interpret threats within their traditional form. The capability of an agency to make comprehensive intelligence estimates for policymakers depends largely on its assessment and analytical capabilities but the ISI and NDS have hardly contributed to their states' policymaking process. They are confused between the traditional principles of counterinsurgency operations and conventional warfare. Their parameters of intelligence information gathering have shrunk.

Public Policy Scholar, Janani Krishnaswamy in her recent research paper spotlighted important facts about the flawed counterterrorism policy and intelligence failure:

Whenever a terrorist attack happens, faulty or inadequate intelligence is cited as a major cause, regardless of whether there happen to be policy failures. However, there are a few exceptions. As a consequence of linking terrorist attacks with inadequate intelligence; the argument of an existing intelligence system not being capable of dealing with immediate threats arises all the time. This unbalanced approach of routinely establishing a strong link between intelligence and counter-terrorism policy is due to the assumption that intelligence analysis normally influences policy decisions leading to a natural deduction that the availability of good intelligence can only lead to effective policies and vice versa. However, this is not to dismiss the need for more capable intelligence machinery. The model inaccurately links flawed counter-terrorist policies to insufficient or erroneous intelligence. The helplessness of the intelligence community to defend any allegations of failure has only reinforced the claim made above. Such an unsound analysis will lead to questions such as why or how policy makers overlook available intelligence.[57]

With the arrival of the ISIS in Afghanistan, the NDS expedited it efforts to professionally counter its network but failed due to some hindrances. The NDS caught in the fight between Indian intelligence (RAW) and Pakistani ISI, which caused huge fatalities and destruction as they all used suicide bomber against each other targets. India is helping Afghanistan to recover from a long imposed civil war, while ISI does not tolerate the existence of Indian diplomatic presence in the country. Former President General Musharaf admitted in his interview with the *Guardian* newspaper that he had ordered ISI to train suicide bombers and use them against civilians and government installations inside Afghanistan. Mr. Musharaf vowed that his government had decided to counter Indian influence in Afghanistan and destabilize the Karzai government.

On 29 March 2016, the NDS Chief warned that ISI was trying to expand the war in Afghanistan.[58] Mr. Massoud Andrabi told Afghan parliament that Pakistan army controls some parts of Afghanistan. However, Mullah Mansour Dadullah, a former Taliban commander, released a video addressing his complaints about the Taliban and Pakistan's intelligence service to Afghan Islamic Press. Mr. Dadullah's

---

57 Public Policy Scholar, Janani Krishnaswamy in her recent research paper (Why Intelligence Fails-2013, Policy Report No 3, the Hindu Centre for Politics and Public Policy.
58 On 29 March 2016, the NDS Chief warned that Pakistani intelligence agency (ISI) was trying to expand parameter of war in Afghanistan. Mr. Massoud Andrabi told Afghan parliament that Pakistan army controls some parts of Afghanistan, *ToloNews report*.

interview was recorded just days after his followers and the Taliban clashed in Zabul province. Mr. Dadullah accused the current Taliban leadership of being "lecherous, rakish and malicious" and described "intelligence networks," which presumably include Pakistan's Inter-Services Intelligence (ISI), as "dirty and disgraced," according to a translation of the Afghan Islamic Press article. Additionally, he claimed:

"We have tried from the very first moments of jihad to give control of the Islamic army to a religious, brave, independent and free Muslim. Ever since the relation between His Excellency Amir al-Momenin [Leader of the Faithful] Mullah Mohammad Omar Mujahid was disconnected and lecherous, rakish and malicious people had entered in the middle, we have raised our voice of truth. Now, the situation is very clear and you see that in the name of the new Amir al-Momenin [Mullah Mansour], the sincere Muslims and Mujahedeen are being deceived again.......We openly made a decision once again and in consultation with religious scholars, and we clearly declared our separation from those lying lecher people, who kept the killing of His Excellency Amir al-Momenin Mullah Mohammad Omar Mujahid for over two years from all the Muslims and who imposed their hated thoughts in the form of the decrees of the Leader Mullah [Omar] on all the Islamic world. We cannot accept Akhtar Mohammad Mansour as the new Amir based on consultation with and fatwa by the religious scholars."Dadullah said. Dissident Taliban commander claims Pakistani intelligence ordered him to conduct assassinations, attacks in Afghanistan".[59]

On June 24 2015, Afghanistan's intelligence service said that a Pakistani intelligence officer helped Taliban carrying out an attack on parliament. The agency spokesman Hassib Sediqqi said that an officer in Inter-Services Intelligence helped the Haqqani network carrying out the attack outside parliament in Kabul, which killed two people and wounded more than 30 as lawmakers were meeting inside.[60]

On 10 December 2015, ToloNews reported the resignation of the chief of National Directorate of Security (NDS), Mr. Rahmatullah Nabil. Mr. Nabil won vote of confidence from the parliament with 154 votes, 58 against, 22 ballots blank, and nine invalid, in January 2015. Shortly after the Pak-Afghan leaders agreed to revive the controversial Afghan peace talks, Mr. Nabil issued a rare statement and said that innocent Afghan civilians were martyred and beheaded in Kandahar airfield, Khanshin district of Helmand, Takhar and Badakhshan at the sometimes Nawaz Sharif was delivering his speech, calling the enemy of Afghanistan as Pakistan's enemy.[61]

59 *Long War Journal*, 07 September 2015
60 AP, June 24, 2015
61 NDS chief resignation, NDS chief Nabil steps down, *ToloNews*, 10 December 2015

In parts of his message, ToloNews reported, Mr. Nabil criticized President Ghani for his remarks in Islamabad, saying: "At least 1,000 liters of blood of our innocent people spilled." Frustrated with the growing interference of Pakistan in internal affairs of Afghanistan, and President Ghani's unprofessional approach towards Pakistan, Mr. Nabil questioned regarding the 5000-year-old history of Afghanistan saying it had kneeled to a 60-year-old history. Mr. Nabil also added that Pakistani Taliban chief Mullah Fazlullah has been residing in Pakistan in ISI's guesthouses during the past several months and years, insisting that Mullah Fazlullah was part of ISI projects. Mullah Akhtar Mansoor had been enjoying the escort and legion of ISI bodyguards in presence of Colonel Rana—his fake name "Rabbani." They were busy drawing future plans to kill our innocent people in Quetta's bypass area, Pakistan. And Sarajuddin Haqqani he said, was enjoying a party of his son from his third wife in Hayatabad area of Peshawar Pakistan. Thanks God I was not present there, Mr. Nabil said.[62]

Moreover, in an interview at his office in Kabul, Mr. Massoud said the confidence expressed by Ghani and Abdullah, does not reflect political and military realities. Citing U.S. military figures, the U.S. Special Inspector for Afghanistan Reconstruction (USSIAR), a watchdog, reported that the Afghan government controls just 72% of the country's 407 districts, believed to be the lowest figure in years. Taliban insurgents continued fighting government forces through a bloody winter, defying the usual lull in violence that comes in Afghanistan's colder months and prompting U.S. military officials to reconsider reducing the U.S. troop presence as the White House had planned.[63]

Former Interior Minister, Mr. Noor-ul-Haq Ulomi, resigned due to an ethnic conflagration and some pressures from foreign intelligence agencies operating inside Afghanistan. "Look at the current state of the nation: the economy is weak, people continue to suffer from joblessness, there are still social problems, there is still political infighting even at the highest level," he said. However, official sources in Pakistan claimed that Afghanistan's National Directorate of Security (NDS) and India's Research and Analysis Wing (RAW) were stepping up terrorist activities on Pakistani soil to aid and abet more deadly terror attacks. Intelligence inputs acquired through communication intercepts and human intelligence sources revealed that NDS was planning to focus on Khyber Pakhtunkhwa, settled areas of the tribal belt, Gilgit Baltistan and Baluchistan. However NDS was also assisting RAW in Baluchistan to sustain its operations linked to Baloch separatist groups. The Indian agency had also to focus on Punjab and Sindh.

---

62 Ibid.
63 The US *Watch Dog Report*

"Indian agency would also launch its sleeper cells with the help of NDS in Khyber Pakhtunkhwa and tribal areas. The members of the cells are being recruited from Afghanistan, mainly from militant groups fled away from Pakistan during Swat, South Waziristan operations and the militants crossed the Durand Line during Operation Zarb-e-Azb, Khyber-1 and Khyber-2." The sources claimed that members of the sleeper cells were selected from the unknown foot soldiers of the outlawed TTP and their affililates scattered in Afghan provinces of Kunar, Nangarhar, Nuristan and Badakshan. The RAW is running training camps with the nod of its Afghan counterpart in the said provinces for "brainwashing" programs of the newly-selected sleepers to launch the same when the time comes."[64] Inter Services Intelligence warned.

The NDS Chief's briefing to Afghan parliament over cooperation with Pakistan's security services to take out the targets threatening the security of both the countries spoke volumes of their sincerity concerning joint efforts. Security experts were of the opinion that Pakistani government should not only share the details of few with Afghan government concerning their involvement in terror activities on Pakistani soil, but it should also share information relating to NDS–RAW nexus.[65]

Inspector General of Frontier Corps Baluchistan, Major General Sher Afgan also warned in a press briefing that Afghan and Indian intelligence agencies were fuelling terrorism in Baluchistan. In 2016, NDS confirmed the presence of Islamic State leaders Hafiz Saeed Khan and Shahidullah Shahid, formerly members of TTP both Pakistani nationals, who were killed in Nangarhar province in US drone strikes. There was a lot of news indicating that Rahmatullah Nabil, leader of the National Directorate of Security was harboring Latif Mehsud, one of the Tehreek-i-Taliban Pakistan leaders. Afghan media were surprised at the rapid and fundamental changes in NDS policy, which in recent years sharply criticized the ISI for harboring leaders of the Islamic Emirate of Afghanistan, and for aiding and abetting the Afghan Taliban and other militant groups who fought in Afghanistan. Incidentally, Mr. Nabil refused to sign the memorandum with ISI. Former Afghan President Hamid Karzai described the agreement as "a blow to the national interests of Afghanistan." In November 2014 the head of the NDS, Rahmatullah Nabil, informed parliament that there was an "overwhelming wave of violence" in the country and he recorded 107 places where the fortified hideouts of militants were found in the provinces around Kabul.[66]

---

64 NDS-RAW nexus fuelling terrorism in Pakistan, *The Nation*, September 28, 2015

65 Ibid.

66 Natalya Zamarayeva, *Pakistan – Afghanistan: an Intelligence War in the Making?* 15.06.2015

After the fall of the Taliban regime in 2001, Pakistan started pressuring Afghanistan and international community for excluding India from the reconstruction efforts, while Afghan government did not hear Pakistan's complaints about the establishment of the Indian consulates in Afghanistan. These consulates, ISI warned, facilitated terrorists to carry out attacks in Pakistan, but Afghanistan said the basic objectives of these consulates were to provide basic facilities to the local governments and civilian population. New York Times reported Pakistan's double game in Afghanistan:

> Pakistan's double game has long frustrated American officials, and it has grown worse. There are now efforts in Washington to exert more pressure on the Pakistan Army. Senator Bob Corker, Republican of Tennessee, chairman of the Senate Foreign Relations Committee, has wisely barred the use of American aid to underwrite Pakistan's purchase of eight F-16 jet fighters. Pakistan will still be allowed to purchase the planes, but at a cost of $700 million instead of about $380 million.[67]

Pakistan's Ambassador to the UN, Mr. Jilani, rejected the allegations made in a *New York Times* editorial, which implicated Pakistan for the mess in Afghanistan, and termed Islamabad a "duplicitous" and "dangerous" partner for the United States and Afghanistan. In a statement that was a rejoinder to the NYT indictment, Mr. Jilani came out hard against the organization, questioning what he called its "partisanship." He said the situation in Afghanistan was a "collective failure of the international community." "The May 12 editorial about Pakistan's role in Afghanistan is biased and negates the complex history of this prolonged conflict. "Allegations of duplicity and double game were extremely painful as Pakistan has suffered the most due to the war in Afghanistan. Pakistan cannot be held responsible for the mess in Afghanistan which is the result of the collective failure of the international community," Jilani said.[68]

However, the same day, Hindustan Times reported Afghan President Ashraf Ghani described Pakistani Taliban as the "greatest threat to the region" and said his country was facing an "undeclared war" from Pakistan, which did not accept his offer of peace. Delivering a well-received lecture on the theme "Fifth Wave of Political Violence" at the Royal United Services Institute, Mr. Ghani expressed frustration at Afghanistan becoming a battleground for fighters from various countries, but mainly from Pakistan. "Who fights in my country? Chinese, Chechens, Uzbeks, Tajiks, but the greatest one of course is a huge movement from Pakistan. The madrassa, a long-time instrument of Pakistani intelligence, has been training people from the ethnic minorities of northern Afghanistan alongside its standard clientele

---

67 *New York Times* reported (12 May 2016) Pakistan's double game in Afghanistan
68 On 13 May 2016

of Pashtuns. The aim is still to win control of northern Afghanistan through these young graduates. From there they have their eyes on Central Asia and western China. Pakistani clerics are educating and radicalizing Chinese Uighurs as well, along with Central Asians from the former Soviet republics.

The escalating violence between India and Pakistan and their support to extremist groups inside Afghanistan threaten to get worse after the recent Pathankot and Bacha Khan University attacks. Pakistan, for instance, alleges that India, with the support of Afghan intelligence agencies, covertly finances the Pakistani Taliban and the Baloch National Army (BLA). India thinks Pakistan facilitated terror attacks on it consulate in Mazar-e-Sharif, and on the airbase in Pathankot, while Pakistan says India was behind the attack on its consulate in Jalalabad. This blame game among the three states has given a chance to terrorist organizations to inflict fatalities on civilians and security forces.

Meanwhile, Indian Defense Minister warned that those who had inflicted pain on India would also feel the pain. This was a limpid warning to Pakistan that Indian agencies would do the same as the terrorists had done in Patankot. The ISI said that India trained and financed the Tehreek-e-Taliban Pakistan and provided with financial assistance to the Islamic State (ISIS) leadership as well. India said Pakistan's concerns were based on controversies. Afghanistan too has concerns about Pakistan's support to the Haqqani network. The three states were in deep water and had nothing to convince their citizens on security issues.

On 21 May 2016, *Dawn* reported a US air strike killed Afghan terrorist leader Mullah Akhtar Mansour in a remote area along the Pak–Afghan border. "Today, the US Department of Defense conducted a precision air strike, targeting Mullah Mansour in a remote area in the Pakistan-Afghan border region," said Pentagon Press Secretary Peter Cook. He said the President of the United States had authorized the air strike and that Pakistan and Afghanistan were both notified of it. "Mullah Mansour was the leader of the Afghan Taliban terrorist network. The Pentagon said that since the death of Mullah Omar and Mullah Mansour's assumption of leadership, the Taliban had conducted many attacks that resulted in the deaths of thousands of Afghan civilians and security forces as well as numerous US and coalition personnel."[69]

Pakistan's alleged involvement in Afghanistan raised serious questions. What does Pakistan want to teach India in Afghanistan? The question needs a thorough investigation on the trilateral level in order to crystallize the basic agenda of this proxy war on the Afghan soil. The Taliban war in Afghanistan intensified as the second phase of reconciliation talks ended with no results. Security situation in

---

69 On 21 May 2016, Dawn reported a US air strike killed Afghan terrorist leader Mullah Akhtar Mansour in a remote area along the Pak–Afghan border

Helmand, Kunduz, Jalalabad and Kabul remained challenging as ISIS and Pakistani militia groups (Lashkar-e-Tayyaba, Lashkar-e-Jhangvi and TTP) entered a decisive war against the Unity Government.

Terrorists wanted to maintain high pressure on Kabul to gain control of some important provinces bordering Pakistan in order to clear their supply line. In 2015, more than 10,000 terrorist and security incidents recorded. Defense Minister Masoom Stanekzai told Afghan parliament that with the withdrawal of foreign forces and the military operation in Waziristan, insecurity in Afghanistan had increased. He said regional rivalries had led to the creation of extremist forces in the country.[70]

Mr. Stanekzai regretted on the deteriorating security in the north and said that Tajik, Uzbek, Chechen, Afghan and Pakistani extremists had made the north insecure through Ghanzni, Zabul, Faryab and Chitral, and added that there were some powerful Afghan commanders and leaders who transported Taliban and the IS fighters in their vehicles to Northern Afghanistan, and settle them along the Russian and Chinese borders. Mr. Mirdad Salangi, head of parliament's internal security commission, criticized the government for its inability to manage the war against terrorists and warned that the next fighting season would be a hard one for the shrinking Afghan army.[71]

NATO commanders also warned that the next season of fighting would be dangerous. Experts viewed this warning as a total failure of the US and NATO forces in fighting insurgents, or they want to shift the parameter of the war closer to the Russian and Chinese borders. On January 20, 2016, terrorists attacked the bus of a local television channel, ToloNews in Kabul and killed seven of its anchors. The incident occurred after a suicide bomber detonated explosives near the bus. In Jalalabad province, Afghan commanders warned that the terror networks of Mangal Bagh, ISIS and Lashkar-e-Tayyaba were spread across the region. Mr Mangal Bagh joined hands with ISIS military command in Shinwari district against the Afghan government.[72]

A commander of Mangal Bagh group in Achin district told an Afghan journalist that his group had held a meeting with the leadership of ISIS to further organize attacks against the Afghan security forces. As the security situation was deteriorating by the day, President Ashraf Ghani appointed a former general, Abdul Jabbar Qahraman, as a special security commander of Helmand province. Mr Qahraman was member of the lower house of parliament, who served under the Dr. Najibullah administration in the 1980s. "We are working on the professionalization of intelligence and a coordination plan to fight militants because we can improve the security situation

70 *Daily Times*, 26 January 2016
71 *ToloNews* 13 January 2016
72 *ToloNews* 20 January 2016

using intelligence techniques within limited resources," General Qahraman said.[73]

On 09 January 2016, Afghan Parliament summoned key security officials to explain the growing threat of Taliban and Islamic State (ISIS) as the Afghan National Army failed to professionalize counterinsurgency operations across the country. Defense Minister, Muhammad Masoom Stanekzai, Interior Minister Noorulhaq Uloomi and Director General NDS Major Masood Andrabi failed to positively respond to the questions of parliamentarians about the capability of Afghan security forces. According to a report of NATO headquarters, in 2016, security situation in Afghanistan was poised to deteriorate as the Afghan National Army lost a third of its troops. Despite multibillion dollar funds, the ANA remains an entity hardly of carrying out the functions of a military force, the report noted. The report further noted that out 101 units only one is battle-ready, while 38 units are incompetent. The report added that more than 8,000 ANA soldiers were killed in the fight against Taliban last year.[74]

In fact, the Obama administration failed to create a fundamentally workable set of transition policy and train a professional army for Afghanistan. Moreover, political horse-trading over the appointment of high-ranking police officers and the ANA commanders prompted deep crisis for the Afghan security forces fighting the Islamic State and Taliban in Helmand and parts of Northern provinces. The two Presidents divided security forces on ethnic and political bases and appoint their own men in the provinces under their control respectively. No doubt, a controversial election process shaped a political patronage system but blind allegiance and obedience of the police and ANA officers to their masters are logic consequences of war criminals to consolidate their own power within the Unity Government.

The two Presidents maintained their own agendas, and introduced patronage system in security sectors. All military commanders are answerable to their political masters and war criminals with conflicting priorities rather than to the state and government. On 29 December, Afghan police commanders loyal to a specific political group refused to fight against Taliban in Helmand. In the end of 2014, more than 100 Afghan police joined Taliban. The crisis further complicated as the ANA is not treading professionally.

In December 2015, in the fight against Taliban and Islamic State, the ANA carried out 377 military and 110 surveillance operations,

---

73 *Daily Times*, 26 January 2016
74 On 09 January 2016, Afghan Parliament summoned key security officials to explain the growing threat of Taliban and Islamic State (ISIS) as the Afghan National Army failed to professionalize counterinsurgency operations across the country. Defense Minister, Muhammad Masoom Stanekzai, Interior Minister Noorulhaq Uloomi and Director General NDS Major Masood Andrabi failed to positively respond to the questions of parliamentarians about the capability of Afghan security forces. *ToloNews report*.

and more than 200 military operations were carried out in Helmand, Ghazni, Faryab, Kunduz and Jalalabad provinces, but the result was very poor. Militants became more strong and gained control on more districts across the country. In Jalalabad, Paktika, Faryab, Helmand, Ghazni, Kunduz, Aruzgan and Sari-pul provinces, more than 370 terror-related incidents occurred, in which 2,000 innocent civilians, 1,600 Taliban and 2010 ANA were soldiers killed and injured.[75]

The attack on Indian consulate in Balkh province remained a question mark as the RAMA and NDS could not find any clue of the involvement of foreign intelligence in it. However, The Taliban and Daesh beheaded and kidnapped over 50 soldiers in Badakhshan province when their request for logistic support was turned down by the Afghan Defense Ministry. However, in Wardak province, more than 30 ANA soldiers deserted, in Kandahar, Paktia, Laghman, Kunduz and Kunar provinces, countless marooned soldiers joined Taliban ranks. Government lost control over the Jalalabad, Nuristan and Kunar provinces because Afghan National Army lost civilian support, and failed to attract young people for recruitment. Majority of jobless people join Daesh and the Taliban to support their families while Afghan Ministers, members of parliament, army generals and corrupt officials continue to purchase expensive houses in the UK, US, Canada, Australia, Germany and Dubai.[76]

On 02 December 2015, Deputy Speaker of the Afghan Lower House of Parliament accused the unity government and its National Security Council for supporting the Islamic State (ISIS), and warned if he presented the documents to parliament, the government would collapse. He showed a CD on the floor of Parliament and said some pressures prevent him to air the CD, but said he would show the CD to certain people at certain time because he did not want the division of Afghan nation. Mr. Zair Qadeer said terrorist need to face the wrath of his Lashkar, adding that the government in Kabul did not help the incarcerated men and women in Daesh private prisons. Mr. Qadeer's bray came after the uprising civilians under his command beheaded four members of the Islamic State (ISIS) for revenge—Daesh had earlier cut off heads of four civilian in Achin district of Jalalabad province. Later on the governor of Jalalabad confirmed that the beheaded four Daesh fighters belonged to Tirah Valley and two other were from the Orakzai Agency of Khyber Pakhtunkhwa province of Pakistan.[77]

---

75 *Daily Times*, 11 January 2016
76 *Daily Times*, 06 January 2016
77 On 02 December 2015, Deputy Speaker of the Afghan Lower House of Parliament accused the unity government and its National Security Council for supporting the Islamic State (ISIS), and warned if he presented the documents to parliament, the government would collapse. He showed a CD on the floor of Parliament and said some pressures prevent him to air the CD, but said he would show the CD to certain people at certain time because he did not want the division of Afghan nation. *ToloNews report.*

CHAPTER 6. THE RAW AND NDS OPERATIONS IN BALUCHISTAN

On 25 March 2016, a day after Pakistani security forces claimed the arrest of a suspected Research and Analysis Wing (RAW) agent in Baluchistan, Commander of Southern Command, Lt Gen Amer Riaz accused elements sitting in London and Geneva of hatching conspiracies against the stability of Pakistan. Speaking at a Yum-i-Shuhada event, the Commander said, RAW agent was in contact with separatist elements in Baluchistan and was involved in a number of terrorist and subversive activities in the province. "Our enemies do not want development and prosperity in Baluchistan," said Gen Aamer Riaz. The RAW officer was shifted to Islamabad for interrogation. He was suspected of involvement in various acts of terrorism and other subversive activities in the province. Foreign Secretary Aizaz Chaudhry, shared details with the Indian High Commissioner. Mr. Chaudhry lodged a strong protest over the RAW officer's spying activities in Baluchistan and Karachi, making it clear that that was unacceptable.[78]

During the last 15 years war on terrorism in Afghanistan, Pakistan and India have been engaged in an intense intelligence war-targeting their diplomatic missions in Kabul and blaming each other of sponsoring terrorist groups in Baluchistan and Kashmir. India believes Pakistan supports Kashmiri groups including Lashkar-i-Toiba and Hezbul Mujahedeen to carry out attacks against its armed forces, while Pakistan understands that India supports TTP, Daesh and Baloch nationalists to disrupt its peace efforts in Baluchistan province. The two states are also involved in an unending proxy war in Afghanistan, where they also turned Afghan society into two rival camps.

The Karzai administration open-heartedly offered India an opportunity to establish its terror recruitment camps against its

78 *Dawn*, 25 March 2016

traditional enemy, Pakistan. This was a golden opportunity where India trained Baloch fighters and sent them back to Pakistan to carry out suicide attacks. Terrorist incidents in Patan Kot, Uri and Baluchistan exacerbated the level of tension between the two states. Indian Interior Minister immediately issued a statement, in which he termed Pakistan a terrorist state, while Indian Defense Minister Manohar Parrikar and other extremist Hindu leaders demanded the change of no first use policy of nuclear weapons against Pakistan. Those statements set forth a hot debate among nuclear experts.

The arrest of Indian intelligence officers in Baluchistan generated many controversial debates that exposed the country involvement with terrorist groups in the region. Director ISPR, General Bajwa confirmed Mr. Yadav motive to sabotage the CPEC, reviving traditional terror-related operations, and constituting a new force to carry out attacks against government and civilian installations. India's intentions about the CPECT became crystal clear from the statement of Indian Prime Minister, Narendra Modi in China where he strongly bashed the CPEC and called the project unacceptable.

On 14 January 2017, China handed over two ships to the Pakistan Navy for joint security along the sea route of the China-Pakistan Economic Corridor (CPEC). Recently built in China and equipped with state-of-the-art guns, the ships became part of the navy. Chinese officials, who reached Gwadar aboard the ships, handed them over to their Pakistani counterparts at a ceremony at the Gwadar port. Commander of the Pakistan Fleet Vice Admiral Arifullah Hussaini received the ships which have been named after two nearby rivers Hingol and Basol. Director General of the Pakistan Maritime Security Agency Rear Admiral Jamil Akhter, Commander West Commodore Mohammad Waris and top naval and civilian officials were present on the occasion. "The Chinese ships have become part of the Pakistan Navy from today," Vice Admiral Hussaini said, adding that the navy would become stronger with the induction of the ships.

At present, with the commencement of the CPEC journey through Baluchistan, the Indian intelligence war entered in a new phase. Border tension between Pakistan in India and the massive deployment of Indian forces in Kashmir further caused in the exacerbation of terror-related incidents from a across the border in Baluchistan and Khyber Pakhtunkhawa provinces.

The links between India and local terrorist groups cannot be ruled out as the groups continue to challenge the writ of the government in Afghanistan. On 08 August 2016, the motive of India behind the killing of innocent Pashtuns and Baluchs in Baluchistan was an attempt to sabotage the CPEC project. Chief Minister of Baluchistan accused RAW of being behind the attack. Pakistan understands that Baloch insurgent receive training in camps in Afghanistan, organized by Indian intelligence. Director General Intelligence Bureau (IB) Aftab Sultan told senate standing committee that his agency arrested several Indian agents. The nexus between the Indian National Security Advisor, Mr Ajit Doval and the Islamic State (ISIS) has already been reported in international press while Pakistan often complained about the Indian involvement in Baluchistan. In a recent statement, Pakistan's military establishment directly accused Indian intelligence agencies of sponsoring terrorism in the country and that it could result in increased tension between the two states.

On 15 May 2016, the accusation came at a meeting of corps commanders in Rawalpindi. They took serious notice of the Indian intelligence involvement in Baluchistan. Defence Minister Khawaja Asif in his television interview warned that RAW is an enemy organization and that it had been formed to undermine Pakistan.[79] On 08 September 2016, Pakistan's foreign office accused India of financing terrorism in Pakistan, saying that "open evidence is available on India's involvement in subversive activities".[80] On 18 September 2016, the Guardian reported Indian Home Minister directly accused Pakistan's involvement in a deadly raid on a Kashmir army base that killed 17 Indian soldiers. He also labeled Pakistan a terrorist state.[81]

Mr. Rajnath Singh said Pakistan is responsible for the attack. "I am deeply disappointed with Pakistan's continued and direct support to terrorism and terrorist groups", he said. However, On 26 October 2016, Pakistan conveyed to the US that Indian intelligence (RAW) and Afghanistan's National Directorate of Security (NDS) are patronizing terrorist groups to attack soft targets in the country.[82] However, the intelligence war between India and Pakistan intensified when Pakistan called its diplomatic staff from Delhi and India reciprocated at the same manner. Pakistan's foreign office condemned the arrest of its embassy staff in India. On 03 November 2016, Pakistan foreign office said: "As you are aware, a number of Indian diplomats and staff belonging to Indian intelligence agencies RAW and IB have been found involved in coordinating terrorist and subversive activities in Pakistan under the garb of diplomatic assignments".[83]

On 26 October 2016, Daily Times reported the details of 110-pages Baluchistan inquiry report, in which judge Qazi Faez Isa suggested that Terrorist organizations must not be permitted to hold meetings and people must be informed about the reasons for banning such organizations.[84] The inquiry report was submitted to a three-judge Supreme Court bench headed by Chief Justice Anwar Zaheer Jamali. The commission was formed by the Supreme Court on 06 October 2016 to investigate the Aug 8 suicide attack on Quetta's Civil Hospital,

79 Dawn, 15 May 2016
80 Ibid
81 18 September 2016, the Guardian
82 On 26 October 2016, Pakistan conveyed to the US that Indian intelligence (RAW) and Afghanistan's National Directorate of Security (NDS) are patronizing terrorist groups to attack soft targets in the country.
83 Daily Times, On 27 October 2016
84 26 October 2016, Daily Times

in which at least 74 people, mostly lawyers, had lost their lives. The commission regretted that Interior Minister Chaudhry Nisar Ali Khan had on 21 October 2016 met Maulana Mohammad Ahmed Ludhianvi, the head of three banned organisations — Sipah-i-Sahaba Pakistan, Millat-i-Islamia and Ahle Sunnat Wal Jamaat — to listen to his demands and conceded to them as per media reports.

However, on 14 January 2017, Interior Minister Chaudhry Nisar Ali Khan said it was unfair to link everything to Ahle Sunnat Wal Jamaat (ASWJ) chief Maulana Ahmad Ludhianvi. Talking to media representatives in Kallar Syedan, a sub-district of Rawalpindi, he admitted that there were photographs of him meeting leaders of proscribed organizations. He countered the criticism coming from the Pakistan People's Party (PPP) by saying, "Which PPP leader did not meet leaders of proscribed organizations in their time?" He said that people with links to terrorist organizations had been eliminated or jailed, while those remaining had fled abroad, "but members of groups proscribed on sectarian grounds who have no case against them still resided in the country. "How is it fair to link everything to Maulana Ludhianvi?"[85]

On 15 January 2017, in his Dawn article, Muhammad Amir Rana hammered Pakistan's Interior Minister meeting with extremist groups: "State has to take constitutional, legal and security measures to deal with its enemies. But when our state functionaries appear to have lost the ability to recognize the enemy within us, it can be inferred that the enemy has accomplished its job. Interior Minister Chaudhry Nisar Ali Khan's refusal to classify sectarian organizations as terrorist groups—apparently to justify his controversial meeting with the leader of a banned group — reflects deep-rooted sectarian and ideological ambiguities that persist in state institutions as well as in the minds of our leaders".[86]

On 06 December 2016, Dawn reported National Security Adviser Lt Gen Nasir Khan Janjua conveyed a message to the US ambassador David Hale in a meeting. The meeting was held to discuss the terrorist attack on Police Training College Quetta, counter-terrorism operations and cross-border attacks. Mr. Janjua also emphasized on the need to break the nexus between terrorist groups operation under the supervision of NDS and RAW.[87] In October 2016, a terrorist attack on the police training academy in Quetta left 60 people dead, most

---

85 Daily Times, 14 January 2017, Interior Minister Chaudhry Nisar Ali Khan said it was unfair to link everything to Ahle Sunnat Wal Jamaat (ASWJ) chief Maulana Ahmad Ludhianvi. Talking to media representatives in Kallar Syedan, a sub-district of Rawalpindi, he admitted that there were photographs of him meeting leaders of proscribed organizations.

86 On 15 January 2017, in his Dawn article, Muhammad Amir Rana hammered Pakistan's Interior Minister meeting with extremist groups and hammered his stance

87 06 December 2016, Dawn reported National Security Adviser Lt Gen Nasir Khan Janjua conveyed a message to the US ambassador David Hale in a meeting.

of whom were young cadets. Before this, in August 2016, terrorists attacked the Civil Hospital in Quetta that killed 73 people, mostly young lawyers. However, Senators blame intelligence agencies over Quetta carnage.

On 08 August 2016, taking part in the debate of attack on Quetta's Civil Hospital that killed over 70 people, mostly lawyers, members of the upper house criticized the federal government for its alleged failure to implement the National Action Plan (NAP) against terrorism that had been announced after the 2014 assault on the Army Public School in Peshawar. The senators belonging to Baluchistan and Khyber Pakhtunkhwa took exception to the statements made by Army Chief Gen Raheel Sharif and Prime Minister Nawaz Sharif that the Quetta suicide bombing was basically an attack on the China-Pakistan Economic Corridor, saying "the project does not exist in the two provinces".[88]

Playing the Baluchistan card represented a big shift for India. Initially, Modi's election in 2014 prompted expectations that Delhi would take a much less conciliatory line with Pakistan. But, to the surprise of some, beginning with the invitation of Pakistan Prime Minister Nawaz Sharif to Modi's inauguration, the Modi government appeared relatively open to exploring approaches to reconciliation while several militant separatist groups supported by India are responsible for various attacks against Pakistani security forces and construction workers. In addition, Baluchistan has seen numerous attacks by Islamist militant groups, including the August bombing of the government hospital in the province's capital Quetta, which was carried out by Pakistani Taliban groups. Thousands of innocent men, women and children have died in this unjust, unfair and one-sided war launched by terrorists against Pakistan.

The emergence of Russia and China as economic and military powers changed the concept of political rapprochement and diplomatic mechanism in South and Central Asia. China is deeply involved in Afghanistan, while Russia wants to revive its old contacts in the country, and extend hand of friendship to Pakistan, exerting more pressure on the US and NATO forces to leave the country. Now, Russia has become a strong competitive stakeholder in Afghanistan by providing arms and training to its own Taliban group to dismantle the terrorist network of the Islamic State and form a new political alliance in the country.

Both China and Russia also established contacts with former communist leaders. Chinese and Russian Intelligence agencies are closely watching the operational mood of the ISIS and its collaboration with other terrorist organizations. They face multifaceted threats from the ISIS that trains Russian and Chinese Muslims in Afghanistan. In Moscow conference, President Putin special representative warned: "There are several camps operated by Islamic State in Afghanistan

---

88 08 August 2016, Dawn

that train people from Central Asia and some regions of Russia....
The rise of Islamic State in Afghanistan is a high priority threat. He
also added that there is a wide national variety of instructors in those
camps".

On 11 August 2015, Express Tribune reported Inspector General of
Frontier Corps (FC) Baluchistan Major General Sher Afgan said that
spy agencies including India's Research and Analysis Wing (RAW)
and Afghanistan's National Directorate of Security (NDS) were
fuelling terrorism in Baluchistan to destabilize Pakistan. Talking
to journalists at FC Headquarters, he said there had been a sharp
decline in incidents of terrorism in Baluchistan following the targeted
operation of security forces against terrorists. He added that the
operation might continue till terrorism is eliminated. "The incidents
are comparatively less than last year," he said. "Besides the Kalat and
Turbat incidents, there were no major incidents of terrorism that
took place; neither any railway track nor train was attacked."[89]

However, India which has already invested billions of dollars
in Afghanistan, signed a wide-ranging strategic agreement with
that country on 05 October 2011. It also included the training of
Afghan security forces, while assisting Kabul in diversified projects.
Apparently, it is open strategic agreement, but secretly, India seeks
to further strengthen its grip in Afghanistan to get strategic depth
against Islamabad. Besides, with the cooperation of Afghan President
Hamid Karzai and Afghan intelligence-National Directorate of
Security (NDS) and with the tactical assistance of American CIA and
Israeli MOSSAD, RAW has well-established anti-Pakistan espionage
network in Afghanistan. India is also in collusion with the Balochi
separatist leaders who took shelter in Afghanistan.

For example, on July 23, 2008, in an interview with the BBC from
Afghanistan, Brahmdagh Bugti stated that they "have the right to
accept foreign arms and ammunition from anywhere including India."
The RAW has quite often been blamed by Pakistani law-enforcement
agencies for being involved in subversive activities in Pakistan.
Pakistani military leadership often raised the issue of activities of
foreign governments and intelligence agencies in Pakistan. Former
army chief Gen Sharif during a visit to Quetta on April 15 warned:
"foreign governments and intelligence agencies" against their
involvement in the insurgency in Baluchistan, but on that occasion he
did not explicitly name RAW.[90]

---

89 On 11 August 2015, *Express Tribune* reported Inspector General of Frontier
Corps (FC) Baluchistan Major General Sher Afgan said that spy agencies
including India's Research and Analysis Wing (RAW) and Afghanistan's
National Directorate of Security (NDS) were fuelling terrorism in Baluchistan
to destabilize Pakistan.
90 The military leadership often raised the issue of activities of foreign
governments and intelligence agencies in Pakistan. Army Chief Gen Raheel
Sharif during a visit to Quetta on April 15 warned "foreign governments and

Pakistan got a firm stance against RAW's activities in Baluchistan and Afghanistan, where at a meeting by the Corps Commander, held at the General Headquarters on 5 May 2016, General Raheel Sharif accused RAW of supporting terrorism in Pakistan. Foreign Secretary Aizaz Ahmad Chaudhry, also spotlighted the RAW involvement in various terrorist activities and said the matter had been taken up a number of times with India, through diplomatic channels. Chinese authorities also disclosed that RAW intends to sabotage the China-Pakistan Economic Corridor (CPEC). Pakistan is a traditional enemy of India, but the country leadership never thought about the terror network of their agencies inside Afghanistan.[91]

The ISI told its government that the harassment of Pakistani officials in Afghanistan started after President Ashraf Ghani, Chief Executive Dr Abdullah Abdullah and the NDS blamed Pakistan for the deadly terrorist attacks in Kabul and the rest of the country. Pakistan strongly condemned the attacks, but Afghan authorities claimed that ISI was behind these attacks. On August 23, Afghan Ambassador Janan Mosazai was told by the Foreign Office in Islamabad to ensure the safety and security of Pakistan embassy officials and nationals in Afghanistan. On 26 March 2016, in his article published in the Wire, Manoj Joshi explained the strategic interests of India in Pakistan and Afghanistan, and the some facts about the arrested Indian agent in Pakistan:

> India has important strategic interests in Pakistan, including in the Baluchistan region. Baluchistan is of interest principally because of the stepped up naval activities of the Chinese in Gwadar and the plans for the China-Pakistan Economic Corridor. For the past two decades, India has made no secret of its activities in Iranian Baluchistan. It has sought to develop the port of Chabahar for alternative routes to Afghanistan and Central Asia. It has used its consulate in Zahedan, which is near the Pakistan border, to keep an eye on Pakistani activity there and support Indian interests. All this is done, of course, under the watchful eyes of the Iranian authorities who, no doubt, have their red-lines on what the Indians can do and what they cannot. Looking at the case of Commander (retired) Kulbhushan Jadhav, the arrested India man that Pakistan says is a 'RAW officer', it is worthwhile recalling the legendary CIA counter-intelligence officer James Jesus Angleton's description of intelligence craft as "a wilderness of mirrors." Finding out where the truth lies is next to impossible, and reality is what you want to believe.[92]

---

intelligence agencies" against their involvement in the insurgency in Baluchistan, but on that occasion he did not explicitly name RAW. *Dawn* 31 March 2016
91 On August 23, Afghan Ambassador Janan Mosazai was told by the Foreign Office in Islamabad to ensure the safety and security of Pakistan embassy officials and nationals in Afghanistan. *The news*, September 20, 2015
92 *The Wire*, On 26 March 2016 Manoj Joshi

On 11 May 2015, the News International reported Indian spy agency, Research and Analysis Wing (RAW) established yet another desk with a special allocation of a huge sum of money at its headquarters on Lodhi Road, New Delhi, to scuttle the China-Pakistan Economic Corridor (CPEC). Rajinder Khanna, the Chief of the agency, was personally supervising the desk as he reports to Prime Minister Narendra Modi directly and seeks instructions from him. The newspaper reported.[93]

Pakistani authorities said the war on terror concreted the way for India to conduct clandestine operations. These stealthy terrorist activities in Pakistan were being conducted in conjunction with Afghan-India Intelligence agency RAMA (Riyast-i-Amoor-o-Amanat-i-Milliyah). The RAW is using Afghan soil for carrying out massive terrorist activities against Pakistan. Daily *Dawn* reported three arrested militants of Tehrik-i-Taliban Pakistan namely Khurram Ishtiaq, Ghulam Mustafa and Shamim disclosed that RAW was funding suicide bomb attacks in Pakistan and that the Indian intelligence agency channelled Rs680 million through its links with the Afghan secret agency, RAMA.[94]

Pakistani newspapers were spreading misunderstanding about the role of India in Afghanistan, while Afghan government and its intelligence agencies have long standing worries that Pakistani intelligence (ISI) have been carrying out operation inside Afghanistan through Afghan Taliban since 2004. This was further confirmed by many reports and books recently published in the United Kingdom. Writer Sandy Gall (2012) in his book elucidated the ISI involvement in Afghanistan, and noted the allegations of Afghanistan that ISI had been recruiting fighters and suicide bombers for the Afghan Taliban among the 1.7 million registered and 1–2 million unregistered Afghan refugees living in refugee camps and settlements along the Afghan-Pakistan border in Pakistan, many of whom have lived there since the Soviet war in Afghanistan.

An Afghan refugee living in Pakistan revealed that ISI once asked him to either receive training to join the Afghan Taliban or to leave the country. He explains: "It is a step by step process. First they come, they talk to you. They ask you for the information.... Then gradually they ask you for people they can train and send [to Afghanistan].... They say, 'Either you do what we say, or you leave the country. Another Afghan refugee, Mr. Janat Gul, told the UN Office for the Coordination of Humanitarian Affairs, that Afghan refugees which had been successfully recruited by the ISI were taken to Pakistani training camps which had previously been used during the times of the Soviet war in Afghanistan.

93 *The News*, 11 May 2015
94ARY *News* Blog: Indian RAW-sponsored terrorism in Pakistan, Dr. Iqtidar Cheema, 11 June 2014 http://blogs.arynews.tv/indian-RAW-sponsored-terrorism-pakistan/

On 24 June 2015, *Dawn* reported Afghanistan's intelligence service warned that an ISI officer helped the Taliban carry out an attack on parliament. Afghan intelligence services spokesman Hassib Sediqqi said that the officer in Inter-Services Intelligence helped the Haqqani network carry out the attack outside parliament in Kabul, which killed two people and wounded more than 30 as lawmakers were meeting inside. Mr. Sediqqi said the suicide car bomb used in attack was manufactured in Peshawar, adding that Afghan authorities were made aware of the attack on June 10 and had deployed extra security.[95]

Afghan intelligence warned that Pakistan used terrorists as proxies to counter India's growing influence in Afghanistan, according to a set of documents released by WikiLeaks from the hacked personal email account of Central Intelligence Agency (CIA) director, John Brennan. The documents released by the whistle-blower website contained reports on Afghanistan and Pakistan, and also ideas for US policy towards Iran. Three days after Barack Obama was elected US President in November 2008, Mr. Brennan wrote to him in a position-cum- strategy paper that Pakistan uses the Taliban to counter India in Afghanistan. "Pakistan's desire to counter India's growing influence in Afghanistan and concerns about US long-term commitments to Afghanistan increase Pakistan's interest in hedging its bets by ensuring that it will be able to have a working relationship with the Taliban to balance Indian and Iranian interests if the US withdraws." Mr. Brennan wrote on 07 November 2008.

At that time, Mr. Brennan was a top foreign policy and counter-terrorism adviser to President Obama, administration. Mr. Brennan was in the running to be CIA Director, but the post, however, went to Leon Panetta. In January 2013, President Obama nominated Mr. Brennan as CIA Director. His views on Pakistan were disclosed in a 13-page executive summary of key findings and recommendations on Afghanistan and Pakistan. Mr. Brennan, in the summary, said efforts in the Federally Administered Tribal Areas (FATA) had been challenged by Pakistan's ambivalence and perhaps outright support for, the Taliban. "While the US Intelligence Community differs on the extent of the relationships, at least some elements of Pakistan's military and intelligence services appear to be ambivalent about the anti-Taliban and anti-militant mission in the FATA, in part due to their history of close ties to the Taliban in Afghanistan's conflict with the Soviet Union and Pakistan's use of militant proxies in its conflict with India," he wrote.

A new document, made public by the nongovernmental National Security Archive at George Washington University claimed that an "unidentified" Pakistani intelligence officer paid $200,000 to the Haqqani network to carry out a suicide attack on a U.S. Central Intelligence Agency (CIA) base in eastern Afghanistan in 2009. The Haqqani network is a militant group active on both sides of

95 On 24 June 2015, *Dawn*

the Pakistan-Afghanistan border and is closely linked with the Taliban. The attack occurred at Forward Operating Base Chapman in Afghanistan's Khost province on December 30, 2009, and was carried out by a Jordanian double agent loyal to militants affiliated with al-Qaeda, Humam Khalil al-Balawi. Seven people working with or for the CIA died, making the attack the second-deadliest ever incident in CIA history.[96]

Former Chief of Army Staff General Raheel Sharif, speaking at the Peace and Prosperity seminar said that Indian intelligence agency RAW was actively involved in destabilizing Pakistan. "Hostile intelligence agencies are averse to China-Pakistan Economic Corridor (CPEC)," said the chief of army staff. "Let me make it clear that we will not allow anyone to create impediments and turbulence in any part of Pakistan", added General Raheel Sharif. He urged those involved in such activities to leave the approach of confrontation and focus on cooperation instead. Referring to CPEC as a corridor of peace and prosperity, he added that CPEC was the grand manifestation of the deep-rooted ties between China and Pakistan. General Raheel also touched upon the ongoing counter-insurgency operation, and acknowledged that Pakistan had come a long was in its struggle for stability and development.

"I take pride in mentioning the strong resolve and sacrifices offered by the people, intelligence and law enforcement agencies, and our gallant armed forces. "Operation Zarb-i-Azb is not just an operation, but a wholesome concept. It ultimately aims at breaking the syndicate of terrorism, extremism and corruption," emphasized referring to CPEC. "We look forward to the emergence of modern infrastructure, special economic zones, health facilities and universities which will bring enduring benefits for our people." He also emphasized on the sustainability of the project, which would only come with good management and transparency.[97]

Indian intelligence agency RAW established a special cell at its Headquarters in New Delhi to sabotage China-Pakistan Economic Corridor (CPEC) project, and the plan was executed via Afghanistan, said Pakistan's Secretary of Defense Gen (retd) Alam Khattak. "RAW and Afghan NDS have launched joint secret operations against Pakistan by using three Indian consulates in Jalalabad, Kandahar and Mazar e Sharif," Khattak said. "The three consulates in Afghanistan are providing weapons, money, training and other logistical support to agents for subversive activities in FATA, Baluchistan and Karachi," Khattak added. Secretary of Defense flanked by senior Defense officials

---

96*A new document*, National Security Archive at George Washington University, claimed that an unidentified Pakistani intelligence officer paid $200,000 to the Haqqani network to carry out a suicide attack on CIA base in Afghanistan.
97 *Dawn* 12 April 2016

was briefing Senate Defense committee which met at Parliament House.[98]

On 25 June 2015, Express Tribune reported Pakistan Foreign Office dismissed Afghan intelligence claims that an officer of Pakistan's spy agency, the Inter-Services Intelligence, and the Haqqani Network were involved in the attack on the Afghan parliament. Afghanistan's intelligence agency, the National Directorate of Security (NDS), alleged that the brazen attack on the parliament building in Kabul was planned in Peshawar. "We reject these allegations. These allegations have been levelled against ISI and its officers in the past as well," Foreign Ministry spokesperson Qazi Khalilullah said.[99]

However, on 13 February 2015, Dawn reported Mr. Musharaf's interview with the Guardian in which he said that during his tenure as the head of state, Pakistan had tried to undermine the government of former Afghan president Hamid Karzai because Karzai had helped "India stab Pakistan in the back." However, the former army chief was of the view that the time had come to fully cooperate with Afghan President Ashraf Ghani Ahmadzai who he believed was the last hope for peace in the region. Mr. Musharaf revealed that: "Obviously we were looking for some groups to counter this Indian action against Pakistan, Definitely they were in contact, and they should be. In President Karzai's times, yes, indeed, he was damaging Pakistan and therefore we were working against his interest. Obviously we had to protect our own interest," Musharraf said.[100]

98 Dawn 14, 04, 2016
99 25 June 2015, Express Tribune
100 13 February 2015, Dawn

Chapter 7 National Directorate of Security (NDS) and India's Intelligence War in Pakistan and Afghanistan

The nexus between India's Research and Analysis Wing (RAW) and Afghanistan's National Directorate of Security (NDS) has been a permanent source of tension for Islamabad since 2001. In January 2017, After the Kabul and Kandahar attacks, some Afghan experts viewed it as foreign intelligence-led attacks-facilitated by some wolves within the Unity Government, some affixed to sweeping generalization that Russian and Chinese intelligence agencies are behind it, and some blamed Pakistan based Quetta Shura and the Haqqani network for their involvement. Islamabad rejected the Kabul's claims about militant safe havens in the Federally Administrated Tribal Areas; Pakistan's Foreign Office Spokesman Nafees Zakaria said his country did not allow its territory to be used for attacks against any other country.

"Afghanistan was infested with many terrorist organizations due to instability there, which created space for the terrorist elements such as Haqqani network's leadership, Tehrik-e-Taliban Afghanistan, Tehrik-e-Taliban Pakistan, Daesh, Al-Qaeda, Jamaatul Ahraar, etc. It is, therefore, not appropriate to blame others for the adversities due to the deteriorating security situation in Afghanistan. The oft-repeated claims about safe havens are, therefore, more of rhetoric than anything else," he said. The spokesperson said: "Pakistan remains committed to peace efforts in Afghanistan as it is not only in the interest of the region but more importantly, Pakistan. It is unfortunate that our sincere efforts towards stability in Afghanistan are being maligned."[101]

---

101 The News International, Islamabad 14 January 2017, Pakistan expressed concern over the nexus of Afghan and Indian spy agencies for militancy inside Pakistan. "We wish to re-emphasize that some foreign elements are exploiting the situation and using the Afghan soil against Pakistan, in particular, and the region, at large. The activities of Indian RAW and NDS nexus remains a matter of deep concern to Pakistan", said the Foreign Office spokesman.

Chief Minister Baluchistan Nawab Sanaullah Zehri sternly criticized Indian intelligence agency 'Research and Analysis Wing' (RAW) and Afghanistan's spy agency 'National Directorate of Security' (NDS) for providing funds to anti state-elements in Pakistan. While talking to delegations in Quetta, Zehri said that geographical and strategic importance of Baluchistan and Gwadar port were thorn in enemy's sides. However, in his Independence Day speech, Indian Prime Minister Narendra Modi accused Pakistan of sponsoring terrorism and committing rights abuses in its Baluchistan province.

In this chapter, I want to spotlight some important fact of India's intelligence war in Afghanistan and Pakistan, which caused hostilities, fatalities, and mistrust between the two neighboring states. Before going to the real argument, I want to describe some facts of the failures and incompetency of Indian intelligence agencies during the last three decades. There have been tenacious efforts in India to introduce security sector reforms in order to bring intelligence agencies under democratic control, and streamline its networks across the border, but notwithstanding the last reform proposals of the Naresh Chandra Committee report (2012), democratic governments in the country failed to bill the cat. Since the end of the cold war and the disintegration of Soviet Union in 1990s, internal conflicts in the country deeply impacted the performance of its intelligence mechanism, where terrorist groups introduced new tactics, which were new to RAW and Intelligence Bureau.[102]

The three decades fight of Research and Analysis Wing (RAW) and the IB with domestic separatism and international terrorism brought about many changes in the attitude of its stakeholders and policy makers, to control their self designed operational strategies that caused misunderstanding between India and its neighbors. In states, like Kashmir, Orissa, Chhattisgarh, Jharkhand, and Assam, several separatist and terrorist groups emerged with new tactics, while the recent Patankot terrorist attacks generated a new debate about the failed strategies, weak security approach, and power politics within the intelligence infrastructure. These and other incidents showed that intelligence review committees, reports and political parties were right in their criticism against the operational flaws of the agencies.[103]

The operational incompetence of the Indian intelligence has now become legendary as it failed to defend the country during the Kargil, Mumbai and Pathankot attacks. They even get away from violence infected regions such as Kashmir and Assam. This way of intelligence mechanism raised many questions including the waste of money and resources. The involvement of Indian intelligence agencies in Afghanistan, Bangladesh and Nepal, generated controversial debate in print and electronic media. In Afghanistan, there are speculations that Indian intelligence use the country against Pakistan, recruit Afghans

102 The crisis of Indian Intelligence, Daily Times, 06 September 2016
103 Ibid, 09 September 2016, Sri Lankan Guardian

and Pakistanis to carryout terrorist attacks in Baluchistan, and further its national interests. Afghan military and political leadership has often expressed the same concern in their private meetings that their country serves the interests of India in the region.[104]

The two-decade experience of the country with terrorism has brought out what in another area is called the "last mile problem". In States of the North-east, in Maoist-affected Orissa, Chattisgarh and Jharkhand and other states of the Union affected by terrorism, the big weakness is the quality of local policing and intelligence gathering. This is an area where reform ideas can be mooted by the Union government, but their adoption and implementation requires the States to come on board, and this is where they are most reluctant.[105]

Terror attacks, whether in Assam or Kashmir have exacerbated by the day, which lead policy maker to the conclusion that the involvement of intelligence agencies in a proxy wars across borders causes major terror-related incident in the country. Amidst all these failures and incomplete intelligence stories, Prime Minister Narendra Modi decided to bring his own team of experts, in order to introduce security sector reforms and bring intelligence under democratic control, but he also needs to understand the difficulties faced by his precursors.[106]

He also needs to find out why RAW and the IB lack cryptanalysts who break enemy codes and ciphers despite India's aggrandizement in the field of computer technologies. This deficit is in stark contrast to the regional trends, where state agencies have been hiring ever-greater number of experts. In his Indian Express article (2014) Praveen Swami noted: "India's over five-year efforts to monitor encrypted traffic-run by the mainly military-staffed National Technical Research Organization-has failed to make progress in decrypting even chat programs used by terrorists, like Viber and Skype".[107]

The Kargil Review Committee found that human intelligence aspect of Indian intelligence agencies was weak. During the Kargil war, RAW succeeded in intercepting the telephone conversation between General Pervez Musharaf and his Chief of General Staff Lt Gen Aziz, which provided crucial evidence to international media that terrorist operation was being controlled from military headquarters in Rawalpindi. Experts perceive it a major intelligence success, but the Kargil Review Committee also criticized military intelligence for its failure related to the absence of update and accurate intelligence information on the induction and de-induction of military battalions,

---

104 Ibid
105 Maoist Movement in India: An Overview, Sandeep Kumar Dubey, 06 August 2013, Institute of Defense Studies and Analysis.
106 Policy Report No. 3: Why Intelligence Fails, Janani Krishnaswamy, The Hindu Centre for Politics and Public Policy, 2013
107 Indian Express article (2014) Praveen Swami

and the lack of expertise to spotlight military battalions in the Kargil area in 1998.[108]

The committee further criticized the lack of fresh information, which make impossible for an intelligence agency to make accurate judgment of the looming threat. According to Indian intellectual circles, rivalry among the intelligence agencies, the issue of appointment in war zones, or violence infected areas has badly affected the counterterrorism efforts across the country. In a country like India, where credit snatching influences intelligence analysis, there is no way to judge the accuracy of collected intelligence information.[109]

Any intelligent state that wants to prevent its system from decaying needs statecraft, which is comprised on economic power, professional intelligence, strong military and mature diplomacy. The case is quite different in India where emerging contradictions in the state system, and the failure of intelligence and internal security strategies generated a countrywide debate in which experts deeply criticized the waste of financial resources by the Indian intelligence agencies in an unnecessary proxy war against Pakistan. India is spending huge amount of money on its secret agencies to make them competent and professional, but the lack of authentic information, trained manpower, intelligence sharing on law enforcement level, and between centre and provinces, and political involvement, vanish all sincere efforts.

The Kargil and Pathankot attacks were intelligence failure because the RAW's recruitment procedure was deeply odd that could not spotlight ISI's intelligence units' activities in parts of the region. Intelligence reforms become the most controversial issue as reform committees were under pressure from political parties to procrastinate the reforms process. In fact, the challenges India faces to control its intelligence agencies, and introduce security sector reforms have become more complicated when stakeholders refused to change the culture of spying on their own people. India is fully involved in Afghanistan. From military planning to intelligence operations, and foreign policy issues, the country interfere in every legal and political issue of the state. Afghan policy makers perceive such interference of the Indian government in a failed state like Afghanistan, and its proxy war against its traditional enemy, against the interest of the country.[110]

Reaction to the RAW and NDS clandestine operations are too irksome for the Afghan population when Pakistan translates its inner pain into military, trade and economic action. However the extension of its intelligence operations over a large area across the country

---

108 Policy Report No. 3: Why Intelligence Fails, Janani Krishnaswamy, the Hindu Centre for Politics and Public Policy, 2013
109 Ibid
110 After Uri, a look at why intelligence failures happen, By Pradip R Sagar, Indian Express, 24 September 2016

raises many questions including the large scale recruitment of young men and women in its secret training camps. Moreover, India has changed the interface of relationship from all Afghan nations to a specific mafia groups in Northern parts of the country, which causes ethnic conflagration. The country's approach towards the Afghan nation has largely been a function of the desire to undermine the political and military influence of Pakistan, China and Iran. In view of the exponentially growing Taliban and ISIS military power in Afghanistan, Washington also showed propensity to use the services of Indian satellite in Afghanistan to get quicker weather information, crucial for the transportation of its military assets.

Pakistani politicians and intelligentsia raised the question of financing terrorism in Pakistan from Afghanistan. They believed that RAW provides arms and military training to TTP and Baluch insurgents, while Afghans were thinking on the same line that India was fighting its own proxy war against Pakistan, which is against the interests of their country. This useless clandestine war of the Indian intelligence in Afghanistan forced Pakistan's military establishment to translate it anger into action.[111]

On 13 February 2015, former military dictator Gen Pervez Musharaf admitted that during his tenure Pakistan had tried to undermine the Karzai government due to his propensity towards India. This statement deeply impacted the heart and mind of those Afghans who view Pakistan as a friendly neighbor, but understand that everything is not going on right direction in their own country.[112]

Pakistan's Foreign Office accused India of financing terrorism in the country, while on 03, 09 2016, former Interior Minister Rehman Malik blamed India for fomenting unrest in Baluchistan.[113] However, on his turn, Pakistan's Army Chief Gen Raheel Sharif warned that his army was fully aware of India's nefarious designs. Making special mention of Prime Minister Modi and his intelligence agency, RAW, Gen Raheel warned that armed forces were fully capable to defend their country. "We don't care what the world says, but we are fighting for our survival", he said. Pakistani politicians, clerics and government officials in their statements raised the issue of the collaboration of Indian and Afghan intelligence agencies that reached to an alarming level.[114]

This collaboration became bigger hindrance that prevented the collaboration between the Inter Services Intelligence (ISI) and National Directorate of Security (NDS) in 2015 and 2016. Pakistan's Defence Secretary also spotlighted RAW's special cell in New Delhi to sabotage China Pakistan Economic Corridor (CPEC) project via

111 The crisis of Indian Intelligence, Daily Times, 06 September 2016
112 The Guardian, 13 February 2015
113 03, 09 2016, former Interior Minister Rehman Malik blamed India for fomenting unrest in Baluchistan, Daily Times
114 Ibid

Afghanistan. General Khattak claimed that RAW and NDS launched joint secret operation using Jalalabad, Kandahar and Mazar-e-Sharif's Indian Consulates. "The three consulates in Afghanistan are providing weapons, money, training and other logistic support to agents for subversive activities in FATA, Baluchistan and Karachi", Gen Khattak said.[115]

This way of helping rebuild Afghanistan by India and Pakistan is absurd and destructive. Pakistan attacks Indian positions in Kashmir while India target army and civilian in Khyber Pakhtunkhawa and Baluchistan. This traditional rivalries between the two states deeply impacted peace process in Afghanistan. With the instruction of the United States, former Afghan President left no stone unturned to make Afghanistan as an India colony in the name of strategic partnership. The NDS took the country into the RAW laps for its own interests. Now, the RAW is using the war torn state for its terrorist operations inside Baluchistan.

On 03 January 2017, Indian army chief in his first interview with NDTV said that surgical strike against Pakistan was necessary. "We have done one surgical strike in PoK. But if we have to do something again, we will do it in a different manner and different style," Gen Rawat said. "We'll surprise the enemy." The Indian army, he explained, was closely watching terrorist movements in the restive Kashmir valley.[116] However, on 04 January 2017, Minister of State for the Ministry of External Affairs V K Singh said the aim of surgical strikes was to send a stern message to Pakistan that India will not accept continued terrorism as new normal.[117]

Speaking at Ministry of External Affairs' mid-term press conference, Singh said, "The aim of surgical strike was to convey to Pakistan that we will not accept continuance of terrorism as the new norm. Our own good faith has been amply demonstrated time and again through repeated initiatives to normalize the relationship. However, as we have often stated, talks and terror cannot go together."

On 06 January 2017, Dawn reported Pakistan's Permanent Representative to the United Nations, Ambassador Maleeha Lodhi, delivered a dossier on India's interference and terrorism in Pakistan, to UN Secretary-General Antonio Guterres, along with a letter from Sartaj Aziz, Adviser to Prime Minister on Foreign Affairs. The dossier was consisted of additional information and proof of Indian intelligence interference in Pakistan and involvement in terrorism—particularly in Baluchistan, FATA and Karachi. In the covering letter sent with the dossier, Sartaj Aziz noted that the arrest of Indian RAW

115 RAW runs special cell to sabotage CPEC, says secretary defence, 14 April 2016

116 On 03 January 2017, Indian army chief in his first interview with NDTV said that surgical strike against Pakistan was necessary.

117 On 04 January 2017, Minister of State for the Ministry of External Affairs V K Singh said the aim of surgical strikes was to send a stern message to Pakistan that India will not accept continued terrorism as new normal

agent Kulbhushan Jadhav from Baluchistan and his confessional statement admitting involvement in activities aimed at destabilizing Pakistan, and support to terrorist elements vindicated Pakistan's longstanding position about India's involvement in such activities.[118]

India was carrying out these activities in clear contravention of the UN Charter and the resolutions of the UN Security Council on counter-terrorism and international conventions on terrorism. "India's hostile intentions towards Pakistan were also borne out by recent statements of its political and military leadership." The adviser added that Pakistan had made a major contribution to global counter terrorism efforts and secured significant gains in its domestic fight against terrorism. "This achievement had come at a great national cost including the lives lost of thousands of civilians and security forces personnel. India's actions threatened to undermine these gains," the UN chief was told.[119]

However, President Ghani in his India visit condemned the sponsor of terrorism by Pakistan. He also threatened the blockage of Pakistan's transit route to Central Asia to show his propensity to the Modi government. In fact his artificial government failed to address the outstanding security challenged, while the nation lost trust over his government. His administration caught in many political and legal crises, and has no crystal clear policy that could improve security across the country. President Ghani did not raise the issue of military assistance with the Indian Prime Minister. Political observer believe that the United States and India fear that providing sophisticated weapons to the Afghan factional army, may possibly fall in the hands of Taliban and ISIS.

The involvement of Indian, Afghan and Pakistani intelligence agencies in the ongoing proxy war prompted the emergence of several ethno-terrorist organization that pose serious challenges to the national security of the three states. To counter these violent groups, multilateral intelligence cooperation can be a new light while this way of cooperation gives nations courage to tackle their national security challenges. The emergence of ISIS and Taliban and their suicide attacks against military and civilian installations forced Pakistan and Afghanistan to consider and develop new working relationship, but unfortunately, the changing foreign policy approach of the Afghan unity government vanished all efforts.

The recent violent bray of the Afghan and Indian leaders about the terrorist infiltration from Pakistan before and after the Uri attacks, received no positive response in print and electronic media in South

---

118 On 06 January 2017, Dawn reported Pakistan's Permanent Representative to the United Nations, Ambassador Maleeha Lodhi, delivered a dossier on India's interference and terrorism in Pakistan, to UN Secretary-General Antonio Guterres, along with a letter from Sartaj Aziz, Adviser to Prime Minister on Foreign Affairs.
119 Ibid

Asia, due to their own sponsorship of various terrorist and extremist outfits. The three heads hydra (RAW, RAMA, NDS) has now become out of control and biting every section of Afghan society, supporting insurgents, warlords, TTP, and exporting terrorism across the borders. India is basically operating in Afghanistan through RAW, IB, RAMA, NDS, and Defense Intelligence Agency (DIA) but most of the times the country failed to assess internal adversaries in the country. It funds propaganda machines in the country, which continue to ignite the fire of ethnicity and sectarianism in Afghanistan.

Major portion of funds it has allocated to the intelligence operations was being spent on recruiting young soldiers for jihad in Baluchistan. The unity government intelligence agencies were following the same streak. However, if we look at the performance and deficiencies of the Afghan unity government, we will find some harsh realities. The irony is that the ANA commanders, members of parliament, police commanders, and intelligence agencies purvey arms and ammunition to Taliban, ISIS and transport suicide bombers to their destination in their luxurious vehicles day and night. Afghans are absolutely exhausted with the long term insecurity, unemployment and interference of foreign agencies in the internal affairs of their country. Politicians and parliamentarians recently raised the question of government support to the ISIS and Taliban groups in their debates. Military and intellectual circles have also raised the question of Indian intelligence sponsorship of terrorism across the border. The country channels huge funds to some ethnic groups and war criminals to turn Afghanistan into its formal or informal colony in order to control foreign and domestic policies of the country.

India did not stop here; the country uses Afghanistan against China and Pakistan by establishing a commando force to disrupt the Pak-China economic corridor. This overt and covert war cannot succeed as the ISI's "S" branch is in full control of the networks of extremist organizations within India, but the fact of the matter is that ISI is facing numerous challenges in its own country. The ISI's sphere of influence and its source of information have badly shrunk due to some of its wrongly designed strategies in its own country.

The interference of India in Afghanistan is too irksome for Pakistan as the country has often asked Afghanistan to restrain Indian intelligence from using its soil, and also accused India of fuelling insurgency in Baluchistan. Pakistani officials understand that Indian intelligence agencies are operating through a network of Indian diplomatic mission dotting Southern and Eastern parts of Afghanistan where training camps of Baloch insurgent are located. India denied the accusations and said it helps to stabilize Afghanistan. The blame game further exacerbated when Baluchistan's Police Chief Muhammad Amlish criticized RAW and NDS for their terrorist activities in the province. The blame-game between Pakistan, India and Afghanistan created the atmosphere of distrust.

The so called unity government in Afghanistan lost confidence and legitimacy. In September and October 2016, more than 15,000 Afghan army soldiers and officers deserted due to the non-payment of their three months salaries from the Defense Ministry. In Aruzgan province, the same policy was repeated. Consequently, the police and military commanders sold more than 150 military check posts and weapons at the hands of Taliban and received million dollars and gifts.

No one is safe in the failing state; everyone is trying to leave the country. Businessmen are on the run, while women and children are being incarcerated by Taliban and Daesh forces and use them as a human shield against the ANA. Corruption is rampant and justice is expansive. Nepotism and warlordism is all times high while 70% of the state and government affairs are being run online because most of the Minister and officials live abroad or use face book to monitor the situation. Police and military commanders facilitate Taliban and Daesh fighter in attacks against the army and police convoys. On 03 July 2016, Tolonews reported the investigation of 10 important Police commander over the attack that targeted a convoy of police recruits in Kabul.

For Russia and China, one of the leading security challenges is the aggravation of war in Afghanistan, where crisis phenomena continue to grow. The most violent threat is posed by the exponentially growing influence of ISIS Khorasan group in the country that controls more than 70 districts, where it trains and equips fighters from Chinese and Russian Central Asia. These political and strategic developments forced Russia and China to reactivate their policies towards Afghanistan in the political and military spheres.

Moscow and Beijing are trying to deploy more intelligence units from Badakhshan to swat region, and from Gilgit-Baltistan to Tajikistan to intercept the infiltration of the ISIS terrorists into Central Asia. However, the altercation of Afghanistan and the rise of Daesh group is a part of Russia's relations with the United States where competition between the two powers has been accompanied by partial cooperation. Having realized security threat from the ISIS and the expansion of NATO eastwards, President Putin organized an Afghan Taliban group—funded and adorned with modern weapons on the one hand, and reincarnated KGB, and merged all domestic and foreign intelligence agencies into one agency (MGB) on the other. This process was named the reorganization and reinvention of intelligence infrastructure.

On September 19 2016, newspapers reported a potentially massive reorganization among Russian security and intelligence services. The reorganization would combine the FSB, SVR and FSO into a new "Ministry of State Security," or MGB. The MGB was the name of Josef Stalin's intelligence agency and secret police force from 1946 to 1953 and the predecessor to the KGB—an ominous historical throwback. The MGB will strengthen Putin's personal control and solidify the system he created. An article in Politico.eu says that the new MGB, which recycles a name used for the Soviet intelligence agency from 1946 to 1953, will eventually employ 250,000 people, as many as the old KGB at the height of its power, but no source is given for that information. While critics might see the proposal as another step in Russia's reconstruction of the totalitarian machinery of the Soviet Union, the MGB has the potential to become a monstrous power structure that will further restrict civil liberties in Russia.

Secret links between the Taliban, Northern Alliance and Russian intelligence are a matter of great concern for NATO and the Afghan government. The Russian government tried to reach every religious and political group, and warlords in the Afghan state institutions to persuade them that Russia was no longer a threat to the national security of Afghanistan. The country needs broader cooperation from Pakistan and Afghanistan in the fight against ISIS terrorists in Central Asia. On October 1, 2015, Afghan President Ashraf Ghani requested military equipment from Russia for the Afghan army.[120]

However, Russian envoy to Kabul, Zamir Kabulove admitted that Taliban's interests objectively coincide with Russian interests. This development was seen in Afghanistan as an intelligence success of Russian and failure of the CIA and Pentagon's modern surveillance and intelligence system. Afghan and the US policy makers are now increasingly worried that any deepening of ties between Taliban and Russian intelligence could further complicate security situation. The failure of US government to adopt a consistent policy on Pakistan and its military needs prompted deep discontent in relations between the two states.

The United States allowed India's civilian and military intelligence agencies to establish terror networks and training camps in Afghanistan. These terror networks recruited thousands Baloch insurgents to carry out attacks against Pakistan's security forces in Baluchistan province, which resulted in spoiling relations between Afghanistan and Pakistan. This unfriendly policy forced Pakistan to approach China and Russia for their support against the Indian aggression on its soil.

Thus, after four decades of hostility, Pakistan improved relations with Russia and signed important agreements with the country. However, Chinese intelligence also reinvented its old Afghan contacts. It approached Taliban leadership through Pakistan and retrieved the sympathy of Haqqani group inside Afghanistan. In 2015, Taliban and the Afghan government representative met in China to discuss the prospect of peace in the country. The involvement of Chinese intelligence in the Afghan theatre strengthened, and Beijing was involved in all peace talks. The involvement of Indian intelligence (RAW) in Afghanistan and its terror attacks inside Pakistan is seen

---

120 On 01 October 2015, Afghan President Ashraf Ghani requested military equipment from Russia for the Afghan army

in China as a great threat, as the country wants to complete the CPEC project within a peaceful environment.

This policy of the US and NATO allies towards Pakistan and Afghanistan prompted the emergence of Russia and China as competent stakeholders in the region. If we look at the performance of the US and NATO intelligence in Afghanistan, their operational mechanism has not been so successful during the last 15 years. Interestingly, the US says its intelligence network in Afghanistan is one of the largest in the world, but if we read the report of Major General Michael Flynn (2010), we can better judge the failures and successes of US intelligence in Afghanistan. Moreover, Russian intelligence specialists recently indicated that CIA has been unable to identify the actual aspect of rising threats in the country. The US and NATO intelligence agencies are preoccupied with information gathering, but they lacked processing skills and failed to provide vital general information about the insurgents' nests. They collect human intelligence information through espionage, but spies are unable to reach remote areas in Afghanistan. It means they gather information only from cities, while insurgents are based in villages and mountainous regions.

More than 15 years into the battlefield in Afghanistan, US intelligence agencies have only been marginally relevant to the fight against Taliban. They focused on information collection but failed to answer fundamental questions about the environment in which the US and NATO allies' agencies operated. They arrested countless people like farmers, shopkeepers, religious clerics and political workers, put them in prisons, tortured and humiliated, but these tactical intelligence approaches and wrongly designed strategies could not bring about changes in their minds. General Mike Flynn noted these and other challenges in his report:

"This problem and its consequences exist at every level of the US intelligence hierarchy, from ground operation up to headquarters in Kabul and the United States. At the battalion level and below, intelligence officers know a great deal about their local Afghan districts but are generally too understaffed to gather, store, disseminate, and digest the substantial body of crucial information that exists outside traditional intelligence channel. With insufficient number of analysts and guidance from commanders, battalion S-2 shops rarely gather, process, and write up quality assessment on countless items, such as census, and patrol briefs, minutes from Shuras with local farmers and tribal leaders, after-action reports from civil affairs officers and Provincial Reconstruction Teams (PRTs), polling data and atmosphere reports from psychological operations and female engagement teams, and translated summaries of radio broadcasts that influence local farmers, not to mention the field observations of Afghan soldiers, United Nation Officials, and non-governmental organizations (NGO)."[121]

121 Fixing Intel: A Blueprint for Making Intelligence Relevant in Afghanistan, By Major General Michael T. Flynn, USA Captain Matt Pottinger, USMC Paul D. Batchelor, DIA, January 2010

CHAPTER 8. AFGHAN SATELLITE STATE: INTELLIGENCE AND WEAK SECURITY APPROACH

In February 2016, the US Intelligence Chief admitted the failure of his agency in bringing peace and stability to Afghanistan. Former intelligence advisor to President Obama, James Clapper told the US Senate that the war-hit country was at serious risk. "Waning political cohesion, increasingly assertive local powerbrokers, financial shortfalls, and sustained countrywide Taliban attacks are eroding stability," Clapper said. In 2015, due to the high rate of desertion, Afghan police and army retreated from important check posts in Helmand. More than 34,000 police officers deserted due to the lack of weapons and logistic support. The failed and wrongly designed military operation strategies to eliminate Taliban groups further jeopardized the security of the country as a growing number of Pakistani sectarian groups continue to enter southern and eastern parts of Afghanistan.[122]

In the Heart of Asia Conference, the Afghan President raised the question of Pakistan's support to terrorist networks operating inside Afghanistan. The Unity Government was close to collapse due to internal ethnic and sectarian conflagration. There were speculations that the expanding periphery of violence in northern and southern parts of the country, and the lack of coordination between security forces and the police, and between the police and NDS meant that the staggering body of the government can any time collapse. However, wide-ranging differences between the two presidents also reached to the point of no return.[123]

---

122 *ToloNews* 10 February 2016
123 Challenges of the Afghan satellite state, in Afghanistan there are different national security and counterterrorism approaches, priorities and mechanism that contradict each other *Daily Times*, 09 April 2016

On 01 March 2016, Dr. Abdullah raised the question of citizen alienation from the state. He criticized President Ghani for his weak national security approach, and warned that the way government is tackling violence is ultimately wrong. Dr Abdullah pointed to the shrinking writ of the government in several parts in the north, where warlords and foreign-sponsored commanders of private militias did not accept the authority of the Kabul government. The performance of government has been poor in 2016; high-ranking officers from the police department and the ANA command openly criticized the Unity government for its failed war strategies.[124]

Politicians raised the question of coordination and a professional approach to national security. Coordination between government organs was in shambles; those who were appointed by Mr. Ghani did not accept Dr. Abdullah's instructions, and those who belonged to Dr. Abdullah's camp did not obey the orders of the President and Vice President General Abdul Rashid Dostum. Public confidence in government remained low. Contradiction in statements of army, intelligence, and police commanders and the presidential palace about the strength of Islamic State (ISIS) created a new conundrum. Afghan army denied the challenge of ISIS while President Ashraf Ghani conceded its strong presence in Afghanistan before the US Congress: "IS is already sending advance guards to southern and western Afghanistan to test our vulnerabilities." The government, in all, had failed to deliver security and support to both domestic and international investors. The Achilles heel was that Mr. Ghani warned that if the level of US forces did not increase, his government may possibly collapse.[125]

There were different national security and counterterrorism approaches, priorities and mechanism that contradicted each other. Majority of people in the northern parts of Afghanistan perceived the Taliban as a terrorist organization, while the Unity Government in Kabul perceived them as a political opposition. Interestingly, those who fought against the Taliban in northern, eastern and southern provinces were removed from their services by the Unity Government in 2015 and 2016. However, Special Advisor to President, Ahmad Zia Massoud and Dr Abdullah were against the Taliban, while the national security advisor supported the Taliban and ISIS groups. General Dostum said Taliban were a terrorist group, while the other group perceived them as political opposition. In Helmand, Urozgan and Kunar provinces, government ordered Afghan army commanders to leave their military posts to the Taliban. In Mazar-e-Sharif, Kunduz, Baghlan and Badakhshan provinces fight against the Taliban had intensified but government targeted specific forces.

On 16 May 2016, Afghanistan signed a draft agreement with the Hezb-e-Islami in a move the government hoped could lead to

124 Ibid
125 Ibid

a full peace accord with one of the most notorious war criminal in the insurgency. Hezb-e-Islami leader Mr. Gulbuddin Hekmatyar is a notorious war criminal who killed thousands in Kabul. Human rights groups have already accused his group of widespread abuses, particularly during civil war in the early 1990s. The United States also linked the group to al Qaeda and the Taliban and put the war criminal (Hekmatyar) on its designated terrorist list. Mohammad Khan (war criminal), deputy to Chief Executive Dr. Abdullah, said the draft accord was a positive step but more work was needed for a final deal. In 2003, the U.S. State Department included Mr. Hekmatyar on its terrorist list, accusing him of participating in and supporting attacks by al Qaeda and the Taliban.[126]

The basic responsibility of the Afghan government was to deliver education, security, good governance, and the requirements of critical national infrastructure, but unfortunately, the writ of the government was poorly existed in the provinces. Government was engaged in business with war criminals, and unnecessarily altered the nature of the state through the introduction of informal politics. In one of his Brooking Institute research paper, Robert I Robert spotlighted some aspects of weak and failed states:

> Weak states include a broad continuum of states that are: inherently weak because of geographical, physical, or fundamental economic constraints; basically strong, but temporarily or situational weak because of internal antagonism, management flaws, greed, despotism, or external attacks; and a mixture of the two. Weak states typically harbor ethnic, religious, linguistic, or other inter-communal tensions that have not yet, or not yet thoroughly, become overtly violent. Failed states are tense, deeply conflicted, dangerous, and contested bitterly by warring factions.[127]

The incompetency, insufficiency and state legitimacy had widely been discussed by Afghan media since the establishment of the Unity Government, but the illegitimate influence of warlords and war criminals in state institution, and policy-making process led to the disintegration of state institutions, which have been unable to deliver services to the citizens since 2015. The poppy cultivation has now become a part of traditional economy, which criminalized and containerized the whole financial market in Afghanistan.

Afghan politicians, military commanders and civil society expressed deep concern about the suspension of the Constitution by the unity government, which developed a negative political and military approach towards stability and governance challenges in the country. They criticized both the Presidents who acted ultra-vires and followed the streak of the road map provided to them by US

---

126 Ibid
127 Afghanistan Signs Draft Pact with HIA, *Daily Outlook Afghanistan*, May 19, 2016

Secretary of State John Kerry in 2014, which led the country towards anarchy, insecurity, mass migration and dismemberment. In dozens of remote districts and provinces, tribal leaders, MPs and members of local councils also refused to accept the unconstitutional acts of the unity government as both the Presidents allegedly promoted a foreign agenda, supported terrorism, and appointed their cronies on important posts, which they think was a clear violation of Article 66 of the Afghan constitution. However, President Ghani, while assuming office, took the following oath according to Article 63 of the Constitution:

> In the name of God, Most Gracious, Most Merciful, I swear by the name of God Almighty that I shall obey and protect the holy religion of Islam, respect and supervise the implementation of the Constitution as well as other laws, safeguard the independence, national sovereignty and territorial integrity of Afghanistan, and in seeking God Almighty's help and support of the nation, shall exert my efforts towards the prosperity and progress of the people of Afghanistan.[128]

Contrary to two important points of this article, Afghan lawyer Mr. Miftahuddin Haroon said that the president neither supervised the implementation of the Constitution, nor tried to provide food, economic and physical security to the people of Afghanistan. Having referred to the constitutional obligations of the president, legal experts argued: "In Article 64 of the Constitution, the President had to determine the fundamental lines of the policy of the country but he didn't, and also violated Article 150 of the Constitution as he didn't make draft proposals for the amendment in Constitution, and did not convene a Loya Jirga (Grand Assembly) through a presidential decree."[129]

From the very beginning, the two Presidents violated the Constitution and affixed to their ethnic and sectarian policies. Article 66 of the Constitution indicates: "During the term of office, the presidential position shall not be used for linguistic, sectarian, tribal and religious as well as party considerations," but President Ghani and Abdullah appointed their aids, ethnic and sectarian leaders, and war criminals who promote their own agendas. Under the terms of the John Kerry road map, Mr. Ghani was bound to share power with Dr Abdullah, and share key posts such as the police, governors, army, interior and foreign ministries. On December 24, 2014, President Ghani said no illegal act was acceptable but his way of governance was illegal. He also said that terrorists had no place in Afghanistan, but his Ministers and advisors provided sanctuaries to the Taliban and Islamic State (IS) leaders across the country.[130]

---

128 Afghan constitution, article 63
129 Afghan constitution, article 64
130 *Failed States Collapsed States, Weak States: Causes and Indicators.* Robert I Robert

The potential gains of the Taliban in Helmand, and ISIS in Jalalabad, Kunar and Nuristan, the capture of Kunduz, Sangin and parts of Badakhshan province, kidnapping for ransom, and the emergence of Taliban group in Paktika province, all raised serious questions over the legitimacy of the Unity Government and weakness of its intelligence agencies. Moreover, an Afghan army commander abruptly revealed that his office had confirmed information about the existence of 200 foreign militants in Kunduz city, and more than 3,000 militants in the entire province, where the Taliban established check points in villages and towns, and targeted Afghan forces. In 2015, the Taliban defeated the Afghan security forces and captured dozens of districts in various provinces, including the Kunduz. The UN report on civilians' deaths seemingly exposed the incompetence of the Afghan armed forces that could not defend the country. At least 3,545 people were killed and more than 7,457 injured in the year 2015, the report said.[131]

In its annual report on the Protection of Civilians in Armed Conflict (PCAC), the United Nations Assistances Mission in Afghanistan (UNAMA) warned that suicide attacks and fighting in cities and towns were the main causes behind collateral damage. Military experts in Kabul predicted that the coming spring war as being more brutal as ISIS is planning to dispatch more than 50,000 fighters to Afghanistan this year.[132]

As security continued to deteriorate, Afghan leaders became irritated and discontented about Pakistan's support to the Haqqani network, which kills Afghans on daily basis. For example, former President Sebghatullah Mujaddidi said: "The invaders destroyed Afghan cities, villages and all infrastructures in addition to killing and injuring millions of Afghans. Now, Allah may save us from our enemy Pakistan, which wants to kill our people in the name of the Taliban." Sometimes they threatened to declare jihad against Pakistan and sometimes they accused Pakistan army of invading and destroying Afghan cities, towns and villages, but they have never declared jihad against corruption, corrupt mafia groups and war criminals that have killed and kidnapped thousands of innocent Afghan civilians during the last two decades.

During his Iran visit, Mr. Ghani mentioned the presence of IS in his country. However, in his India visit, Mr. Ghani warned of the ISIS was threat to regional security: "With all apologies to Microsoft, if al Qaeda was Window One, ISIS is Window Five. Terrorism is fast changing its ecology and morphology, and its communication strategies."[133]

---

131 On December 24, 2014, President Ghani said no illegal act is acceptable but his way of governance is illegal.

132 *The Guardian*, 16 February 2016

133 On February 17, 2016, a member of Afghan parliament from Baghlan province, Mr. Moheidin Mehdi, warned: "As the situation is deterioration in Baghlan

The re-engagement of the Taliban and their allegiance to ISIS gave a tough time to the Afghan army commanders. On April 28, 2015, the Long War Journal reported that ISIS's Khurasan chapter had established training camps in Logar province. However, the governor of Kunduz told journalists that ISIS had taken control of several villages in the province. The ISIS's recent video of Kunduz attacks exposed the false claims of army commanders and showed its fighters in control of Afghan security forces, outposts, captured security personnel, vehicles and weapons seized during the fighting. The video also showed several US-supplied Humvees used by the Afghan army and 150 Ford pickup trucks used by the Afghan police that had been taken during the fighting. The video claimed that ISIS fighters captured assault rifles, machine guns and an assortment of ammunition.[134]

Moreover, the Chief of the Kunduz Provincial Council told reporters that more than 2,000 Taliban fighters attacked the district of Imam Sahib, where the government had lost contact with more than 500 soldiers. The Taliban claimed that their forces had killed dozens of Afghan soldiers, police and Arbakis, including top-ranking officers and commanders, and that they had captured 55 security personnel. Afghan Interior Minister, General Noorul Haq Ulomi, accused Afghan police commanders for their tacit support to ISIS's fight against the Afghan army. On May 3, 2015, Pajhwok news agency reported Taliban had captured 13 check posts in Badakhshan province while Afghan parliament warned that the writ of the government did not exist in 31 provinces.[135]

On 15 May 2016, Afghanistan's main intelligence agency (NDS) initiated a secretive unit in southern Helmand Province with the aim of taking advantage of divisions within the Taliban movement. According to government officials, the goal was to weaken the increasing threat posed by the insurgency by using the Taliban's own tactics. The militants boasted of placing agents among security forces to carry out so-called insider attacks. The initiative comes at a time when fledgling Afghan forces are struggling to stop the Taliban from taking over large swathes of Helmand and other areas across the country.

Abdul Jabbar Qahraman, President Ashraf Ghani's special envoy for security affairs in the southern province, gave confirmation of the existence of the unit, whose members wear no uniform, but he declined to elaborate. "The idea for the creation of the new contingent, which dresses like local Helmandis, was mine," he said, Mr. Qahraman is a former commander who fought for the Soviet-backed government in southern Afghanistan in the 1980s. The Helmand police Chief Abdul Rahman Sarjang said the 300-strong unit, created and equipped by

---

province, I have been informed that between 40,000 and 50,000 [IS] terrorists will be dispatched to Afghanistan from Turkey," the MP told *Fars News Agency*.
134 28 April, 2015, the *Long War Journal*
135 03 May, 2015, the *Pajhwok news agency*

the National Directorate of Security (NDS), had conducted several operations and have so far proved a success.

The NDS headquarters in Kabul did not respond to several requests for comment, although an official—who declined to be identified—at the agency in Helmand confirmed the unit's existence and the broad outlines of how it operates. The Taliban themselves confirmed the unit's existence but dismissed claims that it was successful in exploiting internal divisions, calling such suggestions "propaganda." "It is true that this contingent exists and operates mysteriously in some parts of Helmand," said Qari Yousuf Ahmadi, the Taliban's main spokesman in southern Afghanistan. "We have very strong intelligence and find those who want to infiltrate our ranks."

On April 27, 2015, senators blasted the Unity Government over insecurity in the country. "If the Bilateral Security Agreement (BSA) does not work, it must be terminated," Senator Gulalai Akbari said. Moreover, the governor of Paktika province accused National Security Advisor Mr. Muhammad Haneef Atmar of providing $200,000 to the IS leadership in Bermal district while, according to a New York Times report, an Afghan army soldier, whose left leg had been blown off by a bomb in Lashkar Gah district of Helmand province, had sold his 11-year-old daughter, Noor Bibi, for only $3,000 to treat his wounds. Conversely, on March 25, 2015, Afghan President Ashraf Ghani abruptly showed sympathy with the Taliban and said, "Some members of the Taliban have legitimate grievances given the torture and ill treatment they have suffered and it is necessary to find ways to apologise and heal national wounds." In response to his statement, the inspector general Kadahar police, Abdul Raziq, accused the unity government by saying that the president and his cabinet members were working on the dismemberment plan of the country.[136]

On April 27, 2015, Afghan parliamentarians also accused acting governors of various provinces of involvement in facilitating ISIS forces against the Afghan army. They voiced concerns over the alleged collusion of acting governors and district chiefs with militants. "I swear that the acting governors and district chiefs are involved in promoting terrorism and I have enough proof of that," an MP from Balkh province, Mr. Rahman Rahmani, said. Afghan senators also repudiated the unity government for facilitating thousands of ISIS fighters in destabilizing the country. "Thousands of unknown rebels were entering the western Herat province from the other side of the Durand Line every day to go to the Northern provinces and disturb security there," said Ghulam Faruq Majroh, an MP from Herat province. Another MP from Takhar province said that more than 1,500 Tehreek-e-Taliban Pakistan (TTP) fighters were arriving in the province on a daily basis. I hope the Afghan army would respond

---

136 *New York Times* report (May 2, 2015), Tolo News, 27 April 2015

to the spring operation of the Taliban and ISIS with a strong resolve because a good year is determined by its spring.[137]

137 ToloNews, On April 27, 2015

CHAPTER 9. AFGHAN STATE, LAW ENFORCEMENT AGENCIES, INTELLIGENCE AND NATIONAL SECURITY CHALLENGES

The Unity Government never took interest in addressing poverty, security, law and order and the mass desertion of Afghan national army officers. During the years 2015 and 2016, hundreds of Afghan army soldiers and officers joined Islamic State (ISIS) amidst deep frustration and financial problems. The issue of their salaries not being paid led to indiscipline. In 2013, an International Security Assistance Force (ISAF) commander revealed that in Nuristan province, more than 100 Afghan army soldiers had sold their weapons because they had not received their salaries on time. Their salaries had been pending for three to four months in the Defense and Interior Ministries and sometimes they were even denied pay.

The children of soldiers and officers were out of school and their family members had no access to medical treatment and housing, and received death threats from the military command of the Taliban and ISIS groups. According to newly declassified data provided by the top US commander in Afghanistan, General John Campbell, to the Special Inspector General for Afghanistan's reconstruction, from January to November 2014, the Afghan national army shrank from 190,000 to 169,000 members. This means that 20,000 soldiers and officers have joined the ISIS, Taliban or regional militias, and are now fighting against their Afghan army brothers. The debate over the high desertion rate of the Afghan army soldiers is irksome. The main problem has been the failure to arrest or punish the deserters. Ministry of Defense also did not promote qualified officers. The lack of clear rules concerning appointments and promotions facilitated the spread of nepotism. Nepotism within the military command and selling of positions is a matter of deep concern.[138]

---

138 *Sputnik News* 03 March 2015

The Afghan national army declined, deserted, humiliated and underestimated by both the Pentagon and the Unity Government; the force stood at just 170,000 personnel, the lowest in Afghan history. This consecutive attrition was causing deep pain and frustration. From 2013 to 2014, more than 40,000 personnel were dropped from the Afghan army due to their ethnic backgrounds. In 2011, former President Hamid Karzai expressed deep concern over political interference in the ministry of Defense. The majority of politically appointed jihadists and Talibanized generals have never attended any military training school.[139]

Having covered the strategic inconsideration of the Unity Government, Afghan Defense Ministry issued a statement maintaining that the 20,000 figure in fact makes up just three percent of the military and includes soldiers who were killed or injured in the line of duty. However, experts termed this statement baseless and said that the main factor behind the worrying attrition trend of the Afghan national army was a poor management on the part of Ministry of Defense. The corrupt generals of the Afghan national army shamelessly introduced a contract system within the security forces where soldiers join the army by signing a contract for a specific period of time. They were free to leave the army or withdraw from the contract anytime they want. This meant they could leave the Afghan national army and can sign a contract with any criminal or regional militia including ISIS or Taliban military commands. Afghan army commanders were making money and continued to purchase expensive properties in and outside the country.[140]

This heartbreaking news of the mass desertion among the Afghan national army's soldiers and officers became a bigger challenge for the Ghani–Abdullah unity government and raised serious questions about the future of the ethnically divided army. President Ghani was under severe criticism from the Afghan military command as he systematically ignored the importance of many political and military challenges. He never noticed the exponential network of ISIS across the country while the issue of Daesh and the fatalities inflicted by Lashkar-e-Tayyaba in Helmand and Kunar provinces was a matter of deep concern.

He was also accused of removing senior diplomats from the foreign office and competent executive officers from various government departments without reason. According to the Afghan news agency Pajhwok's report, relatives of government officials and members of parliament held key posts in Afghanistan's embassies abroad where most of them sought political asylum. The Ministry of Foreign Affairs' spokesman, Ahmad Shakib Mustaghni, told Pajhwok that appointment in his ministry was based on nepotism. "There is no law that bars those relatives working here," he said.

139 *ToloNews,* 2014
140 *New Yorker* 07 March 2016

However, President Ghani assured his critics that the appointed officers on the basis of nepotism would be removed in due course. Mr. Ghani said he had directed the ministry of foreign affairs to prepare the list of officials appointed on nepotism basis after which they would be made to go. The alliance of war criminals with the government and their engineering of the 2014 election took the country towards the edge of a major catastrophe, producing a highly fragile national unity government. More importantly, it left huge scars. Public trust in the government was significantly undermined.

These consecutive intelligence failures and lack of a sharing mechanism prompted the emergence of Islamic State (ISIS) in Afghanistan and Pakistan. By virtue of US intelligence failure, the rising power of ISIS in Afghanistan posed a potential security threat to Russia. Against this backdrop, Russian intelligence (FSB) moved forward to fill the gap. The agency quickly reorganized its old contacts in Central Asia and Afghanistan. On October 28, 2015, spokeswoman of the Russian foreign ministry said that Russia was working with the Taliban to gain intelligence information against IS networks in Afghanistan.[141]

The NATO expansion in Europe close to the border of Russia, war in Syria and its military buildup in Afghanistan forced President Putin to sign a new Defense strategy document on January 1, 2016: "The buildup of the military potential of NATO and vesting it with global functions implemented in violation of the norms of international law, boosting military activity of the bloc's countries, further expansion of the alliance and the approach of its military infrastructure to Russian borders create a threat to national security," the document warned. However, in view of the ISIS threat to their national security, Russia and China deployed their intelligence units along Afghanistan's borders. On January 4, 2016, China adopted its first counter-terrorism law to control the emerging insurgent forces and IS influence in the Xinjiang region.[142]

The NATO alliance also failed to train a professional army for Afghanistan. The consecutive bombardment of weddings, schools, homes and hospitals by the US and NATO, humiliation and torture, rape and urination over dead bodies, painted an ugly picture of western human rights and democratic culture in Afghanistan. These unprofessional tactics and low-quality intelligence operations by the international community gave space to the Inter-Services Intelligence (ISI), and Russian intelligence agencies to strengthen their networks across Afghanistan. The ISI and Iran's Ministry of Intelligence (MI) restored their old contacts by using professional means and tactics. Consequently, the performance of the National Directorate of Security (NDS) was in shambles. It could not counter the ISI, MI, and Taliban and IS networks within the Afghan army and police ranks.

141 *ToloNews,* October 28, 2015
142 *Press TV* 01 January 2016

In 2015, the speed of the blame game slowed as diplomatic rapprochement began between the two states. President Ghani visited Islamabad twice. Islamabad showed its willingness to bring Taliban to the negotiating table but Afghan leaders called its stance absurd and demanded a paradigm shift in Islamabad's policy towards Afghanistan. These events occurred only in one year; government and politicians in Pakistan admitted that ISIS had established dozens of networks in Punjab and Balochistan provinces.[143]

President Ashraf Ghani, who sternly denounced warlordism 10 years ago, now surrenders to war criminals' demands shamelessly. The President's indecision to tackle warlordism was considered hoodwinking and circumvention. Lacking a coherent and prioritized policy on corruption and national security issues created misunderstandings about the so-called anti-corruption and anti-terrorism strategies of his government. Afghan National Army (ANA) continued to desert, shrink and be squeezed due to lack of funds and modern weapons needed to defeat the Taliban insurgents and ISIS. Private criminal militias are in control of 70 percent of the territory of the state and are posing a perpetual threat to the existence of the ANA.

Afghanistan's National Unity Government (NUG) was teetering on the brink in 2016. Internal political turmoil worsened as differences over the power-sharing formula intensified between the two Presidents. Ethnic conflagration also increased. Ethno-sectarian violence and the brinkmanship of the ruling class deteriorated. The exponentially growing power of the Daesh (ISIS) and the incompetency of Afghan intelligence (NDS) to counter it were severely criticized by civil society. In Northern and Eastern Afghanistan, the Taliban's influence increased. Pandora's box opened with the abrupt diatribe of Afghan Vice President Abdul Rashid Dostum hammering President Ashraf Ghani for his wrongly designed ethnic policy, nepotism and power monopoly.

Mr. Dostum censured Dr. Abdullah for his failure to act independently. He also expressed dissatisfaction over the ethnic policy of the president and said: "If you speak in Pashtu with President Ghani, you will be a good person, and if you speak Pashtu and you are from the Logar province, then you are a very good person."[144]

Mr. Dostum also accused the NDS Chief Muhammad Masoom Stanekzai for making things worse, and criticized unmerited appointments in the armed forces saying: "The corps commander for the north does not deserve his post, and he wants to paint General Dostum as a weak leader in the north and isolate him with their inappropriate behavior... The jihadist figures appointed by President Ghani and Mr. Abdullah on key military posts had never seen a

---

143 On 13 February 2015, the former President, Pervez Musharraf, told The Guardian that in President Karzai's time, the ISI cultivated the Taliban after 2001
144 ToloNews, 25 October 2016

military base, and could not command even 100 soldiers. We have many experienced generals in our country who are out of job. Why aren't they appointed on military posts? The 50 percent distribution of power is totally wrong, and this way of governance leads soldiers to death."[145]

However, President's Special Advisor for Governance Reforms, Ahmad Zia Massoud, accused the UNG of nepotism, and warned that this policy may further exacerbate ethnic tensions: "What is good in this that I am in government as a Tajik and I bring all Tajiks to government? This creates a reaction. And what is good in this that a Pashtun is head of the state and then he appoints all Pashtuns in government offices? This is not good, and it creates a reaction from other ethnic groups."[146]

In response to the Vice President's accusations, the office of the president termed the outburst as unexpected and said that such accusations did not befit General Dostum. At present, Afghanistan has become a typical case of ethnic discrimination. Ethnic groups are more powerful in arms and fighting capabilities than the factional army of the country. In majority provinces, every powerful government official and military commander appoints members of his own ethnic groups to strengthen his position. In intelligence agencies like the NDS and RAMA and defense intelligence, Tajiks and Pashtuns are dominant, while Hazara and Uzbeks have one percent representation.

In 2016, clashes broke out when Tajiks demanded the reburial of the late king, Habibullah Khan Kalakani. This action prompted intense rivalry between ethnic groups. On 01 September 2016, the funeral ceremony turned violent in Kabul, in which at least one person was killed and several others were injured. The king's supporters were mainly Tajiks who were later attacked by General Dostum's supporters.

The role of state and private media was seen suspicious as it covered language-related topics. Television and radio channels spread prejudice, racism and discrimination day and night. Ethnic tension between Pashtuns and Hazaras and between Tajiks and Pashtuns in Northern provinces was openly discussed in talk shows. The tension renewed memories of the country's long-running ethnic conflict that culminated in 1990s, and continued till the end of the Taliban regime in 2001. The ethnic politics of the NUG failed. Mr. Abdullah openly criticized Mr. Ghani for his ethnic favoritism. In Mazar-e-Sharif, Kunduz, Ghor, Baghlan and Takhar provinces, Pashtuns were

---

145 Pajhwok, 25 October 2016,
146 Daily Times, 05 November 2016, The Afghan army is joining IS, Daily Times, March 10, 2015, and a report of SIGAR, Afghan National Army: DOD Has Taken Steps to Remedy Poor Management of Vehicle Maintenance Program, Special Inspector General for Afghanistan Reconstruction, SIGAR 16-49 Audit Report, July 2016.

humiliated, and their land was grabbed by Uzbek and Tajik war criminals.

Afghanistan was now caught up in a much broader series of violence. Afghan scholar, Dr Zaman Stanizai, views the current ethnic conflict in the country as an unidentified and an unaddressed issue: "The current Afghan crisis is neither correctly identified nor adequately addressed. Pashtuns, who constitute the cohesive core of the otherwise ethnically diverse Afghan society, have earned the distinction of the most resistant for a reason. Like any other majority in any other state, they shoulder a heavier responsibility. The alienation of the majority will neither win hearts and minds nor will it help build institutions for a viable democracy."[147]

The controversial role of Indian government also caused ethnic discrimination when India started providing millions of dollars to warlords and regional groups. Indian agencies—RAW, IB and Defense Intelligence Agency—were making things worse, and created a strong opposition against the NUG in its efforts of rapprochement with Pakistan and China. Afghanistan was a bad victim of the proxy war between Pakistan and India, but with the inclination of Afghan government towards India, things gone from bad to worse. India has been supporting the Northern Alliance since 1990s, which resulted in the return of war criminals into Afghanistan's body politic. India secretly furthers its agenda to transform Afghanistan into its permanent colony by 'recruiting' thousands of young Afghans to study in Indian colleges and universities. Some Afghan politicians warn that India needs to balance its policy towards the Pashtuns, as the country has heavily invested in non-Pashtun groups. Only eight percent scholarship for Pashtuns exposes India's ethnic role in Afghanistan.

Ethnic violence created a hostile environment across Afghanistan. Pashtuns were being subjected to violence and torture in northern Afghanistan. Afghans who returned from Pakistan faced violence and harassment, and were struggling to survive in their own country, but regional warlords were not willing to allow them to return to their hometowns. There were more than two million internally displaced Afghans who also faced the wrath of war criminals and private militia commanders. Afghanistan was a facing a complex humanitarian crisis and the National Unity Government (NUG) was harshly accused of failing and not fulfilling their promises given during election. As a result of poverty and joblessness, the Social insecurity such as robbery, kidnapping and explosions in all parts of the country including the capital became a common practice. On the other hand the illegitimate crisis widely debated in the media. The legitimacy of the National Unity Government (NUG) derived from a political agreement expired. Around 70% Afghan citizens were dissatisfied with NUG government; as they defied all types of threats to go to the

---

147 From Identity Crisis to Identity in Crisis in Afghanistan, Zaman Stanizai, the Middle East Institute Policy Brief No. 27 December 2009

polls under tough conditions but they have been compelled to pay $3 billion in bribe in a year. As a result day to day people are getting more

Altercations over the agro-land in northern Afghanistan intensified as returnees claimed their occupied land, but without original documents, they were unable to repossess their land. Social media and private channels, repeatedly, illustrated public anger over the inconsideration of government vis-à-vis the armed forces of the country. In 2016, more than 16,000 Afghan soldiers and officers were killed and injured, and all but 2,600 joined Taliban and Daesh groups. In insider attacks 300 soldiers and officers were killed and 200 injured.[148]

---

148 Ethnic violence has created a hostile environment across Afghanistan. Pashtuns are being subjected to violence and torture in northern Afghanistan. Afghans who returned from Pakistan face violence and harassment, and are struggling to survive in their own country, but regional warlords are not willing to allow them to return to their hometowns. There are more than two million internally displaced Afghans who also face the wrath of war criminals and private militia commanders. Daily Times, 05 November 2016

CHAPTER 10 . TORTURE, CUSTODIAL DEATH, AND ABUSE OF DETAINEES
IN KHAD AND NDS SECRET PRISONS

Numerous reports published by international human rights
organizations envisaged the torture tactics of Afghan intelligence
agencies (KHAD and NDS) in their secret prisons. The NDS and
KHAD have a notorious record of killing, torture and inhuman
treatment of political opponents and terror suspects. In September
2014, in his short statement before the UNAMA research team, an
NDS officer admitted that his agency tortured detainees in its private
secret prisons: "As a National Directorate of Security (NDS) human
rights officer, I do not have the necessary conditions to carry out my
work. There is a general spirit of impunity for human rights violations.
The NDS Director is not cooperative and the other colleagues shrug
their shoulders and advise me to 'just leave it.' Nobody at NDS
actively stops me from doing my work but there is passive resistance,
inaction and denial of logistical support. My reports, which I send to
my supervisors in Kabul, are not acted on."[149]
    In Afghan constitution, torture has been defined as an illegal
act. The 2003 constitution's penal-code (1) say that torture against
detainees and everyone is illegal: "Torture is already illegal under the
2003 Constitution, the Penal Code (1) and the Convention against
Torture which Afghanistan ratified in 1987. However, successive
Afghan governments have honored legal bans on torture almost
entirely in the breach. In that sense, this new decree does not change
the legal situation. However, if the President were to follow it through
seriously, it could act as a wake-up call to the government itself and

---

149 Update on the Treatment of Conflict Related Detainees in Afghan Custody:
Accountability and   implementation of Presidential Decree 129, United
Nations Assistance Mission in Afghanistan Office of the United Nations High
Commissioner for Human Rights February 2015 Kabul, Afghanistan. http://
www.ohchr.org/Documents/Countries/AF/UNAMA_OHCHR_Detention_
Report_Feb2015.pdf

as an important, public signal of a change in what is expected and what will be tolerated in the behavior of state officials".[150]

The research team of UNAMA found solid evidence of torture in the NDS secret prisons. According to the report, detainees receive ill-treatment in the NDS prisons, and they are not allowed to treat their wounds:

"The 2011 and 2013 reports found sufficiently credible and reliable evidence that approximately half of the conflict-related detainees interviewed had experienced torture or ill-treatment during interrogation–mainly to obtain confessions or information–in detention facilities run by the NDS and ANP. UNAMA found that torture was used systematically within several NDS and ANP facilities and noted the Government of Afghanistan's position that torture and ill-treatment of detainees was not an institutional or Government policy. The reports noted measures taken by the International Security Assistance Force (ISAF) to address torture in Afghan custody including suspension of detainee transfers to ANP and NDS locations identified as practicing systematic torture and roll-out of a detention facility certification review process".[151]

Afghan constitution guarantees the right of life, and does not allow anyone to kill or torture detainees. The UK Home Office country report on prison conditions in Afghanistan spotlighted some important points: "The 2004 Afghan Constitution, in Article 23, asserts the right to life, envisaging at the same time the possibility of its deprivation by the provision of law. However, in accordance with Article 396 of Afghanistan's Constitution, a convict sentenced to death can appeal to two higher courts and Article 129 of the Constitution establishes that "...All final decisions of the courts shall be enforced, except for capital punishment, which shall require presidential approval."[152]

The US Department of State (USSD) noted in its Human Rights report covering 2014 that: "The general directorate of prisons and detention centers (GDPDC), part of the Ministry of Interior, has responsibility for all civilian-run prisons (for both men and women) and civilian detention centers, including the large national prison at Pul-e-Charkhi. The Ministry of Justice's juvenile rehabilitation directorate (JRD) is responsible for all juvenile rehabilitation centers. The ANP [Afghan National Police], which is under the Ministry of Interior and the NDS [national directorate of security] also run short-term detention facilities at the provincial and district levels, usually collocated with their headquarters facilities. The Ministry of Defense

---

150 Clark, Kate: *Torture, Illegal Armed Groups: Signs of Possible Afghan Government Action?* 22. February 2013.
151 United Nations Assistance Mission in Afghanistan Office of the *United Nations High Commissioner for Human Rights* February 2015 Kabul, Afghanistan
152 *The UK Home Office Country Information and Guidance Afghanistan:* Prison conditions Version 1.0 September 2015

runs the Afghan National Detention Facilities at Parwan and Pul-e-Charkhi."[153]

This issue has also been reported by the UN report (Update on the Treatment of Conflict-Related Detainees in Afghan Custody: "Accountability and Implementation of Presidential Decree 129, United Nations Assistance Mission in Afghanistan Office of the United Nations High Commissioner for Human Rights, February 2015, Kabul, Afghanistan) with details:

> In Kabul, of the 112 detainees interviewed who had been held at one or more of three facilities, namely NDS Department 124, 40 and the NDS Kabul provincial facility, 36 detainees (32 per cent) experienced torture or ill-treatment with most incidents occurring in Department 124.40 Fewer incidents of torture were observed at NDS Department 4041 although of the 73 detainees interviewed, 29 were found to have experienced torture or ill-treatment in other NDS facilities prior to their transfer to Department 40. At the NDS Kabul provincial facility, nine of 33 detainees interviewed (27 per cent) were subjected to torture or ill-treatment.[154]

> The legal prohibition against using evidence gained through torture as the basis for prosecution or conviction at trial and a detainee's right to mandatory access to Defense counsel was found to be routinely violated by judges and prosecutors. The government of Afghanistan has shown it is serious about addressing torture and ill-treatment through Presidential Decree 129 and other measures. Further efforts are needed to fully end and prevent its use, reinforce the prohibition of torture and improve accountability.[155]

Amnesty International (2015/2016) expressed deep concern about the power abuse of NDS officers who illegally torture and abuse detainees in their secret prisons. The NDS authorities detained Afghans for acts that were not terror related acts under the Afghan law. According to the detailed report of the American University Washington College of Law 2014 on inhuman treatment and torture of detainees by the NDS authorities:

"Prisoners report being beaten with several kinds of instruments and abused in a variety of ways. Many prisoners reported being deprived of sleep and required to stand for prolonged periods.... In other cases, too, such treatment was exacerbated by prisoners being

---

153 *US Department of State, Country Report on Human Rights* Practices 2014, Afghanistan, 26 June 2015, Section 1c. Prison and Detention Center Conditions
154 *United Nations Assistance Mission in Afghanistan Office of the United Nations High Commissioner for Human Rights* February 2015 Kabul, Afghanistan
155 UNAMA report on the Treatment of Conflict-Related Detainees in Afghan Custody: Accountability and Implementation of Presidential Decree 129. *Afghanistan Annual Report* 2014, Protection of Civilians in Armed Conflict 25 February 2015

exposed to sun or forced to stand in water or snow.... Some prisoners reported being only threatened with electric shock torture, but many others reported being subjected to it, apparently quite routinely at an early stage as well as later stages of their interrogation. The most common electric shock torture device is referred to as the "telephone": a small machine that looks like an old-fashioned telephone with wires that are attached to the victim's body and a handle which is turned or pulled to apply the current. Other prisoners simply referred to a small box with wires coming out of it.... Several other forms of serious physical abuse were reported. These included prisoners having a bottle or in one case a heated wire thrust into the rectum, having fingernails pulled out or needles inserted under them, being cut with a knife, having a chair placed on the stomach or hands and sat upon, being burnt with cigarettes, being scalded with very hot water, and having hair torn out."[156]

The UNAMA investigative researchers noted in their report (2015) some important facts about the torture and investigation mechanism of the National Directorate of Security (NDS). In January 2014, in Shindand district, prisoner No-24 explained his inhuman treatment by the agency investigators: "The NDS punched me in the stomach and hit me with a cable on my back as I was sitting on the floor. One of the two also grabbed my hair and slapped me on the face twice. It was terrible. Then, I was told to sit outside near a wall in the semi-dark. I do not know how long I was out there, but I was called to go in the same room again. I was terrified and completely lost. At one point, they made me lie on my back and raise my feet up with one of them holding them firmly and the other hitting on the sole of my feet. I was screaming. Then, I had to give a confession and say that I am an IED planter and was involved in the IED explosion. Only then they stopped beating me. They showed me a paper and forced me to thumbprint it twice."[157]

However, in December 2014, detainee No 376 in the NDS department 124 also told the UNAMA team about his torture story: "On Saturday three people came to my cell and one of them told me: 'Tell us the full truth and do not force us to beat you up.' They took me from my cell to the upper floor, to a small office. There were three persons. When I entered the room, before even questioning me, one person hit me with a plastic pipe on my legs, back and my hands.

---

156 Finding Patterns through Documentation: Reconstructing the History of Torture and Cruel, Inhuman and Degrading Treatment of Detainees in Afghanistan, Patricia Gossman, *War Crimes Research Office*, March 2014, American University Washington College of Law
157 Update on the Treatment of Conflict Related Detainees in Afghan Custody: Accountability and implementation of Presidential Decree 129, United Nations Assistance Mission in Afghanistan Office of the United Nations High Commissioner for Human Rights February 2015 Kabul, Afghanistan. http://www.ohchr.org/Documents/Countries/AF/UNAMA_OHCHR_Detention_Report_Feb2015.pdf

My nails turned black [from the beatings]. With some pauses, the beating continued for three hours. They demanded that I confess being a Taliban member, and I did because I couldn't take it anymore. Then they asked me to tell them who else was with me. I gave them the name of my cousin. After that they left me. On the second day, nobody interrogated me. On the third day in the morning at 9 o'clock they came and hung me on a wall near the bathroom of the cell block for two hours. I had already confessed, but they still hung me."[158]

Another detainee No-161 in the same department explained his cruel treatment by NDS in these words: "I was taken to NDS Department 124. They started beating me. They kicked me with their boots and they punched me on the first day. On the second day, they also beat me but this time with a water pipe for about two hours. On the third day, they used a machine on my sexual organs. It was like a clip or pliers and they used it to squeeze my sexual parts till I cried. After this, I made a confession I was a Talib. I was scared because they threatened they would destroy my sexual organs. I just said anything and they wrote it down and I put my thumb prints on the papers. I thought I might die if they destroyed my sexual organs."[159]

Moreover in Kandahar and Takhatr provinces, the UNAMA recorded two more torture stories of detainees in the secret prisons of NDS: "I was arrested by NDS Spin Boldak and was slapped repeatedly while in the NDS vehicle. I was taken to NDS Takhtapul (halfway between Spin Boldak and Kandahar) and there three NDS used a cable to beat me on my back, waist and feet. They also tried to choke me by forcing a piece of cloth in my mouth and at the same time clasping my neck. They wanted me to confess I was a Talib and after this I did confess, verbally, to whatever they wanted."[160]

"I was arrested and taken to NDS HQ detention facility in Taloqan city. I was there for 12 days. I was interrogated four times. I told the interrogator everything but he didn't agree with me. Due to that, he started beating me with several electric cables which were about one meter long and about one inch thick. Three times the interrogator who was a tall man together with two other hooded me and laid me down. Two of them held my arms and the third one started beating me on my feet. The interrogator told me if I didn't confess that I learned making IEDs in Pakistan, was involved in terrorist activities and planting IEDs especially in the election sites, he would beat me more and give me electric shocks. I was scared and agreed and he stopped beating me."[161]

In October 2011, a human right department was established in the NDS headquarters to monitor all detention facilities and human

---

158 Ibid
159 Ibid
160 Ibid
161 UNAMA, Detainee 394, NDS Spin Boldak, December 2013 and Detainee No-202, April 2014

rights violations. In January 2012 it was named the "Human Rights Monitoring Sub-Directorate" with a plan to have a permanent presence in 16 provinces with officers responsible for training NDS officials on human rights issues. In 2013 NDS merged the Human Rights Monitoring Sub-Directorate with other NDS 'policy-related' units into its Department 47 responsible for Foreign Affairs, Protocol, Human Rights, Gender and Women Affairs.

The Treatment of Conflict-Related Detainees in Afghanistan: Independent Human Rights Commission (AIHRC), Open Society Foundations March 17, 2012

Executive Summary

In recent months, the Afghan intelligence service has come under increased scrutiny and criticism for its use of torture and other violations of detainees 'rights. This report raises significant, new areas of concern, including previously undocumented facilities where torture is taking place and the abuse of detainees transferred by international forces. The report is based on long-term, regular detainee monitoring conducted by the Afghanistan Independent Human Rights Commission (AIHRC), as legally mandated under the Constitution of Afghanistan, as well as on interviews with more than 100 conflict-related detainees between February 2011 and January 2012 (Dalwa 1389-Jadi 1390), conducted with the assistance of the Open Society Foundations. The AIHRC monitors interviewed detainees in the National Directorate of Security (NDS) and Ministry of Interior (MOI) facilities while Open Society researchers interviewed detainees who had been previously held by the NDS and had either been transferred to MOI facilities or released.

Researchers found credible evidence of torture at nine NDS facilities and several Afghan National Police (ANP) facilities, including beatings, suspension from the ceiling, electric shocks, threatened or actual sexual abuse, and other forms of mental and physical abuse, which were routinely used to obtain confessions or other information.[162] Four of the NDS facilities where torture was documented were also identified by a recent United Nations report as practicing torture. Monitors also found evidence of torture at five additional NDS facilities.

Several specific methods of torture that have been previously denied by the NDS, such as the use of electric shock, abuse of genitals, and threats of sexual abuse, were confirmed in interviews, providing even further evidence that these methods of torture have been used by NDS officials. Research also uncovered widespread and deliberate violations of detainees' fundamental due process rights, including the right to counsel, and family notification, which contributed to increasing the risk of torture and other abuse.

Researchers also examined the transfer of detainees from international forces to the Afghan government. In response to an October 2011 (Mizan 1390) UN report, International Security Assistance Forces (ISAF) suspended all detainee transfers to facilities of concern, initiated a regime to address problems identified at these facilities, and proposed an ambitious monitoring program to cover all detainees transferred by ISAF. Efforts by ISAF and troop contributing nations with national monitoring programs are welcome and can have a positive impact. But concerns raised in this report, including evidence of off-site abuse, and detainees 'fear of reprisals for disclosing abuse, suggest that a post-transfer monitoring system may not be sufficient to meet the obligations that ISAF nations have under international law.[163]

The largest remaining gap in detainee monitoring is the lack of monitoring of U.S. forces outside the ISAF chain of command. Despite the high number of detainees transferred by U.S. forces, particularly by the Combined Forces Special Operations Component Command–Afghanistan (CFSOCC–A), which are not subject to the recently initiated ISAF monitoring program, the United States has yet to adopt a mechanism to monitor detainees transferred to Afghan custody.[164]

Researchers found credible evidence that some U.S.-transferred detainees have been subjected to torture by Afghan officials, underscoring the need for such a monitoring program. Ten cases were documented of individuals detained by U.S. forces between May 2010 (Saur 1389) and January 2012 (Jadi.1390), and then transferred to NDS facilities where they alleged they were subsequently tortured. In four

---

162 Locations include NDS Kabul Department 90/124, NDS Herat, NDS Kandahar, NDS Laghman, NDS Badakhshan, NDS Helmand, NDS Kabul Department 17/40, NDS Nangarhar, and NDS Wardak, as well as ANP Kandahar headquarters and several ANP Kandahar checkpoints

163 It should be noted that most of the cases of torture and abuse in NDS detention facilities documented by the AIHRC and the Open Society Foundations pre-date implementation of ISAF's six-phase remediation plan and inspections regime.

164 CFSOCC-A, along with all USFOR-A forces are subject to the transfer prohibitions and other aspects of the ISAF six-phase plan. However, they are not subject to ISAF detainee monitoring, phase V of the ISAF six-phase plan.

of these cases, individuals reported that they were held for some period of time at a detention facility located at or near Bagram Air Base, and in at least three cases individuals were transferred to NDS Kandahar after the suspension of transfers to the facility by all ISAF and U.S. forces. These cases raise serious concerns regarding U.S. policies on detainee transfers, particularly transfers by non-ISAF U.S. forces and U.S. special operations forces, and whether appropriate safeguards exist to protect detainees 'rights and ensure that the United States is not complicit in torture.

The Afghan government has stated that it is committed to addressing concerns about the torture of detainees, and has largely responded positively to increased demands for access to facilities. The government has also recently established a human rights unit within the NDS to investigate allegations of abuse, all of which is strongly welcomed. However, research for this report indicates that the Afghan government has thus far largely failed to hold individuals responsible for detainee abuse accountable. In some cases, instead of dismissing and prosecuting responsible officials, the Afghan government has simply reassigned officials to other detention facilities. AIHRC monitors also continue to face challenges accessing some NDS facilities, including Department 90/124.

While the Afghan government faces immense security and capacity challenges, this does not mean that torture is justifiable, or inevitable. The prohibition on torture is absolute under both Afghan and international law. The use of torture is a violation of fundamental human rights, and seriously damages the legitimacy of the Afghan government and its allies. The Afghan government has long made clear its demand for sovereignty over the detention of conflict-related detainees in Afghanistan. As the Afghan government assumes greater responsibility for security as well as detentions, and the drawdown of U.S. and other ISAF nations 'troops accelerates, the challenges associated with properly holding and prosecuting conflict-related detainees will only become more pressing for the government. Urgent action is required, and the Afghan government, with the support of its international partners, must take immediate, effective steps to address mistreatment and torture of conflict-related detainees.

Key Recommendations

Government of Afghanistan

1. Investigate and hold to account all those who are responsible for torture, including commanding officers. End the practice of moving rather than removing officials responsible for torture and make public or provide to AIHRC the results of investigations and actions taken.

2. Ensure AIHRC has full, unfettered, and confidential access to all NDS detainees and facilities, including NDS Kabul Department 90/124, as legally mandated under the Constitution of Afghanistan. Ensure NDS officials permit AIHRC monitors to conduct unannounced visits to all NDS facilities.

3. Provide the NDS Human Rights Unit with the authority and resources necessary to effectively investigate allegations of abuse and ensure those responsible are held to account.

4. Cease holding detainees incommunicado. Notify family members of detainee's arrest immediately or as soon as practicably possible, ensure access to legal counsel, and permit family members to visit detainees. Transfer all detainees to MOI custody within 72 hours, inform detainees of the reason for their arrest within 24 hours, and ensure all detentions beyond 72 hours are authorized by a prosecutor or judge.

5. Ensure defense lawyers have access to detainees and all NDS detention facilities at all stages of detention as well as proper access to the findings of investigations and evidence against clients.

ISAF and Nations Contributing Troops

1. Make use of ISAF suspension and remediation policies to work with the Afghan government to adopt measures that will protect all detainees from abuse, such as full, unfettered access by AIHRC, detainee access to defense counsel, and accountability for detainee abuse.

2. Ensure no detainee is transferred into facilities where there is real risk of torture. Where detainee transfers have been suspended by ISAF due to credible allegations of torture, ensure resumption of transfers to a facility occur only when there is sufficient information to determine that there is no real risk of torture at that facility.

The United States

1. Support the NDS and the Afghan government to ensure all detainees are free from torture. Work with the NDS to identify critical deficiencies in resources, and provide appropriate technical and financial assistance to help ensure detainee treatment and interrogations comply with Afghan and international law.

2. Ensure all U.S. forces, including U.S. Special Operations Forces and intelligence agency personnel, comply with U.S. detainee transfer policies and international law and are covered by the AIHRC detainee monitoring program.

List of Abbreviations

ADF	Australian Defence Forces
AIHRC	Afghanistan Independent Human Rights Commission
ALP	Afghan Local Police
ANBP	Afghan National Border Police
ANP	Afghan National Police
ANSF	Afghan National Security Forces
BTIF	Bagram Theater Internment Facility
CAT	Convention Against Torture
CFSOCC-A	Combined Forces Special Operations Component Command-Afghanistan
CJIATF-435	Combined Joint Interagency Task Force-435, the unit overseeing detention operations at DFIP
COM-ISAF	Commander of ISAF; currently General John R. Allen
DFIP	Detention Facility In Parwan
DOT	Detainee Oversight Team, the unit responsible for implementing the UK's detainee monitoring program
DRB	Detainee Review Board
ICPC	Interim Criminal Procedure Code
ILF	International Law Foundation
ISAF	International Security Assistance Force
JCC	Juvenile Corrections Center
JSOC	United States Joint Special Operations Command
MOI	Ministry of the Interior
MOJ	Ministry of Justice
MoU	Memorandum of Understanding
NDS	National Directorate of Security
OEF	Operation Enduring Freedom
RC	Regional Command, ISAF's largest sub-national command units
SIT	Special Investigations Team, a division of the AIHRC
TCN	Troop Contributing Nation
UNAMA	United Nations Assistance Mission in Afghanistan
USFOR-A	United States Forces in Afghanistan

Introduction

Every year throughout Afghanistan, thousands of individuals are detained by Afghan and international forces in connection with the armed conflict. As the conflict has intensified, the number of individuals detained on national security grounds has increased, with the vast majority ending up in the custody of the National Directorate of Security (NDS), Afghanistan's intelligence agency. Accused of sensitive, national security-related crimes and often held in prolonged, incommunicado detention by intelligence officials, these conflict-related detainees are particularly vulnerable to torture and mistreatment.

The Afghanistan Independent Human Rights Commission (AIHRC), has regularly monitored detainee treatment and detention conditions since 2002 (0831), and along with other national and international human rights groups, has raised concerns about detainee abuse, as well as the potential complicity of international forces. Following a United Nations Assistance Mission in Afghanistan (UNAMA) report in October 2011 (Mizan 1390), which exposed the depth and breadth of abuse, the Afghan government and its international partners have demonstrated a new level of engagement on this issue.[165]

This report is based on interviews conducted by the AIHRC between February 2011 and January 2012 (Dalwa 1389-Jadi 1390), with assistance from the Open Society Foundations. The report raises significant, new areas of concern, including torture at facilities not previously identified, and continued transfers by U.S. and other international military forces that put detainees at risk of torture. The report assesses recent steps taken by the Afghan government to end abuse and hold perpetrators accountable, raising concerns that assurances have not been matched by action. It also examines whether international forces are doing enough to ensure that the detainees they transfer to the Afghan government are not at risk of torture.

While comprehensive reform will take time, with sustained attention, the coming months represent a critical opportunity to maintain the momentum of reform and ensure implementation of policies and programs that will successfully address detainee abuse.

II. Background

National Directorate of Security (NDS)

The NDS is Afghanistan's principle intelligence organization, with primary responsibility for handling conflict-related detainees. The NDS also receives conflict-related detainees transferred from international military forces and other Afghan National Security Forces (ANSF). Though the NDS has primary responsibility for national security cases, other Afghan security forces, like the Afghan National Police (ANP) and Afghan Local Police (ALP), also arrest and detain conflict-related detainees. While mistreatment is a problem for detainees throughout the Afghan justice system, research and experience have shown that conflict-related detainees are particularly vulnerable to abuse and torture.

---

165 *United Nations Assistance Mission in Afghanistan,* Treatment of Conflict-Related Detainees in Afghan Custody, October 2011, http://unama.unmissions.org/Portals/UNAMA/Documents/October10_%202011_UNAMA_Detention_Full-Report_ENG.pdf,hereinafter "UNAMA, Conflict-Related Detainees in Afghan Custody

International Military Forces

International Security Assistance Forces (ISAF) continues to regularly detain and transfer individuals to Afghan custody. Under ISAF's "96-hour rule," individuals detained during ISAF operations are generally released or transferred to Afghan authorities within 96 hours. There is significant diversity in detention policies and practices among ISAF nations. The United States detains thousands of individuals all across Afghanistan, with the majority held in the Detention Facility in Parwan (DFIP) as well as a number of "temporary" detention sites, including a secretive U.S. screening facility at Bagram Air Base run by the U.S. Joint Special Operations Command (JSOC).[166]

Meanwhile, nations with a much smaller troop presence like Denmark may detain only a handful of individuals in a given year, and transfer all of those detained to the Afghan authorities. Some nations, like Germany, claim that they don't take part in detentions themselves, yet nevertheless participate in military operations with Afghan forces in which individuals are arrested and detained.

III. Methodology

Afghanistan Independent Human Rights Commission (AIHRC) is a constitutionally-established, independent national human rights institution which is mandated under Afghan law to monitor the situation of human rights in the country, promote and protect human rights, investigate and verify cases of human rights violations, and take measures for the improvement and promotion of human rights in Afghanistan.

The Open Society Foundations is a nongovernmental organization that works throughout the world to build vibrant and tolerant democracies whose governments are accountable to their citizens. The Open Society's Regional Policy Initiative on Afghanistan and Pakistan, which partnered with the AIHRC on this report, works with national civil society organizations in Afghanistan and Pakistan to conduct research, reporting, and advocacy on conflict-related human rights and policy issues.

As part of its mandate, the AIHRC conducts regular monitoring of confinement conditions and detainee treatment in Afghan detention facilities. The AIHRC conducts visits to detention facilities where

---

166 Open Society Foundations, Confinement Conditions at a U.S. Screening Facility on Bagram Air Base, October 14, 2010 (22 Mizan 1389), http://www.soros.org/resources/articles_publications/publications/confinement-conditions-20101014/confinement-conditions-20101014.pdf; *hereinafter "OSF, Confinement Conditions at a U.S. Screening Facility"+; Kimberly Dozier, "Terror Suspects Held for Weeks in Secret," Associated Press, April 8, 2011 (19 Hamal 1390), http://abcnews.go.com/International/wireStory?id=13325716 [hereinafter "Dozier, Terror Suspects Held for Weeks'

it inspects conditions of confinement and conducts interviews with detainees as well as officials responsible for overseeing detention facilities.

This report is based on interviews with detainees conducted by the AIHRC between February 2011 and January 2012 (Dalwa 1389-Jadi 1390). Interviews were conducted as part of AIHRC's regular monitoring of NDS and MOI facilities by provincial monitoring and investigation teams. The AIHRC Special Investigations Team (SIT) also conducted interviews with detainees over this time period through 10 monitoring missions to NDS and MOI detention facilities. Together, AIHRC monitoring visits covered 12 NDS and 11 MOI detention facilities during the research period. During this period, the AIHRC has been denied access to detainees in NDS Kabul Department 90/124 and in NDS Kunar.

In total, over 100 current or former NDS detainees were interviewed in the research period. 103 interviews were conducted by the AIHRC with detainees while in NDS custody or MOJ/MOI custody and 15 interviews were conducted with recently released detainees by researchers.[167] Interviews with detainees were conducted individually, confidentially, and in private, without the interference or presence of government officials in almost all cases. However, NDS officials prevented the AIHRC from conducting unannounced visits. AIHRC monitors were required to provide NDS officials with one or more days 'notice before monitoring visits were conducted. Informed consent was provided to use information provided by interviewees in this report. For security reasons and to protect interviewees 'identities, all the names of detainees featured in this report have been replaced with pseudonyms or numbers.

Interviews were also conducted with 20 Defense lawyers and legal aid organization directors, 15 detention facility officials, as well as other Afghan and foreign government officials. Most defense lawyers and government officials asked not to be named in this report.

Researchers made efforts to verify the credibility of detainees 'statements, though given the limitations of access and the need to protect the identities of interviewees, this was often challenging. In some cases interviewers observed scars or other physical signs of abuse. In other cases, where possible, the interviewers sought to verify and corroborate information through interviews with witnesses, lawyers, government officials, and doctors. Interviews were also conducted with multiple detainees at each facility, so that a picture of consistent and credible allegations could be built.

These findings are also consistent with the general picture of detainee abuse that has been documented by the AIHRC from 2002 to 2011, prior to this specific research period. Detainees interviewed

---

167 On December 17, 2011 (26 Qaws 1390), President Karzai signed a decree that would transfer control of prisons from the Ministry of Justice to the Ministry of Interior, effective January 10, 2012 (20 Jadi 1390).

at different times and in different locations also provided accounts of torture and abuse that were largely consistent with each other. In many cases, detainees described near identical methods of abuse, for example the use of suspension and tools like electric cables for beatings, as well as similarities in substance and patterns of questioning.

Evidence documented during interviews was also consistent with reports of torture received by UNAMA. Researchers verified that the detainees interviewed for this report were different than those interviewed by UNAMA—only four detainees interviewed for this report were also interviewed by UNAMA. Researchers found evidence of torture in many of the same locations as UNAMA, and methods of torture that were near identical to those documented by UNAMA, including suspension, beating, threats of sexual abuse, abuse of genitals, and electric shock.

IV. Torture and Mistreatment of Conflict-Related Detainees in Afghanistan

Between February 2011 and January 2012 (Dalwa 1389-Jadi 1390), researchers documented a significant number of cases of torture and other cruel, inhuman or degrading treatment of conflict-related detainees by NDS and ANP officials at 11 different detention facilities in Afghanistan. Several specific patterns and methods were identified, including electric shock, threats of sexual abuse, and abuse of detainees 'genitals, as well as torture at undisclosed locations.

In recent years, the Afghan government has taken a number of positive steps to address general weaknesses in the justice sector. The Afghan government has also adopted several measures to improve detainee treatment within NDS, particularly after reports of abuse. These measures have included training of NDS staff and the creation of two new monitoring bodies—a government committee to investigate and assess concerns raised by the recent UNAMA detentions report, and a human rights unit, which will have access to and oversight of detainees under interrogation in NDS facilities.[168]Though the Afghan government has made progress on reforms, and expressed a commitment to protecting detainees' rights, this report's findings indicate that torture continues to be a major problem in many facilities and requires further urgent action by the Afghan government and international partners to address the depth and breadth of detainee abuse.

---

168 *UNAMA, Conflict- Related Detainees in Afghan Custody*, supra note 3. 8 Convention against Torture and Other Cruel, Inhuman or Degrading Treatment or Punishment (*Convention against Torture or CAT*), adopted December 10, 1984 (19 Qaws 1363), G.A. res. 39/46, annex, 39 U.N. GAOR Supp. (No. 51) at 197, U.N. Doc. A/39/51 (1984), entered into force June 26, 1987

Methods of Torture

Under international law, torture is defined as —any act by which severe pain or suffering, whether physical or mental, is intentionally inflicted on a person for such purposes as obtaining from him or a third person information or a confession, punishing him for an act he or a third person has committed or is suspected of having committed, or intimidating or coercing him or a third person, or for any reason based on discrimination of any kind.[169] Torture occurs when such pain or suffering is inflicted by, at the instigation of, or with the consent or acquiescence of a state official or other person acting in an official capacity.[170] Torture is strictly prohibited by Afghan and international law.[171]

The individuals interviewed for this report were detained or convicted on conflict-related charges.[172] Based on interviews with 118 detainees, researchers found a significant number of cases in which NDS or ANP officials subjected detainees to treatment that constituted torture under international and Afghan law. Detainees were subjected to a variety of abusive interrogative methods by state actors or officials that inflicted severe physical or mental pain and suffering, constituting torture, including:

1. Beating (most often with kicks, punches, electric cables, wooden sticks, and plastic pipes, and rubber hoses)

2. Suspension (being hung by the wrists or ankles from chains on the wall, fixtures, or the ceiling)

3. Electric shock

4. Threatened sexual abuse

---

169 Saratan 1366), art. 3, http://www2.ohchr.org/english/law/cat.htm, *hereinafter "CAT." *Afghanistan ratified CAT* on April 1, 1987 (12 Hamal 1366).

170 9 Id

171 Constitution of Afghanistan, ratified January 26, 2004 (6 Dalwa 1382),Art. 29, http://www.afghanembassy.com.pl/cms/uploads/images/Constitution/The%20 Constitution.pdf. hereinafter "Constitution of Afghanistan"+. According to Article 29 of the Constitution of Afghanistan, "No one shall be allowed to order torture, even for discovering the truth from another individual who is under investigation, arrest, detention or has been convicted to be punished"; see also Afghan Penal Code, Gazette No. 347 (October 7, 1976; 15 Mizan 1355), Art. 275, http://www. asianlii.org/af/legis/laws/clc1976ogn347p1976100613550715a429.txt/cgi-bin/ download.cgi/download/af/legis/laws/clc1976ogn347p1976100613550715a429. pdf [hereinafter "Afghan Penal Code"+.Art. 275criminalizestorture and states that if public officials (including all NDS and ANP officials) torture an accused person for the purpose of obtaining a confession, they shall be sentenced to imprisonment between 5 and 15 years.

172 Conflict-related detainees are most often charged with offenses codified in the Penal Code(1976), the Law on Crimes against Internal and External Security of the Democratic Republic of Afghanistan(1987), and the Law on Combat against Terrorist Offences(2008). The Law on Crimes against Internal and External Security lists the categories of the offenses NDS investigates, including but not limited to national treason, espionage, terrorism, sabotage, propaganda against the government, war propaganda, assisting enemy forces, and organized activity against internal and external security. See Art.1-9, 23

5. Twisting and wrenching of the genitals
6. Forced prolonged standing
7. Burning (with cigarettes)
8. Biting (by interrogators)

Beating was the most frequently reported form of abuse. Beatings were typically administered multiple times and over periods of several days, using a variety of tools including electric cables, plastic pipes, and wooden sticks. Monitors also found that in many of the cases in which detainees were subjected to beating, they were also subjected to suspension by their arms or upside-down by their legs from walls, ceilings, or fixtures for durations lasting up to several hours, and in some cases repeatedly over periods of time lasting up to several weeks.[173] Several of these methods have been specifically and emphatically denied by the NDS, including electric shock, threatened sexual abuse, and abuse of genitals. This report's findings contradict these denials by the NDS, and confirm that these methods of torture have been used by NDS officials to interrogate detainees.[174]

Monitors also found credible evidence of torture in NDS facilities in Herat, Kandahar, Laghman, and in NDS Kabul Department 90/124.Credible evidence of torture was found in NDS facilities in Kabul Department 17/40, Nangarhar, Badakhshan, Wardak, and Helmand; in ANP facilities in Kandahar, including the provincial ANP Headquarters; and in the Juvenile Corrections Center (JCC) in Helmand.

Electric Shock

Monitors received 14 credible allegations of NDS detainees being subjected to electric shocks, contradicting an official statement that the use of electric shock is —absolutely non-existent in the NDS.[175] Detainees reported that electric shocks were often administered through wires clipped to their toes. As one detainee held in NDS Department 90/124 explained, —They used to tie my hands and sit me in a chair. They put two clips on my toes then used this machine with electricity [that was] giving electric shock to me. It was very hard. They were laughing, smoking cigarettes, making fun of us. We were screaming, screaming in pain.[176] Another detainee said, —They tied some wires to my two second toes. Then they gave me electric

---

173 Many of these methods are consistent with and corroborate UNAMA's findings, including suspension, beating, electric shock, threatened sexual abuse, forced standing, and twisting and wrenching of the genitals. See UNAMA, Conflict-Related Detainees in Afghan Custody; supra note 3, p. 3.
174 UNAMA, Conflict-Related Detainees in Afghan Custody, supra note 3, p. 61-62.
175 Ibid.
176 Interview with Detainee 99

shocks. It was very bad treatment. So much pain...They kept asking me questions and saying confess, confess![177]

Other detainees told monitors of the use of electric shocks on multiple areas of their bodies. According to one detainee, interrogators administered electric shocks —on my hands, temple, armpits, and testes. They would use around five minutes of electricity to get me to confess.[178] Another detainee said that his interrogators administered electric shocks three times, each time using —a kind of pistol like a gun for the shock. [It was] special electricity and would shock me all over the body...each time they used it, they placed it on different parts of my body.[179]

Detainees described intense pain from the shocks: —It felt like I was half-dead, said one detainee. —My entire body was trembling and shaking, and my heart was beating very quickly, but I wasn't able to move or speak.[180] Another detainee described electric shock as — the worst punishment; it destroyed your manhood, your dignity.[181] In some cases, the pain caused by the electric shocks would cause detainees to lose consciousness. Every time I passed out from the pain, said one detainee who was shocked 12 times in succession. Every time I would go unconscious. Then I would wake up and they would shock me again.[182]

Threats of Sexual Abuse

Monitors found 10 credible reports of NDS officials threatening to sexually abuse detainees. These findings contradict NDS claims that the practice is absolutely non-existent and those officials have never used threats of sexual abuse to interrogate and torture detainees.[183]

Interviewers were told that interrogators used the threat of rape to force detainees to confess. One detainee held in NDS Kandahar stated, —They said they would rape me, and one time they took a stick and dipped it into chilli powder and threatened to insert the stick into my anus. They tried to pull off my pants. When they did that, I confessed to everything they wanted.[184] Other detainees experienced similar threats. One reported that, —They told me they will take off my shalwar [Afghan traditional dress] and rape me unless I confess.[185] Another detainee told interviewers that the interrogators — threatened to stick a plastic bottle up my anus. They asked me how

177 *Interview with Detainee 54*
178 *Interview with Detainee 46*
179 *Interview with Detainee 55*
180 *Interview with Detainee 101*
181 *Interview with Detainee 99*
182 *Interview with Detainee 54*
183 UNAMA, *Conflict Related Detainees in Afghan Custody, supra note* 3, p. 61-62
184 *Interview with Detainee 46*
185 *Interview with Detainee 51*

many children I had, and when I said that I had five children, they said, five is enough for you.' They would tell me, "If you do not tell us the truth, you will get the bottle.' They pulled my trousers down.[186]

Researchers found that the specific threats reportedly used by interrogators were consistent with the findings of UNAMA, including near identical forms of abuse threatened. All three groups received reports from different detainees that interrogators threatened to sexually abuse detainees with sticks coated in chilli powder in NDS Kandahar and with plastic bottles in the NDS Department 90/124.

Abuse of Detainees Genitals

Monitors received reports from eight detainees that their genitals were physically abused by NDS officials. Three detainees in Kandahar, three detainees in NDS Department 90/124, and one detainee in Herat reported that officials had twisted, wrenched, whipped, or otherwise abused their genitals in the course of their interrogations.[187] These reports directly contradict NDS's official statement that abuse such as the —twisting of sexual organs, etc. is —absolutely non-existent in the NDS.[188] One such detainee reported that over a period of seven days, —They whipped my testicles and my penis with a cable several times. There was blood in my urine after. I have no sexual feelings for women anymore. It hurts when I go to the bathroom.[189]

Detainees also reported that interrogators hung weights from their testicles. One detainee described how while in NDS Kandahar, —I was freed and taken to my cell to have some sleep. They gave me a blanket then. But that night, they tortured me. They tied my testicles with a rope and hung an iron weight from the rope. I can't remember exactly how long this lasted, but it was for a long time. The torture made me confess everything...I confessed that I was involved with the Taliban.[190] Another detainee told the monitors that while in NDS Herat, —They took a weight and they tied it to my testicles so that it became very painful.[191]

---

186 *Interview with Detainee 6*

187The findings of this report are also consistent with those of UNAMA, which documented several cases of wrenching or twisting detainees' genitals. Notably, both AIHRC and the Open Society Foundations and UNAMA received reports that interrogators had abused detainees' genitals in NDS Department 90/124 and NDS Kandahar.

188 UNAMA, *Conflict-Related Detainees in Afghan Custody, supra note 3*, 61-62

189 *Interview with Detainee 6*

190 *Interview with Detainee 47*

191 *Interview with Detainee 86*

Detainee Confessions Obtained Using Torture

As noted above, international law defines torture as acts carried out by or with the consent or acquiescence of government officials where pain or suffering is inflicted for the purposes of —obtaining a confession,—punishment, or the—intimidation or coercion of an individual or based on any —discriminatory reasons. According to interviewees for this report, in the vast majority of cases of abuse Afghan state officials inflicted pain for the purpose of obtaining a confession or coercing detainees to provide information. The evidence collected indicates that state officials often utilized specific methods of abuse in conjunction with interrogations, clearly aimed at coercing confessions or information from detainees, constituting torture under international law. This finding is consistent with a past AIHRC report.[192] In its 2009 report, Causes of Torture in Law Enforcement Institutions, the AIHRC stated that —one of the main causes of torture and other inhuman treatment is to obtain confessions and testimonies.[193]

Most detainees interviewed who confessed to crimes reported that they confessed only after being subjected to severe physical abuse. As one detainee described, —I was beaten with cables, and while I was being beaten, I confessed that I was associated with the Taliban...I was under such extreme pressure that I confessed. After it was finished I told them that I only confessed because of the beating.[194] Another detainee reported that he confessed only after interrogators beat him with electric cables, subjected him to electric shocks, and threatened to —open [his] parts if he didn't admit to being a member of the Taliban.[195]

Researchers also found that in most cases, interrogators would stop torturing the detainee after he confessed, indicating that the abuse was carried out for the purpose of obtaining a confession or information. As one detainee explained,—I couldn't last longer than two days before I confessed. NDS just wants to send us to the central jail, and so they want my fingerprint [on the confession]. Once they have that, they will not torture anymore.[196] The detainee was subjected to beatings with electric cables and physical abuse of his genitals before confessing.

---

192 Afghanistan Independent Human Rights Commission, Causes of Torture in Law Enforcement Institutions, AIHRC, April 2009 (Hamal 1388), p. 16, available at: http://www.aihrc.org.af/english/ *hereinafter "AIHRC, Causes of Torture in Law Enforcement Institutions".
193 Likewise, in its October 2011 detentions report, UNAMA found compelling evidence that NDS officials at five facilities had used torture systematically "for the purpose of obtaining confessions and information."See *UNAMA, Conflict-Related Detainees in Afghan Custody; supra note 3, p. 3.*
194 *Interview with Detainee 45*
195 *Interview with Detainee 7*
196 *Interview with Detainee 86*

Another detainee described how he was tortured by officials until he confessed at NDS Department 90/124. —For five days and nights I was hung upside down for long periods of time. They beat me with PVC plastic pipes—they beat me on the back of my legs and everywhere else on my body. I couldn't suffer the beatings and the torture any longer, and I didn't want them to beat me anymore, so I put my fingerprint on the paper. I was in Department 90[/124] for 10 days, and after I gave them my fingerprint they stopped beating me and transferred me to Department 17[/40].[197] Detainees themselves identified a pattern in which abuse stopped once NDS officials obtained a confession: —I think that half of the prisoners are forced to confess like I was. When they arrest us, they torture at the beginning, but then they stop once they have a confession.[198]

Many detainees claimed that they were forced to provide false confessions.[199] One detainee told monitors that he falsely confessed after 25 days of torture including suspension, severe beatings with pipes and cables on his feet, head, and genitals, and threats of sexual abuse. —They tortured me to confess...it was a forced confession. What I said was not true.[200] Another detainee interrogated at NDS Kandahar stated, —I was interrogated three times in NDS. Each time, I was beaten with hands, fists, and cables. One time I was beaten with the cables, and while I was being beaten, I confessed that I was associated with the Taliban. They said, pull off your pants,' and they threatened to penetrate me with a stick [in my anus]. I was under such extreme pressure that I confessed. But the detainee insisted his confession was coerced and false. —After [the torture] was finished

---

197 *Interview with Detainee 12,* Detainees are typically interrogated first in Department 90/124 before being transferred to Department 17/40.

198 *Interview with Detainee 80*

199 There is ample evidence that the use of torture in interrogations can lead to false confessions and unreliable information. See Juan E. Méndez, Report of the UN Special Rapporteur on Torture and Other Cruel, Inhuman or Degrading Treatment or Punishment, *United Nations UN Human Rights Council, February 2011 (Dalwa 1389)*; Saul M. Kassin and Gisli H. Gudjonsson, "The Psychology of Confessions: A Review of the Literature and Issues," *Psychological Science in the Public Interest, Vol. 5, No. 2 (Nov. 2004; Aqrab 1383)*, pp. 33-67;Richard A. Leo and Richard J. Of she,"The Consequences of False Confessions: Deprivations of Liberty and Miscarriages of Justice in the Age of Psychological Interrogation," *The Journal of Criminal Law and Criminology, Vol. 88, No. 2 (Winter 1998)*, pp. 429-496; Barrie Paskins, "What's Wrong with Torture?" *British Journal of International Studies, Vol. 2, No. 2 (July 1976; Saratan 1355)*, pp. 138-148; Christopher Kutz, "Torture, Necessity and Existential Politics," *California Law Review, Vol. 95, No. 1 (February 2007; Dalwa 1385)*, pp. 235-276; Peter Finn and Joby Warrick, "Detainee's Harsh Treatment Foiled No Plots," WashingtonPost,March-29,2009,(9-Hamal1388),http://www.washingtonpost.com/wp-dyn/content/article/2009/03/28/AR2009032802066.html; Dr. Marvin Zalman, Criminal Procedure: Constitution and Society, 2007;"France/Germany/United Kingdom 'No Questions Asked' Intelligence Cooperation with Countries that Torture," *Human Rights Watch, June 2010 (Jawza 1389), http://www.hrw.org/sites/default/files/reports/ct0610webwcover.pdf.*

200 *Interview with Detainee 6*

I told them that I only confessed because of the beating. But they responded to that by beating me again, he said. —I swear by God and by my children that I am innocent.[201]

Failure to Exclude Forced Confessions in Court

Under Afghan law, confessions extracted under torture are not admissible in court.[202] However, interviews with detainees and Defense lawyers (and based on the AIHRC's long standing experience monitoring Afghan courts), suggest that Afghan judges often accept the confessions of detainees even if detainees have told the court that their confessions were forced through the use of torture.

During the research period for this report, several interviewees alleged that they were convicted of crimes based on forced confessions.[203] According to one detainee; he was convicted and imprisoned based on a confession provided after a month and a half of torture by NDS officials. —They would come in and beat me two or three times a day and usually once a night. Every time they would beat me, they would also ask me questions. They put me down and tied my feet, and then they whipped my feet with the cables. The color of my feet was changed to the black of your shirt. One time...they took my trousers down. So of course after this I signed the confession, and I put my name on it and I stamped it, he said. The court accepted the detainee's confession and sentenced him to 16 years in prison.[204] A defense lawyer from Kandahar complained, —We are not happy with the courts. The confession comes from pressure through torture, beatings, etc, and we tell the court that the confession came through such illegal means, and according to the Constitution this is not right. But the judges do not listen to us.[205]

---

201 *Interview with Detainee 45*

202 *Art 30, Constitution of Afghanistan*; Art 5.5 and Art 7, Interim Criminal Procedure Code

203 The admission of forced confessions by Afghan judges has been documented by UNAMA as well, which found in its 2011 detentions report that "even in cases where defense lawyers raise the issue of forced confession through torture, courts usually dismiss the application and allow the confession to be used as evidence." See UNAMA, Conflict Related Detainees in Afghan Custody; supra note 3, p. 7. The UN also observed in its 2009 report on arbitrary detentions that "judges did not necessarily investigate allegations of that evidence, including confessions, were elicited through coercion. The consequence [is] that a number of forced 'confessions' may have been accepted as evidence,"Arbitrary Detention in Afghanistan: A Call for Action, Vol. II, UNAMA, January 2009, [hereinafter UNAMA, Arbitrary Detention in Afghanistan, Vol. II], p. 65

204 *Interview with Detainee 6*

205 *Interview with Defense Lawyer 16*

Locations

The researchers found credible evidence of torture at nine separate NDS facilities:[206]

> NDS Kabul Department 90/124
> NDS Herat
> NDS Kandahar
> NDS Laghman
> NDS Badakhshan
> NDS Lashkar Gah
> NDS Kabul Department 17/40
> NDS Nangarhar
> NDS Wardak

NDS Kabul Department 90/124

Interviews with detainees indicate that torture is a particularly serious problem in NDS Counter-Terrorism Department 90/124 in Kabul.

In NDS Department 90/124, —high-value terror suspects are detained, including those suspected of holding positions of authority in anti-government elements or being involved in high-profile attacks. Although the AIHRC repeatedly requested permission to interview detainees held in NDS Department 90/124, the NDS has refused to grant access.[207] However, monitors interviewed detainees who had been released or transferred from NDS Department 90/124 to other facilities. Out of the 12 detainees interviewed who had been detained in NDS Department 90/124, 11 reported being subjected to abusive interrogation techniques that constituted torture.[208]

Detainees in NDS Department 90/124 reported that they were subjected to a number of different forms of torture. A significant number of detainees reported being suspended and beaten, as well as threatened with sexual abuse. Other forms of abuse were also reported, including burning with cigarettes, and stretching detainees while lying on a wooden board.

Many detainees reported being subjected to repeated, severe beatings during interrogations in NDS Department 90/124. —During

---

206 AIHRC and Open Society Foundations findings of torture in NDS Kabul (Department 90/124), NDS Herat, NDS Kandahar, and NDS Laghman are consistent with UNAMA's findings that torture has been practiced at these specific facilities. Unless otherwise specified, NDS provincial facilities named in this report refer to provincial NDS headquarters facilities, located in the capital city of the province named.

207 UNAMA also reported being denied access to Department 90/124. *UNAMA, Conflict-Related Detainees in Afghan Custody, supra notes* 3, p. 18. Despite repeated requests, NDS has not granted the AIHRC access to NDS Kabul Department 90/124

208 These findings are consistent with UNAMA's finding that torture is systematically practiced at NDS Department 90/124. See id., p. 3

the questionings, I would be hit on the head and body with shoes and books, and they would pull my beard and bang my head against the wall. These beatings happened at least 10 times during my month of interrogation," said one detainee.[209] Another detainee reported, — They would put me on my hands and knees and then hit me on the back with electric cables and one long, heavy pipe. I was only beaten during interrogation times—they wanted me to confess to being a Talib or a suicide bomber. These beatings would happen at least once a day and sometimes more. Once I was beaten four times in one night. I was in such bad shape that I couldn't even walk to the bathroom. I had to crawl...Before I came here [to prison], I had a black beard. Now my beard is half white.[210]

According to detainees held in NDS Department 90/124, such beatings were a common practice in the facility. As one detainee explained, —Many people were being beaten. We were all brought down to the basement. The basement was the torture place. It was like a butcher shop—you could see blood everywhere...You could hear a lot of screaming. Screaming like it was animals screaming. When we would scream, the guards would put their fists under our chins to stop our voices.[211]

Detainees also reported being suspended from the wall or ceiling for several days at a time. One detainee described how he was suspended from the ceiling with his arms shackled and his feet — barely touching the ground for 11 days: —I was only released from the restraints to eat, pray, go to the bathroom, and to be beaten. I begged the interrogators for rest.[212] Another detainee was suspended for seven days.—They kept me blindfolded, and they hung me from the wall so that my feet were not touching the ground, he said. —They would take me down for meal times, and usually they would take me down for prayer time...I was out of my senses during this time—my feet were very swollen from the hanging. I didn't know that it was my feet, they were so swollen and strange looking.[213]

Other detainees who had been detained in NDS Department 90/124 reported being beaten while they were suspended. One detainee reported that he was —hung upside down for a long period of time and received multiple beatings while in this position. The detainee reported that as a result of this treatment, his foot and toe were broken.[214] Several additional forms of torture were also reported by detainees held in NDS Department 90/124. For instance, one detainee described how he was placed on a —long, wooden board and pulled

---

209 *Interview with Detainee 1*
210 *Interview with Detainee 9*
211 *Interview with Detainee 6*
212 *Interview with Detainee 9*
213 *Interview with Detainee 6*
214 *Interview with Detainee 12*

in both directions.[215] Another detainee reported that interrogators would burn his hands with cigarettes during questioning.[216]

The NDS Herat

Researchers also found evidence of torture in NDS Herat, although a monitoring visit on February 13, 2012 (24 Dalwa 1390), found evidence of improvements in detainee treatment. Seven individuals who had been detained at the Herat facility reported that they had been subjected to abuse during interrogations, including beating and suspension.[217] Though most cases occurred prior to the implementation of ISAF inspections in response to the UNAMA report, one case of abuse occurred after the ISAF inspection of NDS Herat. A 15 year-old detainee reported that he was arrested by ALP and then transferred to NDS Herat on or around November 5, 2011 (14 Aqrab 1390). The detainee reported being beaten by NDS officials at NDS Herat for multiple days from November 9, 2011 (18 Aqrab 1390), onwards.

I was beaten with a double twisted electric cable. They hit me on my head until I couldn't feel anything and tears were coming from my eyes.[218] The detainee stated that he was regularly beaten in a container located within the NDS facility. He also described being forced to lie down on his chest and being beaten on his back and backside for one to one and a half hours in a room within or adjacent to the same container. While abusing the detainee, NDS officials demanded that he name members of the Taliban at his school. The detainee stated that his confession was obtained by force after he was too dazed from the beatings with the cable to know what [he] was saying.[219]

Evidence of Torture in Additional NDS Facilities[220]

Two interviewees who were detained in NDS Wardak reported being subjected to torture, including suspension and beatings. One detainee stated, they hung me and used many different forms of torture. It was very severe; they used electric cables, wooden sticks, metal rods, and hung us upside down. They asked questions [saying] tell us the links you have [and that] you are Talib...accept and confess these things. They kicked and slapped me...it was very, very bad

---

215 *Interview with Detainee 9*

216 *Interview with Detainee 2*

217 This finding is consistent with UNAMA's finding of systematic torture at NDS Herat

218 *Interview with Detainee 91*

219 *Id.*

220 Aside from NDS Kandahar, the six NDS facilities listed below are additional to those where UNAMA found evidence of systematic torture.

treatment.[221] Another detainee reported similar practices of beating and suspension, as well as forced standing. —They stood me in front of a wall, tied one leg to the wall and forced me to stand on the other leg. If I couldn't stay up and balance they would beat me...They beat me a lot. They used a rubber hose, rope, and plastic around my feet. They took the binding on my feet and had a pulley attached to the ceiling and hung me upside down, he said. The detainee reported that while he was upside down, the interrogators would —bounce me up and down and slams my head into the ground.[222]

Researchers also found evidence of torture and mistreatment, including beatings, suspension, and biting, in seven cases in Department 17/40 in NDS Kabul, the most recent allegation dating to August 2011 (Asad 1390). One detainee reported beatings, suspensions, and beatings while suspended.[223] Another detainee reported that he was subjected to severe beatings of his lower body during his detention in Department 17/40. He also reported being bitten by interrogators; two bite marks were visible to interviewers on his lower left calf and upper right leg.[224]

Eight detainees in NDS Nangarhar provided credible allegations of torture, including one detainee who recounted how he was repeatedly beaten with a stick over the course of 11 days. After one beating, the detainee reported, he was made to stay outside in the rain, naked, for around 30 minutes. These beatings were so severe, he said, that —it was painful just to have the material of my prison uniform resting on my skin.[225] One detainee also reported being beaten with sticks, and another with sticks and electrical wires.65Another detainee who had been detained in NDS Nangarhar reported that he was subjected to various forms of torture over a period of 20 days including suspension, electric shocks, and severe beatings with a piece of wood.[226]

In NDS Lashkar Gah, monitors documented two credible allegations of torture, both including severe beatings. One detainee alleged that abuse occurred in January 2011 (Jadi 1389), while the other alleged that abuse occurred in October 2011 (Mezan 1390). An additional detainee reported being abused by NDS officials in an NDS facility in Nad Ali district. However, the large majority of detainees interviewed that were held at NDS Lashkar Gah reported no mistreatment. One detainee stated that while in custody in NDS Lashkar Gah, —They [the interrogators] hit me on the back and feet with a solid iron pipe...They also beat us with their fists. They gave us such beatings. They would not give up...they would beat you until you

---

221 *Interview with Detainee 98*
222 *Interview with Detainee 99*
223 *Interview with Detainee 12*
224 *Interview with Detainee 13*
225 *Interview with Detainee 25*
226 *Interview with Detainee 32, 33, and 30*

said that you have relations with the Taliban.[227] The same detainee mentioned that detainees who had been tortured were moved to an isolated room when the facility was visited by outside monitors.— When the authorities came to the NDS, they would keep us—the ones who had been tortured—somewhere else so that we would not be seen. There was an underground room.[228]

Five victims of mistreatment and torture were also interviewed in NDS Badakhshan. One detainee was reportedly tied between two trees and beaten until he lost consciousness. After three days of detention and interrogation by the NDS, he was eventually released. Another detainee was abused at NDS Keshim District (in Badakhshan Province) through kicking, punching, and beatings from officials with the butts of their guns. He was then transferred to NDS Badakhshan, where the head of interrogation beat him with a stick. The head of NDS Keshim District and the head of interrogation of NDS Badakhshan both acknowledged to the AIHRC that they had abused the detainee, and monitors obtained photographic evidence of marks, bruises, and cuts on the detainee's back, legs, and shoulders from the beatings.[229] Four allegations of abuse in NDS Laghman were reported during the research period; the most recent abuse was alleged to have taken place in July 2011(Saratan 1390). AIHRC monitors also received a significant number of credible allegations of abuse in NDS Kandahar—a total of 20 over the course of the research period. AIHRC monitors most recently visited NDS Kandahar in January 2012 (Jadi 1390), and documented 10 credible allegations of abuse.

Torture and Mistreatment at Non-NDS Facilities, Juvenile Corrections Center Helmand

Monitors also found credible evidence of mistreatment at the Juvenile Corrections Center (JCC) in Helmand. It is unclear, however, whether those who reported abuse were themselves conflict-related detainees as NDS LashkarGah regularly transfers juvenile conflict-related detainees to the facility. Reports of abuse at the JCC Helmand included sexual abuse and routine beatings. One detainee reported that there were three juveniles who were regularly raped by the director and the director's son: —They have been used many, many times. Whenever they want to use them they do...It will happen outside the center [pointing to the area behind the building where the detainees are held]. Even in this office they can do it.[230]

227 *Interview with Detainee 24*, It should be noted that this detainee was held in NDS Nangarhar two years ago, though his complaints of abuse are not inconsistent with complaints of more recent detainees.
228 Id.
229 *Interviews with Detainees 104, 105, 106, 107, and 108*
230 Id.

One detainee reported that he had been subjected to multiple beatings with fists and an iron pole: —One time the director made us stand up. After we stood for a long time he yelled, Why are you standing,' and he hit me... [W]e gets hit very hard with the pipe. I have a scar on my back from one beating, he said. A one-inch scar was visible to interviewers on the upper-right side of his back. He continued, —If you look at the buttocks of the other boy prisoners, you will see that they have been hit with the pipe. You will see their scars.[231]

AIHRC officials followed up on the report of sexual abuse, interviewing every detainee at the JCC in Helmand. Their investigation found that the allegations of abuse, including sexual abuse, were credible. AIHRC monitors also received reports that juvenile detainees had been threatened not to speak about mistreatment to AIHRC monitors, and that detainees had in the past been beaten for disclosing abuse to AIHRC monitors. As a result of the AIHRC's findings, the governor of Helmand removed the director of the JCC Helmand on or around July 21, 2011 (30 Saratan 1390). The director was removed from JCC Helmand within days of the AIHRC's investigation—swift action that is welcomes and speaks to the credibility and seriousness of the AIHRC's findings. However, it remains unclear whether the individual was criminally prosecuted for alleged crimes.

Afghan National Police Facilities in Kandahar

Researchers interviewed multiple individuals detained by the Afghan National Police (ANP) in Kandahar who reported being mistreated and tortured while in ANP custody. Detainees were reportedly tortured at a variety of official and unofficial locations including ANP check posts, ANP headquarters, and other ANP facilities in Kandahar. Multiple methods of torture were used and were broadly similar to those reportedly employed by some NDS officials, including beatings with kicks, fists, electric and wire cables; choking; electric shock; and squeezing of testicles.[232] One detainee also reported that he was interrogated and tortured at an unofficial detention facility.

Several detainees reported being tortured while detained at ANP Headquarters. One detainee reported that interrogators —would hold me from the neck until I became unconscious, and then they would kick me very hard. I had to pass urine in the cell, so I was forced to sleep in my own urine. The police [ANP] told me that I should never

---

231 *Interview with Detainee 83*

232 These findings are also consistent with and corroborate UNAMA's documentation of torture and mistreatment in ANP facilities in Kandahar. See UNAMA, *Conflict-Related Detainees in Afghan Custody, supra note 3*, p. 36-37

tell anything that happened there to anyone. They treated us like animals.[233]

Detainees also reported being tortured while in custody at ANP check posts. After being arrested, detainees reported being held at ANP check posts for substantial periods of time, between one and four days, and were not immediately transferred to the provincial headquarters of the ANP or the NDS. It was during this time that detainees were interrogated and subjected to mistreatment and torture. One detainee reported being subjected to beatings, stress positions, and abuse of his genitals while detained at the 9th district police check post. He told researchers that ANP official's —made I lie down on the ground on my stomach and one of the officials sat on my back and started pulling my hand and legs to join them together. [As a result] he broke my left arm. After this they started squeezing my testicles so that I couldn't bear it. They did it so many times that blood came out of one side of my testicles.[234] The detainee stated that ANP officials were torturing him in order to obtain a confession. — Repeatedly they were showing me some AK47s, a rocket launcher, and other explosive materials and saying that I should confess that they were mine, but I hadn't ever seen them before and they were not mine.[235]

Researchers for this report have also received allegations that one detainee died in April 2011 (Hamal 1390) as a result of torture and mistreatment at an ANP checks post. The AIHRC investigated this case at the time of the incident and the findings have also been previously reported by UNAMA.[236] According to interviews with family members, the individual was detained at an ANP check post for several days, where he was kicked and beaten with fists and wire cables. He was then transferred to NDS Kandahar. Around 15 days later, the individual died. At the time of death, the detainee's abdomen was heavily bruised.[237]

A doctor at Mirwais Hospital, the province's main hospital, stated that they have treated a significant number of individuals for injuries sustained while in ANP custody. —Most injury cases we receive are from the police. Sticks, guns, cables, they use all these kinds of things to beat detainees. There is no controlling them—they can do anything and everything to people.[238] The doctor described a recent case of a 60-year-old man who had been severely beaten in ANP custody. According the doctor, the beatings suffered by the man had caused blood vessels in his leg to rupture, leaving his leg without sufficient

233 *Interview with Detainee 44*
234 *Interview with Detainee 44*
235 *Interview with Detainee 48*
236 Id.
237 *UNAMA Detentions Report*
238 Interviews with family members of the deceased detainee and a doctor who treated the deceased detainee. See also, UNAMA, *Conflict -Related Detainees in Afghan Custody, supra note 3*, p. 25.

blood supply. —He was here in the hospital for two nights, and we said we needed to amputate or he would die, but he decided to leave. [He] maybe went to Pakistan, probably Quetta or Peshawar, to get treatment.[239]

Another detainee reported being subjected to severe beatings and electric shock at a location that was not an official ANP detention facility. He stated that he was transferred from ANP headquarters to a provincial government building that was not an official detention facility, where he was detained and interrogated for two days. — They used an electric cable to beat me—30 times, 30 lashes with the cable. They beat me on both sides of my feet, usually on the soles of my feet. Then they beat me with the cables on my head, 27 times they beat me. [I] still [have] marks from this. [I was] bleeding from my hands, feet, and head very badly. Four other people I spoke to [at NDS Kandahar] were also beaten [there].The detainee was also subjected to electric shocks. —It was so much pain; they said confess, confess, they kept asking me questions. Twelve times they shocked me. Every time I passed out from the pain, and they kept asking me questions and saying confess, confess. They took my thumbprint [upon confession].[240] The detainee said he believes the Afghan Border Police (ABP) were responsible for detaining and abusing him at this location before transferring him to NDS Kandahar.

The ANP is playing a prominent role in counter-terrorism and national security cases in Kandahar, including working closely with U.S. and ISAF forces in major operations during 2010 and 2011(1389-1390).[241] Consequently, the ANP appears to be involved in detaining and interrogating a significant number of conflict-related detainees in Kandahar. Researchers found evidence that ANP officials in Kandahar not only engage in torture of detainees but have done so at as many as five sites, one reportedly not an official ANP facility, in some cases for multiple days at a time.

Challenges to Effective Detainee Monitoring

In the course of conducting interviews for this report, researchers found that effective monitoring of NDS and other detention facilities was hindered by several factors, including holding or moving detainees to concealed or secret locations where AIHRC monitors have not been granted access, and detainees' fears of reprisals for reporting torture and mistreatment. The impact of fear of reprisals acting as an impediment to effective detainee interviews, particularly while the detainees remain in custody, has impeded monitoring in Afghanistan

---

239 Id.
240 *Interview with Detainee 54*
241 *Interview with Detainee 54*

and has been cited as a major obstacle by human rights monitors in other parts of the world.[242]

Evidence of Efforts to Conceal Torture

Reports from several detainees indicate that NDS officials may have conducted interrogations and engaged in torture in locations within or close to detention facilities that may not be readily visible or made accessible to outside monitors, such as basements and temporary containers. The reported use of such locations raises concerns that some officials are seeking to evade independent monitoring and conceal detainee abuse.

Monitors received reports of a basement facility in NDS Herat. Five detainees interviewed stated that they were brought to a basement or underground room in NDS Herat for interrogation.[243] One detainee stated that the underground room was in —the old NDS facility, which lies behind the main white office building inside the NDS Herat compound. All five detainees who were taken to the basement were tortured there. Detainees reported that NDS officials used a variety of methods of torture, including suspension by the arms from steel bars and beatings. In one case, a detainee claimed that after being beaten he was immersed in a tub filled with salt water in order to increase the pain from his wounds.[244] The existence of an underground room within the former NDS Herat building was corroborated by another interviewee who stated that he was held in an underground room in the same facility during the Taliban regime.[245]

---

242 Matthieu Aikins, "Our Man in Kandahar," *The Atlantic, November 2011* (Aqrab 1390),http://www.theatlantic.com/magazine/archive/2011/11/aikins/8653/.YaroslavTrofimov, "Surge Focus Is Roads, Police," The Wall Street Journal, December 17, 2009 (26 Qaws 1388),http://online.wsj.com/article/SB126085693657891775.html. Forsberg, Counterinsurgency in Kandahar: Evaluating the 2010 Hamkari Campaign, Institute for the Study of War Studies, December 2010 (Qaws 1389),http://www.understandingwar.org/sites/default/files/Afghanistan%20Report%207_15Dec.pdf.

243 See for example the case of dual Canadian and Syrian citizen Maher Arar, who was tortured in Syrian custody in 2002 despite nine visits by Canadian consular officials as part of diplomatic assurance with the Syrian government. Commission of Inquiry into the Actions of Canadian Officials in Relation to Maher Arar, http://www.sirc-csars.gc.ca/pdfs/cm_arar_rec-eng.pdf, p. 44. See also *Human Rights Watch*, "Diplomatic Assurances against Torture: Questions and Answers," http://www.hrw.org/sites/default/files/related_material/ecaqnal106web.pdf.

244 See also Human Rights Watch, "Diplomatic Assurances against Torture: Questions and Answers,"

245 *Interview with Detainees 87, 94, 95, 96, and 97.* In addition, Detainee 93 said that he has relatives who were abused in a basement facility of NDS Herat, and Detainee 89 said that he knows other prisoners at the Herat central prison who were tortured in such a basement. Neither Detainee 89 nor Detainee 93 was taken to the basement himself, however.

Monitors also received several reports of NDS officials acting to conceal evidence of torture or mistreatment from monitoring organizations. One detainee from Kandahar told the AIHRC that one of his fellow detainees at NDS Kandahar, who had been —beaten hard, was transferred —to some unknown place the day before the AIHRC visited the facility; NDS Kandahar does not permit unannounced visits by AIHRC monitors and requires at least one day notice.[246] Similarly, a detainee in Helmand reported that —when the authorities came to the NDS, they would keep those of us who had been tortured somewhere else so that we would not be seen. There was an underground room, and there were three of us who were kept there.[247]

Detainees Fears of Reprisal for Revealing Evidence of Torture or Mistreatment

Several detainees reported that they feared being subjected to reprisals for discussing mistreatment with monitors. One detainee in NDS Herat, who had reported being subjected to severe beatings and abuse of his genitals, stated at the end of the interview, —I have nothing else to say. They will put me somewhere else after I talk to you. They will disappear me.[248] A detainee at the Juvenile Corrections Center in Helmand reported to the AIHRC that he and his fellow detainees were severely beaten as a consequence of having reported mistreatment at the facility. "We wrote a complaint letter once, but the director found out, and then we got hit very hard with the pipe after that," he said.[249]

Some detainees' fears of reprisal had a direct impact on what they would disclose to monitors. In one case, an official in NDS Parwan repeatedly interrupted an interview conducted by two AIHRC monitors. When the detainee being interviewed began to talk about the conditions and treatment in NDS Parwan, the official repeatedly yelled at the detainee that he should "tell the truth!"[250] Another detainee interviewed by an AIHRC monitor in NDS Laghman indicated that he had been severely beaten by speaking quietly and making hand gestures, refusing to say any more because "[the official] will come back and I will be in trouble."[251]

---

246 *Interview with Detainee 59*
247 *Interview with Detainee 80*
248 *Interview with Detainee 86*
249 *Interview with Detainee 83*
250 *Interview with Detainee 109*
251 *Interview with Detainee 103*

V. International Detainee Transfers, Monitoring, and Joint Operations

Under the general international law principle of non-refoulement, which has a basis in international human rights, refugee, and humanitarian law, states are prohibited from transferring persons under their effective control to the custody of another state if there are substantial grounds to believe the individual would face a real risk of torture or cruel, inhuman or degrading treatment or punishment.[252] ISAF forces continue to regularly detain and transfer individuals to Afghan custody. Under ISAF's —96-hour rule, individuals detained during ISAF operations are generally released or transferred to Afghan authorities within 96 hours. However, in the absence of more detailed, uniform standards and guidelines for detention transfers, in large part due to the multinational structure of ISAF, in which each nation may interpret legal obligations differently, there is significant diversity in detention policies and practices among ISAF nations.

ISAF nations also face very different circumstances and challenges when it comes to detentions. The United States detains thousands of individuals all across Afghanistan, with a majority held in the Detention Facility in Parwan (DFIP, formerly known as the Bagram Theatre Internment Facility). Meanwhile, nations with much smaller

---

252 The principle of non-refoulement is a general principle of international law with a basis in international human rights law, refugee law, and international humanitarian law. Sir Elihu Lauterpacht and Daniel Bethlehem, "The Scope and Content of the Principle of Non-Refoulement: Opinion," in Erika Feller, Volker Turk, and Frances Nicholson (eds.), Refugee Protection in International Law: UNHCR's Global Consultations on International Protection, Cambridge, UK: Cambridge University Press (2003),www.unhcr.org/publ/PUBL/419c75ce4.pdf. See also Convention against Torture and Other Cruel, Inhuman or Degrading Treatment or Punishment (Convention against Torture or CAT), adopted December 10, 1984 (19 Qaws 1363), G.A. res. 39/46, annex, 39 U.N. GAOR Supp. (No. 51) at 197, U.N. Doc. A/39/51 (1984), entered into force June 26, 1987 (5 Saratan 1366), art. 3, http://www2.ohchr.org/english/law/cat.htm; Nigel Rodley, Treatment of Prisoners under International Law, Oxford: Oxford University Press (2009), p. 172; Cordula Drogue, "Transfer of Detainees: Legal Framework, Non-Refoulement, and Contemporary Challenges," International Review of the Red Cross, Vol. 90 No. 871, September 2008 (Sunbola 1387); Emanuela-Chiara Gillar, "There's No Place Like Home: States' Obligations in Relation to Transfers of Persons," International Review of the Red Cross , Vol. 90, No. 871, September 2008 (Sunbola 1387), http://www.icrc.org/eng/assets/files/other/irrc-871-gillard.pdf *hereinafter "Gillar, 'There's No Place Like Home'"+. See also Center for Human Rights and Global Justice, New York University Law School, Minimum Standards for Transfer: International Law Concerning Rendition in the Context of Counter-Terrorism, June 2009 (Jawza 1388), http://www.chrgj.org/projects/docs/legaladvisory.pdf. The Committee Against Torture, the international expert body that monitors states' compliance with CAT, has repeatedly reaffirmed the prohibition on torture is absolute. See UN Committee Against Torture, "Consideration of Reports Submitted by State Parties under Article 19 of the Convention, Conclusions and Recommendations of the Committee Against Torture, France," CAT/C/FRA/CO/3, April 3, 2006 (14 Hamal 1385), http://www.unhchr.ch/tbs/doc.nsf/(Symbol)/CAT.C.FRA.CO.3.En, para. 6.

troop presences, such as Denmark, may detain only a handful of individuals in a given year, with operations, detentions, and transfers confined to a single province. Other nations, such as Germany, claim that they don't take part in detentions themselves, yet nevertheless participate in military operations with Afghan forces in which individuals are arrested and detained.

It is important to note that some U.S. forces in Afghanistan operate as a part of Operation Enduring Freedom (OEF), a U.S. led counter-terrorism coalition that is separate from ISAF forces.[253] Known as U.S. Forces Afghanistan (USFOR-A), most of these non-ISAF U.S. forces are special operations forces and also referred to as Combined Forces Special Operations Component Command-Afghanistan (CFSOCC-A). CFSOCC-A forces frequently conduct operations in which individuals are detained. USFOR-A is under the command of General John Allen, who also serves as the commander of ISAF (COM-ISAF). There are also a number of U.S. military units that operate separately from ISAF and USFOR-A forces, and are not under the command of General Allen.

U.S. detention operations are run by the Combined Joint Interagency Task Force-435 (CJIATF-435). Officially, the United States runs one long-term detention facility, the Detention Facility in Parwan (DFIP), though previous work by the Open Society Foundations shows that a number of —temporary detention sites are also maintained, including the secretive —Tor Jail (—Black Jail) at Bagram Air Base, run by the U.S. Joint Special Operations Command (JSOC).[254] USFOR-A forces do not consider themselves to be bound by ISAF's 96-hour rule, and it is believed that they are permitted to hold interrogate detainees at these temporary detention sites for up to nine weeks before releasing them or transferring them to the DFIP or to Afghan custody.[255]

At least six ISAF troop contributing nations (TCNs) have negotiated separate Memorandums of Understanding (MoUs) with the Afghan government, which govern detention authority and transfers: the United Kingdom, Canada, Australia, Denmark, Norway, and the Netherlands.[256] These MoUs involve varying levels

---

253 *U.S. Department of Defense*, Report on Progress towards Stability and Security in Afghanistan,

254 Open Society Foundations, Confinement Conditions at a U.S. Screening Facility, supra n. 4; Dossier, "Terror Suspects Held for Weeks,"supra note 4.

255 Id

256 *Amnesty International*, Afghanistan: Detainees Transferred to Torture: ISAF Complicity?, November 2007 (Aqrab 1386), http://www.amnesty.ca/amnestynews/upload/ASA110112007.pdf [hereinafter "*Amnesty International*, Afghanistan: Detainees Transferred to Torture"+. See also, Stephen Smith, Minister for Defense, "Detainee Management in Afghanistan," Australian Government, Department of Defense, December 14, 2010 (23 Qaws 1389), http://www.Defense.gov.au/minister/105tpl.cfm??CurrentId=11212 *hereinafter "Stephen Smith, Australian Minister for Defense, 'Detainee Management in Afghanistan'"+;*Memorandum of Understanding Between the Government of the United*

of monitoring of transferred detainees as part of the agreements. However, monitoring programs have varied in quality and suffered from some serious weaknesses, and have been shown in some cases to be insufficient to safeguard against abuse and torture of detainees transferred to Afghan custody.[257] For years, credible allegations of mistreatment and torture of detainees in Afghan custody have surfaced despite the existence of MoUs, including detainees transferred from international forces.[258] As discussed below, while monitoring by international forces of the detainees that they transfer is a welcome step, such measures alone do not necessarily meet the legal obligations of states to ensure that detainees transferred to Afghan custody do not face a real risk of torture.[259]

Kingdom of Great Britain and Northern Ireland and *the Government of the Islamic Republic of Afghanistan* Concerning Transfer by the United Kingdom Armed Forces to Afghan Authorities of Persons Detained in Afghanistan, April 23, 2006 (3 Saur 1385), http://www.publications.parliament.uk/pa/cm200607/cmselect/cmfaff/44/4412.htm#n78,[hereinafter "Transfer MoU between the UK and Afghanistan"+;Government of Canada, "Backgrounder: Canadian Forces Release Statistics on Afghanistan Detainees," September 2, 2011 (11 Sunbola 1390), http://www.afghanistan.gc.ca/canada-afghanistan/news-nouvelles/2010/2010_09_22b.aspx?lang=eng&view=d *hereinafter "Government of Canada, 'Canadian Forces Release Statistics

257 UNAMA, *Conflict- Related Detainees in Afghan Custody, supra notes* 3. See also Report of *the Special Rapporteur on Torture and other Cruel, Inhuman or Degrading Treatment or Punishment, UN Doc.* 60/316, August 30, 2005 (5 Sunbola 1384), para. 46, http://www.unhcr.org/refworld/pdfid/43f30fb40.pdf; Human Rights Institute, Columbia Law School, U.S. Monitoring of Detainee Transfers in Afghanistan: International Standards and Lessons from the U.K. and Canada, December 2010 (Qaws 1389), http://www.law.columbia.edu/ipimages/Human_Rights_Institute/AfghanBriefingPaper%20FINAL.pdf *hereinafter "Human Rights Institute, U.S. Monitoring of Detainee Transfers in Afghanistan"+; Human Rights Institute, Columbia Law School, Promises to Keep: Diplomatic Assurances against Torture in U.S. Terrorism Transfers, December 2010 (Qaws 1389), http://www.law.columbia.edu/ipimages/Human_Rights_Institute/Promises%20to%20Keep.pdf *hereinafter "Human Rights Institute, Promises to Keep

258 *Amnesty International*, Afghanistan: Detainees Transferred to Torture: ISAF Complicity?, November 2007 (Aqrab 1386), supra note102; Andrea Prasow, "Afghan Torture is No Secret," National Post, May 4, 2010 (14 Saur 1389), http://fullcomment.nationalpost.com/2010/05/04/andrea-prasow-afghan-torture-is-no-secret/.

259 The United States ratified CAT subject to an understanding that the phrase "where there are substantial grounds for believing that he would be in danger of being subjected to torture" in Article 3 means "if it is more likely than not that he would be tortured."Resolution of Advice and Consent to Ratification, S. Exec. Rep. No. 101-30, 1990, http://thomas.loc.gov/cgi-bin/ntquery/z?trtys:100TD00020. The U. S. government has taken the view that Article 3 does not impose legal obligations on the United States with respect to individuals who are outside U.S. territory, although it has stated that, as a matter of policy, it will not transfer persons to countries where it is more likely than not that they will be tortured. See Second Periodic Report of the United States of America to the Committee Against Torture, May 6, 2005, para. 30, http://www.state.gov/g/drl/rls/45738.htm. See also Diplomatic Assurances and Rendition to Torture: The Perspective of the State Department's Legal Advisor: Hearing before the Subcomm. on Int'l Organizations, Human Rights, and Oversight, 110th Cong.

ISAF Six-Phase Response Plan

In response to the findings in the UNAMA detentions report, ISAF has begun implementing a six-phase plan to address torture and ill-treatment. The plan includes the suspension of detainee transfers to 16 facilities identified by UNAMA as practicing torture, combined with measures to allow for the resumption of transfers. It should be emphasized that the findings in this report on torture and abuse in NDS detention facilities in most cases pre-date implementation of ISAF's six-phase remediation plan and inspections regime. One allegation of torture in NDS Herat and 14 allegations in NDS Kandahar were received after the implementation of ISAF's response plan. Consequently, aside from these cases, this report's findings should not be used as a basis for judging the effectiveness of ISAF's response plan. More information is needed in coming months to properly assess whether ISAF's inspections, certifications, and other remedial measures have successfully addressed reports of torture and the risk of detainee abuse.[260]

However, as discussed in section IV, research conducted for this report points to serious flaws in the ISAF plan, including abuse outside the 16 facilities identified by UNAMA, and reports of undisclosed locations of detention and interrogation. While the comprehensive monitoring scheme will greatly increase ISAF's awareness of abuses in other facilities, there is clearly a need for more proactive efforts to accurately assess the risk of torture faced by potential transfers. Furthermore, there are U.S. forces and personnel that remain unbound by ISAF remedial actions and proposed monitoring.

ISAF's six-phase plan includes a process of certification for the facilities where torture has been discovered. This involves inspections of implicated facilities, when detainees and staff are interviewed, followed by remedial training of all detention facility staff. An additional inspection is conducted to verify completion of training and review any evidence or allegations of abuse through interviews with detention facility staff and detainees. If there are any credible allegations of abuse, certification of the facility cannot proceed, and the inspections and certifications process is restarted.

After inspections, trainings, and follow up visits are completed, recommendations are made by relevant ISAF officials and field commanders to COM-ISAF, who makes a final determination as to whether to certify a facility for resumption of transfers. As of February 15, 2012 (26 Dalwa 1390),ISAF has certified 13 of 16 facilities, including NDS Herat, NDS Uruzgan, NDS Khost, NDS Takhar, NDS Kapisa, ANP Zhari, AUP Kunduz, AUP Dasht-e-Archi (a district of

---

12 (2008), statement of John B. Bellinger, III, Legal Advisor, State Department, www.fas.org/irp/congress/2008_hr/rendition.pdf.
260 Information on ISAF six-phase response plan based on interviews with several ISAF officials, Kabul city, Kabul Province, November 12, 2011 (21 Aqrab 1390); December 11, 2011 (20 Qaws 1390); January 12, 2012 (22 Jadi 1390).

Kunduz province), and AUP Khost. Four of these certifications are "conditional," which means ISAF determined there was insufficient information to fully certify the facility for resumption of transfers.

Given the smaller size of some facilities and the turnover in detainees, ISAF assessment teams found no detainees to interview at some facilities, and were consequently unable to gather the information necessary to fully certify those facilities for resumption of transfer. These conditionally certified facilities include ANP Arghandab (Kandahar province), ANP Daman (Kandahar province), ANP Kandahar City District 9, and NDS Laghman. This conditional status permits transfer of detainees subject to an immediate (within 72 hours) unannounced site visit to interview detainees regarding their treatment and confinement conditions. Three facilities remain prohibited for detainee transfers: NDS Kabul Department 90/124, NDS Kandahar, and ANP Kandahar City District 2.

Currently, when an individual is captured in a joint ISAF/ANSF operation, ISAF forces accompany the detainee to a facility not among the 16 facilities implicated in abuse by the UNAMA report. ISAF forces obtain assurances from the facility director or commander that the detainee will not be transferred to a detention facility implicated in abuse.

ISAF is also moving forward with a long-term detainee monitoring program that will include facility inspections and monitoring of every detainee captured in ISAF and joint ISAF/ANSF operations, including those transferred outside the 16 previously identified facilities of concern. The focus will be on tracking individual detainees rather than facilities, and commits ISAF to interviewing each transferred detainee on a monthly basis. Each Regional Command will have two officials employed on a full time basis for this purpose. ISAF has not responded to AIHRC and Open Society requests for the number of detainees expected to be covered by this monitoring regime.

Critically, ISAF has adopted a broad, inclusive definition of which detainees will eventually be covered by its protective measures, including its proposed monitoring program. ISAF's protective measures will apply not only to individuals captured and detained by ISAF forces, but to all detainees captured in any combined operation between ISAF forces and ANSF. This definition is broader than the —effective control standard employed by many ISAF TCNs.

ISAF's swift response to UNAMA's report and decision to suspend transfers to all 16 facilities identified by UNAMA is a positive, welcome step. The adoption and implementation of a six-phase plan to address concerns raised by the UNAMA detentions report will help protect the rights of detainees transferred to Afghan custody and encourage Afghan officials to pursue improvements and reform. However, additional information will be required to assess whether ISAF inspections, training, and certifications are in fact ensuring detainees are not subjected to a real risk of torture. ISAF must also work to finalize and clarify its plan for inspecting facilities beyond the 16 identified by UNAMA and its proposal for longer-term detainee monitoring program.

There is also significant concern that international monitoring programs such as ISAF's result in the creation of a —two-tier system, where transferred detainees were free from abuse, while the wider detainee population continued to face mistreatment. Consequently, there should be a priority on ensuring the AIHRC, which is mandated to monitor all detainees in all detention facilities, has full, unfettered access to NDS facilities. It also necessary that the Afghan government and international officials ensure international monitoring programs, including monitoring conducted by ISAF, individual troop contributing nations, and international organizations never substitute or undermine an Afghan-led, national detainee monitoring mechanism, which has both the comprehensiveness of mandate and enduring institutional presence critical to long-term, sustainable improvements in detainee treatment and conditions.

Despite signs of genuine effort, there are also serious concerns as to whether ISAF's inspections regime has been able to adequately and accurately assess the risk of torture in 13 of the 16 facilities within such a short period of time. Experience from elsewhere in the world suggests that eliminating torture can be a slow process, not least because it often rests on changing assumptions within institutions and among officials that abusive methods are effective and necessary. It would be surprising if such attitudes within the NDS had been changed in a matter of months. Going forward, operational constraints, particularly those stemming from reduced troop numbers, must not lead to a lowering of the bar when it comes to meeting states' legal obligations or rigorously assessing the risk of torture detainees will face in Afghan detention facilities.

ISAF's six-phase response plan is a significant, positive effort to address detainee abuse; however, ISAF and TCNs must learn from past mistakes and ensure that whatever remedial actions are taken or monitoring conducted, nations must meet their legal obligations to never subject a detainee to a real risk of torture. Efforts should also be made to ensure the AIHRC, as the national detention monitoring mechanism with a mandate to monitor all detainees, is afforded full, unfettered access to detention facilities.

ISAF Troop Contributing Nations Transferring Detainees to Afghan Custody

United States
Number of transfers: Several thousand
Facilities transferring to: Many, nationally
Monitoring program: None

Though U.S. officials are either unwilling or unable to provide exact figures on detainee transfers, it is clear that the United States currently transfers far more detainees to the Afghan government than any other ISAF nation.[261] The United States is also the only ISAF nation with a long-term detention facility, the Detention Facility in Parwan (DFIP).[262]

According to a cable from the U.S. Embassy in Kabul, leaked by Wikileaks, in 2009 (1388) U.S. forces under ISAF detained 643 individuals and transferred 370 to Afghan custody.[263] Trends from night raids or —kill/capture operations indicate that the number of individuals detained by the United States has increased sharply since then. ISAF and USFOR-A special operations forces together detained over 8,000 individuals between April 2010 and April 2011 (Hamal 1389-1390), a large proportion of which were likely detained by U.S. special operations forces, and marking a substantial increase in the number of detentions.[264] With the population of the United States 'only long-term detention facility, DFIP, currently at around 3,000, these and other figures indicate that the vast majority of those detained by U.S. forces are clearly being either released or handed over to Afghan authorities.[265]

---

261 *U.S. Department of State, Cable,* "Proposed Afghanistan Detainee Monitoring Strategy, U.S. Embassy Kabul, Afghanistan, February 24, 2010 (5 Hoot 1388), http://www.cablegatesearch.net/cable.php?id=10KABUL688 [hereinafter "U.S. Department of State, 'Proposed Afghanistan Detainee Monitoring Strategy.'" In recent years, as the number of U.S. troops has surged and night raids have become an increasingly utilized tactic, the number of individuals detained and transferred to Afghan custody has significantly increased.

262 There have been significant improvements in treatment of detainees in U.S. custody over the past 10 years. While there are still denials of basic rights in terms of due process flaws, there have been very few allegations received regarding mistreatment at DFIP, particularly in recent years. This contrasts with serious reports of abuse and deaths in custody occurring in U.S. detention facilities in earlier days of U.S. detentions in Afghanistan, particularly at the Bagram Theater Internment Facility (BTIF) pre 2006. See Tim Golden, "In U.S. Report, Brutal Details of Two Afghan Inmates' Deaths," *The New York Times,* May 20, 2005 (30 Saur 1384), http://www.nytimes.com/2005/05/20/international/asia/20abuse. html?pagewanted=all; Hilary Andersson, "Afghans 'Abused at Secret Prison' at Bagram Airbase," BBC News, April 15, 2010 (24 Hamal 1389).The AIHRC and the Open Society Foundations have welcomed the opportunity to conduct visitsto DFIP and DRBs when the U.S. government has granted access and Open Society have engaged productively with U.S. officials on a range of detention issues. See Open Society Foundations, "New Detention Rules Show Promise and Problems," April 20, 2010 (31 Hamal 1389), http://blog.soros.org/2010/04/new-detention-rules-show-promise-and-problems/; Open Society Foundations, Confinement Conditions at a U.S. Screening Facility on Bagram Air Base, supra note 4

263 Id.

264 Katherine Tiedemann, "'Kill Capture': A live chat with PBS' *Frontline,*" The Afpak Channel, May 10, 2011 (20 Saur 1390), www.afpak.foreignpolicy.com/posts/2011/05/10/kill_capture_a_live_chat_with_pbs_frontline.

265 Interview with official from U.S. Combined Joint Inter-Agency Task Force 435, January 11, 2012 (21 Jadi 1390). There is also very little turnover in DFIP, which could have accounted for the low number of individuals at DFIP relative

However, the United States remains without a detainee monitoring program to ensure those individuals it transfers to Afghan custody are free from a real risk of torture. Going forward, while U.S. forces under ISAF will be covered by the proposed ISAF detainee monitoring program, transfers from non-ISAF U.S. forces will remain outside the scope of ISAF monitoring — a significant gap that is a serious cause for concern. (See section VI for additional information on U.S. detainee transfers and proposed monitoring program).

United Kingdom
Number of transfers: 20 per month, on average
Facilities transferring to: NDS Lashkar Gah, Helmand
Monitoring Program: Military-civilian Detention Oversight Team (DOT) monitors every transferee.

The United Kingdom currently transfers on average 20 detainees per month, according to one U.K. official.[266] Transfers are ongoing, but following a U.K. High Court decision in June 2010 and subsequent policy decisions taken by the U.K. government, U.K. forces are now transferring only to NDS Lashkar Gah, in Helmand, where most of their forces operate, and to the Afghan Counter-Narcotics Police in Helmand.[267]

The United Kingdom has had detainee monitoring program since 2006, implemented by a Detainee Oversight Team (DOT), comprising of a Royal Military Police officer and a military lawyer. All post-transfer U.K. captured detainees are visited regularly and interviews are conducted in private, although monitoring visits are not unannounced.[268]

---

to the total number of individuals detained by U.S. forces. Between January 2010 (Jadi 1388) and January 2012 (Jadi 1390) approximately 79 percent of detainees transferred to DFIP remain in the facility, while only 21 percent have been transferred to JCIP or released. *Interview with U.S. officials at DFIP*, January 11, 2011 (21 Jadi 1389). Between January-October 2011 (Jadi 1389-Aqrab 1390),the Detainee Review Board (DRB) completed 3,224 cases, including 506 in September (Sunbola 1390), and will reach an estimated 4,600 review boards by the end of the calendar year, with over 550 cases anticipated in October 2011 (Mizan 1390). See *U.S. Department of Defense, Report* on Progress towards Stability and Security in Afghanistan, supra note 4, October 2011 (Mizan 1390),p. 86,http://www.defense.gov/pubs/pdfs/October_2011_Section_1230_Report.pdf.
266 *Interview with UK Government official*, Kabul city, Kabul Province, Afghanistan, October 9, 2011 (17 Mizan 1390)
267 BBC News, "Maya Evans: Peace Activist Wins Legal Aid Court Battle," May 12, 2011 (22 Saur 1390), http://www.bbc.co.uk/news/uk-13371880.
268 Queen in re: Maya Evans v. Sec'y of State for Defense, [2010] EWHC 1445 (Q.B.) (U.K.). See also Memorandum of Understanding between the United Kingdom of Great Britain and Northern Ireland and the Government of the Islamic Republic of Afghanistan, supra note 102. Concerning Transfer by the United Kingdom Armed Forces to Afghan Authorities of Persons Detained in Afghanistan, April 23, 2006 (3 Saur 1385), http://www.publications.parliament.uk/pa/cm200607/cmselect/cmfaff/44/4412.htm#n78.

Detainees are interviewed within 30 days of their transfer to Afghan custody, and then every 30 days thereafter until first conviction; if allegations of abuse are received, follow-up visits are conducted every 15 days. Though the DOT says that it tries to conduct private interviews with detainees, this has not always been permitted by Afghan authorities.[269]

Australia

Number of transfers: 154 between August 1, 2010 (10 Asad 1389) and 2 December 2011 (11 Qaws 1390)[270]

Facilities transferring to: DFIP, NDS TarinKowt, Uruzgan. Monitoring program: Monitor every detainee in Afghan custody and have access to detainees at DFIP

Between August 1, 2010 (10 Asad 1389), and December 2, 2011 (11 Qaws 1390), Australian forces, which operate in Uruzgan province, transferred 53 detainees to Afghan custody at NDS Tarin Kowt and 34 detainees to US custody at the DFIP.[271] After initial screening, Australian forces transfer detainees deemed to be higher-level security risk are transferred to U.S. custody at DFIP, while those deemed as less serious security threats are transferred to NDS Tarin Kowt, the capital of Uruzgan.[272] As NDS has no holding facilities in Tarin Kowt, detainees are physically held at the Attorney-General's office, which is located across the street from the NDS. Australia currently monitors all of the detainees it transfers into Afghan or US custody to assess their ongoing treatment and welfare. Monitoring is conducted via initial visits shortly after their transfer and then on a monthly basis thereafter until the detainee is sentenced by an Afghan court or released from custody.[273]

As part of its monitoring responsibilities for detainees, Australia also inspects the facilities and the conditions where Australian Defense Forces (ADF)-apprehended detainees are held, but do not usually inspect facilities where detainees are not transferred by Australian elements. Monitoring visits in Uruzgan are unannounced, while visits to DFIP are organized in advance due to logistical and access reasons. Visits in Tarin Kowt at all facilities (NDS/Attorney-General's Office and the Tarin Kowt central prison) are conducted in private, while visits to DFIP are recorded in accordance with US requirements.

Allegations of detainee mistreatment are, with the detainee's consent, raised with the detaining authority and, if possible,

---

269 Interview with international official, Kabul city, Kabul Province, Afghanistan, December 11, 2011 (20 Qaws 1390)

270 Information provided by Australian government official, March 17, 2012 (27 Hoot 1390)

271 Ibid.

272 *Interview with Australian government official*, Kabul city, Kabul Province, Afghanistan, October 14, 2011 (22 Mizan 1390).

273 Information provided by Australian government official, March 17, 2012 (27 Hoot 1390).

investigated. Allegations are also reported through the Australian Ambassador, Australian Chain of Command, and to ISAF and relevant human rights organizations. In the event that the Australian Government becomes aware of a credible allegation or reasonable suspicion of detainee mistreatment within a particular detention facility, the Australian government may consider suspending transfers of detainees to that facility pending investigation. Australia halted detainee transfers to NDS TarinKowt for three months from July 2011 in line with ISAF direction.[274]

Canada
Number of transfers: None, last in July 2011 (Saratan 1390)
Facilities transferring to: DFIP
Monitoring program: Monitor all detainees still in Afghan custody and have access to detainees in DFIP

Canada officially ended combat operations in July 2011 (Saratan 1390), and now maintains only a training mission. In December 2011 (Qaws 1390), Canada signed an agreement with the United States to transfer all individuals captured by its forces to U.S. custody at DFIP, though the likelihood of Canada detaining further individuals without combat troops present is low.

Canada first signed a MoU in 2005 with the Afghan government, but included no provision for monitoring or oversight (unlike the Dutch and British MoUs of the time).[275] In 2006, Canadian government officials reported internally that torture was taking place in facilities in Kandahar. In 2009, the former chargé d' affaires in the Canadian Embassy in Kabul, Richard Colvin, told the Canadian House of Commons that, —according to our information, the likelihood is that all the Afghans we handed over were tortured. For interrogators in Kandahar, it was standard operating procedure under political and public pressure in 2007; Canada signed a new MoU to begin detainee monitoring.[276]

---

274 Ibid.
275 *Testimony of Richard Colvin, formerly acting ambassador at the Canadian Embassy in Kabul*, addressing the Canadian House of Commons, November 18, 2009 (27 Aqrab 1388), http://www.parl.gc.ca/HousePublications/Publication. aspx?DocId=4236267&Language=E&Mode=1&Parl=40&Ses=2, hereinafter "Testimony of Richard Colvin
276 See *Testimony of Richard Colvin*, Id. See also First Secretary, Embassy of Canada to the United States, Special Committee on the Canadian Mission in Afghanistan, November 18, 2009 (27 Aqrab 1388),http://www.parl.gc.ca/HousePublications/ Publication.aspx?DocId=4236267&Language=E&Mode=1&Parl=40&Ses=2; Testimony of Andrea Prasow, Senior Counter-Terrorism Counsel, Human Rights Watch, May 5, 2010 (15 Saur 1389), http://www.hrw.org/sitesdefault/files/ related_material/Prasow%20Canada%20Testimony%20May%205%202010. pdf; Amnesty International and BCCLA v. Chief of the Defense Staff, 2008 F.C. 162 (Can.), http://www.haguejusticeportal.net/Docs/NLP/Canada/A.I.Canada_ and_BCCLA_v_Canadian_Defense_Decision_07-02-2008.pdf.

Since 2007, civilian Canadian government officials have conducted post-transfer monitoring visits to assess the conditions of detention and treatment of Canadian-transferred detainees held in Afghan facilities, through regular visits to a limited number of designated detention facilities in Kabul and Kandahar. At least one case of torture was still discovered after the monitoring system was put in place, which, according to Colvin, was due to weaknesses in the monitoring regime, including insufficient human resources.[277]

While Canada no longer has combat forces in Afghanistan, it continues to monitor every detainee that it has previously transferred to Afghan custody, all of whom are now held in the MOI-run Sarpoza prison in Kandahar.

Denmark
Number of transfers: Seven in total[278]
Facilities transferring to: NDS LashkarGah, Helmand
Monitoring program: Monitor all detainees

All detainees captured by Danish forces are transferred to NDS LashkarGah — only seven have been transferred since 2005, five of whom have since been released while two detainees remain in Afghan custody.[279] Danish representatives monitor all detainees from point of transfer to Afghan custody, until release, with regular, unannounced visits and private interviews with the detainees. Visits are conducted by a medical officer and a lawyer.

Meeting International Legal Obligations and Effective Detainee Monitoring

Under the general international law principle of non-refoulement, which has a basis in international human rights, refugee, and humanitarian law, states are prohibited from transferring persons under their effective control to the custody of another state if there are substantial grounds to believe the individual would face a real risk of torture or cruel, inhuman or degrading treatment or punishment.[280]

---

277 *Testimony of Richard Colvin, supra note 121*

278 *Interview with Danish government official, Kabul* city, Kabul province, October 17, 2011 (25 Mizan 1390)

279 *Interview with Danish government official, Kabul city, Kabul province*, October 17, 2011 (25 Mizan 1390).Written email responses of Danish government to Open Society Foundations questions on detention policies and practices, November 28, 2011 (7 Qaws 1390), and December 20, 2011 (29 Qaws 1390). See *also Danish Ministry of Foreign Affairs*, "Denmark in Afghanistan: Detainees," http://www.afghanistan. um.dk/en/menu/DenmarkinAfghanistan/DenmarksIntegratedApproach/ Detainees/; Memorandum of the Understanding between the Ministry of Defense of the Islamic Republic or Afghanistan and the Ministry of Defense of the Kingdom of Denmark concerning the transfer of persons between the Danish Contingent of the International Security Assistance Force and Afghan Authorities, June 8, 2005 (18 Jaws 1384), http://www.afghanistan.um.dk/NR/rdonlyres/97DB19DB-2A1D-4C6E-92A1-742671501049/0/DKAFGoverdragelsesaftale.pdf.

280 The principle of non-refoulement is a general principle of international law with a basis in international human rights law, refugee law, and international humanitarian law. Sir Elihu Lauterpacht and Daniel Bethlehem, "The Scope and

Monitoring programs by ISAF and troop contributing nations are welcome steps and can greatly enhance detainee protection. However, monitoring alone is not sufficient to meet states 'legal obligations and experience has shown that the effectiveness of monitoring depends greatly on the circumstances and varies widely.

Because fulfilling the legal obligation of non-refoulement requires ensuring that every detainee transferred to another state's custody is free from a real risk of torture, post-transfer monitoring alone is insufficient.[281] In order to avoid transferring detainees into circumstances in which they are subject to a real risk of torture, states must assess the risk at a particular facility prior to transfer — post-facto determinations are insufficient. Authoritative legal interpretations and jurisprudence indicate that states should also afford detainees certain procedural guarantees, such as informing the detainee of the decision to transfer and providing them an opportunity to express concerns that transfer would expose them to a real risk of torture or ill-treatment.[282] Guidance from legal authorities and practitioners indicates that properly assessing the risk of torture requires states to implement measures that would —take into account all relevant considerations, such as facility-wide inspections, interviews with

Content of the Principle of Non-refoulement: Opinion," in Erika Feller, Volker Turk and Frances Nicholson (eds.), *Refugee Protection in International Law: UNHCR's Global Consultations on International Protection*, Cambridge, UK: Cambridge University Press (2003), www.unhcr.org/publ/PUBL/419c75ce4.pdf. See also Convention against Torture and Other Cruel, Inhuman or Degrading Treatment or Punishment (Convention against Torture or CAT), adopted December 10, 1984 (19 Qaws 1363), G.A. res. 39/46, annex, 39 U.N. GAOR Supp. (No. 51) at 197, U.N. Doc. A/39/51 (1984), entered into force June 26, 1987 (5 Saratan 1366), art. 3, http://www2.ohchr.org/english/law/cat.htm; Nigel Rodley, Treatment of Prisoners under International Law, Oxford: Oxford University Press (2009), p. 172; Cordula Drogue, "Transfer of Detainees: Legal Framework, Non-Refoulement, and Contemporary Challenges," International Review of the Red Cross, Vol. 90 No. 871, September 2008 (Mizan 1387); Emanuela-Chiara Gillar, "There's No Place Like Home: States' Obligations in Relation to Transfers of Persons," International Review of the Red Cross , Vol. 90, No. 871, September 2008 (Sunbola 1387), http://www.icrc.org/eng/assets/files/other/irrc-871-gillard. pdf *hereinafter "Gillar, 'There's No Place Like Home'"+. See also Center for Human Rights and Global Justice, New York University Law School, Minimum Standards for Transfer: International Law Concerning Rendition in the Context of Counter-Terrorism, June 2009 (Jawza 1388), http://www.chrgj.org/projects/docs/legaladvisory.pdf.

281 The precise definition of non-refoulement and specific obligations for international forces operating in Afghanistan and transferring detainees are beyond the scope of this report; instead, attention is drawn to the issue of whether monitoring programs, in practice and in the particular context of Afghanistan, are sufficient to meet states' obligations under international law. See UN Committee Against Torture (CAT), General Comment No. 1: Implementation of Article 3 of the Convention in the Context of Article 22 (Refoulement and Communications), November 21, 1997 (30 Aqrab 1376), A/53/44, annex IX, http://www.unhcr.org/refworld/docid/453882365.html. See also Emanuela-Chiara Gillar, "There's No Place Like Home," supra note 98.

282 Id.

non-transferred detainees, and the removal of officials responsible for past abuse.[283]

States that do implement monitoring programs must also genuinely assess the effectiveness of such programs in policy terms, mindful of the dynamic and challenging circumstances in Afghanistan, as well as those practices that are critical to effective monitoring. Visits should be unannounced and states must have full access to detainees and facilities. Interviews with detainees should be conducted in private and in confidence.[284] Ideally post-release interviews should also be carried out, when fears of reprisals will be somewhat reduced. Monitors should also assess whether detainees' due process rights are violated, including access to counsel and family members — rights that are critical to protecting detainees from abuse. Monitoring teams should be adequately resourced, and include civilian professionals with expertise and experience in detainee monitoring and interviewing victims of abuse and torture.[285]

In addition, effective and sustainable monitoring systems must be sure to complement and work with national, civilian organizations, like the AIHRC — the national and constitutionally-mandated institution with a long-term commitment to monitoring. Crucially, the AIHRC is an organization committed to monitoring the treatment of all detainees, rather than focusing on those transferred by international forces. States seeking to meet their legal obligations should engage cooperatively with the AIHRC, and ensure its monitors also have full, unfettered access to all detainees and detention facilities.

Joint Operations and Intelligence Sharing

ISAF nations also have legal obligations with respect to detainee treatment arising from their cooperation with Afghan security and intelligence forces. Many ISAF nations conduct combined, or joint operations with Afghan forces, in the course of which individuals may be detained. Following these operations, detainees are often taken into Afghan custody, where they could be at risk of ill-treatment or torture. Some ISAF TCNs, including Germany, have failed to reach agreements with the Afghan government regarding transfers, and have instead adopted a policy of taking part in joint operations with ANSF without —arresting individuals.[286]

---

283 Id. See also Committee against Torture, General Comment No. 1, Implementation of article 3 of the Convention in the context of article 22, November 21, 1997 (30 Aqrab 1376), UN Doc. A/53/44, Annex IX, para. 5-8.

284 See Report of the Special Rapporteur of the Commission on Human Rights on the question of torture and other cruel, inhuman or degrading treatment or punishment, September 1, 2004 (11 Sunbola 1383), UN Doc. A/59/324, para. 41-42.

285 For fuller examination of the minimum requirements for effective detainee monitoring and basis in international law and guidance, see Human Rights Institute, U.S. Monitoring of Detainee Transfers in Afghanistan, supra note 103.

286 *Interview with foreign officials December 2011* (Qaws 1390), Kabul. See also John Goetz, Marcel Rosenbach, and Alexander Szandar, "Germany Handed Prisoners

The participation of Afghan forces in joint operations is in most cases unlikely to absolve international forces of their legal obligations to those individuals captured in such operations. International forces play a critical role in joint operations, from logistical and intelligence assistance to force protection; they are often effectively in the lead during such operations as well as physically present and protecting ANSF soldiers while they take individuals into custody. Consequently, international forces must examine their forces' specific involvement in joint operations to determine whether they have any legal obligations to those captured — a determination that cannot be reduced to the mere presence of Afghan forces during an operation or the fact that it is Afghan forces that physically take individuals into custody. Instead, the degree and nature of international forces' involvement in joint operations must be genuinely assessed to determine whether those detained in the course of operations come within international forces' effective control, thereby triggering legal obligations under the principle of non-refoulement.[287]

In a welcome move, ISAF officials have stated that, as a matter of policy, ISAF protective measures (as opposed to the policy of individual troop contributing nations) will be triggered not just when individuals come under the effective control of ISAF forces, but whenever an individual is captured in combined ISAF/ANSF operations.[288] However, effective control remains the prevailing legal standard applied by each ISAF nation's forces. In interviews for this report, officials from some nations indicated that obligations to those captured in joint operations are taken into account, but no nation would specify how it defines effective control and under what circumstances their forces 'participation in joint operations would trigger obligations undergone-refoulement.

Intelligence sharing is a further concern. Given the widespread use of coercive and abusive interrogation methods by Afghan intelligence officials, there is a significant risk that intelligence gathered by Afghan authorities is gathered through torture. International allies should avoid sharing Afghan intelligence unless they can ensure that in doing so they are in no way complicit with torture or ill-treatment by Afghan authorities, an obligation which arises regardless of whether

---

over to a Government that Tortures," Der Spiegel, November 11, 2008 (21 Aqrab 1387),http://www.spiegel.de/international/world/0,1518,534511,00.html.

287 *U.N. Human Rights Committee, General Comment No. 31* [80]: The Nature of the General Legal Obligation Imposed on States Parties to the Covenant, CCPR/C/21/ Rev.l/Add. 13, May 26, 2004 (4 Jawza 1383), para.12, http://daccess-dds-ny. un.org/doc/UNDOC/GEN/G04/419/56/PDF/G0441956.pdf?OpenElement.   See also U.S. Executive Order 13491, "Ensuring Lawful Interrogations," January 22, 2009 (3 Dalwa 1387), http://www.whitehouse.gov/the_press_office/ EnsuringLawfulInterrogations/.

288 *Interview with ISAF officials, Kabul city, Kabul province, Afghanistan*, December 2011 (Qaws 1390).

detainees were transferred from international forces custody.[289] However, in interviews with various foreign government officials, no ISAF nation indicated that it had implemented measures to ensure that intelligence gathered by Afghan authorities and then shared and utilized by their forces was not obtained through the use of torture.[290]

An ongoing concern is continued cooperation by non-ISAF special operations forces and CIA personnel, who are believed to maintain a relationship with NDS officials, in particular from Department 90/124, which involves visits by some personnel to the department.[291] Although U.S. officials themselves have not been directly implicated in torture, close cooperation between U.S. and Afghan intelligence officials, particularly at NDS Department 90/124, would raise serious concerns that U.S. officials could be complicit in torture and ill-treatment perpetrated by Afghan intelligence officials.

VI. Torture and Mistreatment of U.S. Detainees Transferred to NDS

Researchers documented a number of credible cases in which individuals were detained by U.S. forces and then transferred to Afghan custody, where they were reportedly subjected to torture, including beatings, suspension, and electric shock.

10 cases of individuals detained by U.S. forces transferred to NDS facilities where they reported being tortured between May 2010 and January 2012 (Saur 1389-Jadi 1390).[292] In four of these cases individuals reported being held for some period of time at a detention facility located at or near Bagram Air Base, and in four cases individuals

---

289 130 State parties to the Convention Against Torture (CAT) are obligated "to prevent public authorities and other persons acting in an official capacity from directly committing, instigating, inciting, encouraging, acquiescing in or otherwise participating or being complicit in acts of torture as defined in the Convention," General Comment 2 by the Committee Against Torture on Implementation by State Parties. http://daccess-dds-ny.un.org/doc/UNDOC/GEN/G08/402/62/PDF/G0840262.pdf?OpenElement.

290 Interviews conducted with government officials from the United States, Germany, Denmark, United Kingdom, Canada, and Australia.

291 Interviews with international officials, December 2011 (Qaws 1390). See also: Joshua Paltrow and Julie Tate, "U.S. Officials Had Advance Warning of Abuse at Afghan Prisons Officials Say," The Washington Post, October 30, 2011 (8 Aqrab 1390), http://www.washingtonpost.com/world/asia_pacific/us-had-advance-warning-of-abuse-at-afghan-prisons-officials-say/2011/10/21/gIQA7Dg2VM_story.html.

292 Although detainees described the international soldiers who detained them as Americans, this description may at times be used more generically to describe any soldiers belonging to international forces. However, several factors substantiate the detainees' claims that the forces involved were Americans, including the fact that English was spoken by the forces involved, that detainees report being held at "Bagram" in conditions consistent with the JSOC-run temporary detention facility near Bagram, and that they were detained in areas of responsibility assigned to U.S. forces.

were transferred to NDS Kandahar despite such transfers being suspended by all ISAF as well as USFOR-A forces. These cases are strong evidence that U.S. detainee transfers have in fact been tortured by NDS officials. They raise serious concerns regarding U.S. policies on transfers to NDS, particularly transfers by U.S. special operations forces, and whether appropriate safeguards exist to protect detainees rights and ensure that the United States is not complicit in torture.

U.S. Detainees Transferred to Afghan Custody from "Bagram" and other U.S. Detention Facilities

In four cases, individuals interviewed by researchers for this report said that they were arrested by U.S. forces between May 2010 (Saur 1389) and May 2011 (Saur 1390) and held at —Bagram. All four individuals said that they were then held by the NDS in incommunicado detention, without charge, and subjected to various forms of torture.

There is some uncertainty regarding precisely which facility detainees were at when they describe being held at "Bagram," as this could mean either the long-term U.S. detention facility, DFIP, or the Joint Special Operations Command-run (JSOC) screening or transit detention facility at Bagram Air Base, known as Black Jail or Tor Jail. U.S. officials have stated to the AIHRC and the Open Society Foundations those detainees at DFIP are not transferred directly into NDS facilities, indicating that it is more likely detainees were held at the transit detention facility at Bagram Air Base.[293] Instead, according to the officials, detainees are either released through shuras or are transferred to the Afghan-controlled block at DFIP for prosecution.[294] None of the detainees reported being through a Detainee Review Board (DRB) hearing or a release shura. The U.S. officials would not comment on whether detainees, who are held at JSOC facilities, including the temporary detention facility at Bagram, are subsequently transferred into NDS custody.[295]

Detainees' descriptions of the conditions in which they were held, specifically small, windowless single person cells, excessive light, insufficient water for ablutions before prayer, and noises that interfered with sleep, are consistent with conditions of confinement at the JSOC-run temporary detention or screening facility at or near Bagram Air Field documented in previous Open Society reporting.[296]

---

293 *Interview with U.S. officials, January 11,* 2012 (21 Jadi 1390).

294 A "shura" is a consultation, or meeting; in this case it is a meeting hosted by local leaders to facilitate the release of detainees at .

295 *Various interviews with U.S. officials, Kabul city, Kabul province, Afghanistan,* November and December 2011 (Aqrab-Jadi 1390).

296 Detainees 10, 49, 57, 98, 99, and 100. See Open Society Foundations, "Confinement Conditions at a U.S. Screening Facility," supra note 4. There are also cells for solitary confinement at DFIP, however, according to U.S. officials; individuals are only placed into such cells for disciplinary reasons, if they are a threat to themselves, or for medical reasons. There is no indication that any of these conditions applied in the cases of detainees interviewed by the AIHRC

This facility is located near to both the DFIP and its predecessor, the Bagram Theatre Internment Facility (BTIF), likely producing some confusion. Since detainees are not informed of where they are being held, identifying the location of their detention must be based on their recollections of confinement conditions, physical descriptions, treatment, interrogations, and other details that could help substantiate the exact detention location. Based on this information and information compiled by Open Society on the JSOC temporary detention facility at Bagram, it is likely that all of the four detainees in question spent some time at this facility.[297] Whether the detainees may also have been held at DFIP is less likely.

Of the four detainees transferred from U.S. custody at DFIP or the temporary detention facility at Bagram to NDS, two were transferred to NDS Wardak, one to NDS Laghman, and one to NDS Kabul Department 90/124, where they report being subjected to torture, including beating, suspension, and electric shock.[298] One of the detainees transferred to NDS Wardak was also subsequently transferred to Kabul Department 90/124, where he alleges he was again subjected to torture. Detainees reported being held by the United States at DFIP/Tor Jail anywhere from 20 days to six months.

In two additional cases, interviewees said that they were held by U.S. forces at temporary detention facilities in the provinces of their capture, and then transferred directly to NDS custody, where they were subsequently tortured. Two detainees told the researchers for this report that they were transferred directly from U.S. detention facilities to NDS; one detainee reported being transferred from Jalalabad airfield to NDS Nangarhar, and then to NDS Kabul Department 90/124, where he says he was subjected to torture, including beating and suspension. The other detainee was transferred from a U.S. detention site in Laghman to NDS Laghman, where he reported being tortured by beating and electric shock.[299]

No detainees reported any physical abuse by U.S. forces while in detention in U.S. detention facilities and several noted that they were well-treated, particularly in comparison to their treatment while in Afghan custody. In none of the cases did detainees report being informed of the basis for their arrest and detention by U.S. forces, nor were they provided with specific reasons for their release or transfer by U.S. forces.

According to one detainee who was held at either DFIP or the temporary detention facility at Bagram Air Base for approximately two and a half months, —One day the Americans came and said they were going to release me, they said that they had made a mistake. I

---

and Open Society. Interview with U.S. officials on visit to DFIP, January 11, 2012 (21 Jadi 1390).

297 Id.

298 *Interviews with Detainee 98, Detainee 99, Detainee 100, and Detainee 10*

299 *Interview with Detainee 101*

thought that they would release me from there, but instead they gave me to the NDS. I was so happy at first, I thought I would be free, but I didn't realize this was just the beginning.[300] Another detainee held at —Bagram stated that U.S. forces suggested to him that he was cleared of wrongdoing and would be set free. —The interpreter came in and said we have good news for you, the investigation is over and you will be released. I asked if this was a joke, and he said, no, the U.S. does not joke about these things. But instead of being released, he was handed over to NDS Wardak in Maidan Shar. —They restarted the interrogations. I said, look, I've already been investigated by the U.S, I'm not the one you're looking for.[301] Over the course of the next week, he was repeatedly suspended upside-down from the ceiling and beaten with electric cables, wooden sticks, and metal rods.

Transferred Detainees Subjected to Torture

In all six of the above cases, where individuals were transferred from U.S. custody directly to the NDS, the interviewees said that both Afghans and Americans were present on the raids, and that they were held at U.S. detention facilities where they were interrogated for a short period of time. The first of these arrests was in May 2010 (approximately Saur 1389), and the most recent arrest was in May 2011 (Saur 1390). All six detainees transferred from U.S. to NDS custody reported forms of mistreatment and abuse consistent with accounts provided by other detainees in NDS custody, including suspension, beatings, electric shocks, and denial of medical care. All six cases occurred within the last year and a half.

Two detainees described being suspended while in custody at NDS Wardak.[302] In both cases, the detainees 'feet were bound and tied to a rope, which was threaded through a pulley on the ceiling. Some detainees who were hung upside-down by their feet from the ceiling were also beaten. Another detainee reported being suspended in NDS Kabul Department 90/124. He was hung upside-down by chains attached to cuffs around his ankles and beaten with plastic PVC pipes.[303]

All six detainees reported being beaten multiple times, over periods ranging from one week to many months. The beatings were administered through a variety of methods, including kicking, slapping, punching, and beating with tools such as rubber hoses, electric cables, wooden sticks, and metal rods. Detainees reported being beaten on multiple areas of their body, including the legs, backside, head, and the soles of their feet. Detainees were beaten in

---

300 *Interview with Detainee 99*
301 *Interview with Detainee 98*
302 *Interviews with Detainee 98 and Detainee 99*
303 *Interview with Detainee 100*

a variety of positions, including while standing, sitting and bound in chairs, suspended from the ceiling, and lying face down on the floor or on a bed. Two of the six detainees described their hands being bound, and NDS officials holding their feet out in front of them — in one case binding them to a stick — and being beaten on the soles of their feet.[304]

> They beat me twice a day, once in the morning, once in the evening. They beat me on my arms, my legs, and backside. They used sticks, electric cables, and metal rods. After that you could see the marks, the welts; you could even tell differences between the marks — that this one is from the stick, this one from cable, this one from the metal.[305] Two detainees reported being subjected to electric shocks. —They used to bind my hands and tie me to a chair and put clips on two of my toes. Then they would have this machine for electricity, they would crank it up and give us shocks. It was very hard and we would be screaming in pain.[306] Describing the pain of the electric shocks, another detainee said, "It felt like I was half-dead. All my body was trembling and shaking, and my heart was beating very quickly, but I wasn't able to move or speak."

Upon being transferred to the NDS, none of the six detainees were ever charged or brought before a judge. After having little to no contact with family while in U.S. custody, transfer to the NDS meant many more months of incommunicado detention — a clear violation of detainees 'fundamental due process rights that also substantially increases the risk of torture. The detainees 'families lacked any knowledge of their condition or whereabouts. In two cases, even when family members managed to locate detainees, they reported having to pay bribes to NDS officials to secure their release.

One detainee stated that he was in U.S. custody at—Bagram for approximately six months before being transferred to NDS Kabul, where he remained for an additional three months. It was not until he was released from NDS, dropped off on a main road outside the detention facility, and handed 1,000 Afghanis (approximately U.S.$20), that he could call his family to inform them where he was, after a total of approximately nine months in detention. —My family had no news, no information at all; they didn't know where I was, if I was at Bagram, NDS, or Kabul, or wherever. When I got out I didn't even know where I was. It was somewhere in Kabul, but I don't know the city very well. It was hard to walk. I was dizzy and confused. Some people found me and after I told them what happened they took me to

---

304 *Interview with Detainee 100 and Detainee 101*
305 *Interview with Detainee 98*
306 *Interview with Detainee 99*

a restaurant, gave me some tea and food and I called my brother and I told him to come and find me. He started crying.[307]

These cases highlight a potential practice in which some U.S. forces seem to be detaining, interrogating, and screening individuals and then transferring some of them to Afghan officials and facilities that engage in torture. In four of the cases investigated, detainees were transferred to and subjected to torture at NDS facilities where ISAF has since suspended transfers as a result of reports of abuse, including NDS Laghman and Department 90/124.

U.S. Detainees Transferred to NDS Kandahar despite ISAF/USFOR-A Transfer Suspension

Researchers have documented eleven recent, credible cases in which individuals reported being detained by U.S. forces and subsequently transferred to NDS Kandahar despite a July 2011 (Saratan 1390) order suspending all detainee transfers to NDS Kandahar due to reports of detainee abuse. The most recent transfer reportedly occurred in January 2012 (Jadi 1390).

In July 2011 (Saratan 1390), in response to reports of detainee abuse, COM-ISAF and U.S. Forces-Afghanistan (USFOR-A) issued an order suspending all detainee transfers to NDS Kandahar. According to ISAF and U.S. officials, this order still stands and all U.S. forces under ISAF and USFOR-A commands are prohibited from transferring detainees to NDS Kandahar.[308]

However, eleven detainees interviewed for this report described being detained by U.S. forces and transferred to NDS Kandahar since the COM-ISAF and USFOR-An order. Detainees stated that they were detained by Americans or U.S. forces, or U.S. Special Forces, or sometimes foreign forces, and held for 1–2 days before being transferred to NDS Kandahar. Five detainees stated specifically that they were held at Mullah Omar's House.

Firebase Maholic, also known by its previous name, Camp Gecko, is often locally referred to as Mullah Omar's House, a reference to the facility's well-known past as the residence of Taliban leader Mullah Omar. The facility has been used for many years as a base for the C.I.A. and U.S. special operations forces operating in Kandahar.[309] The base

307 *Interview with Detainee 98*

308 *Interview with ISAF official, Kabul city, Kabul province*, December 11, 2011 (20 Qaws 1390)

309 Interview with credible source, December 20, 2011 (29 Qaws 1390), confirming that U.S. intelligence personnel and U.S. Special Forces have operated out of this facility for several years, training Afghan forces and cooperating with Afghan forces on night raids and other operations. See also "U.S. Special Forces Using Former Taliban Base," Fox News, February 1, 2007 (12 Dalwa 1385), http://www.foxnews.com/story/0,2933,249501,00.html; Dexter Filkins, Mark Mazzetti, and James Risen, "Brother of Afghan Leader Said to be Paid by C.I.A.," *The New York Times*, October 27, 2009 (5 Aqrab 1388), http://www.nytimes.com/2009/10/28/

is also reportedly home to Afghan forces including the paramilitary unit known as the —Kandahar Strike Force. According to reports, the Kandahar Strike Force was assembled and trained by U.S. special operations and C.I.A. personnel and continues to work closely with U.S. special operations and intelligence personnel conducting raids and other operations targeting insurgents.[310]

One detainee interviewed by the AIHRC reported being arrested by U.S. forces and abused by Afghan forces while in the presence of Americans at Firebase Maholic. "I was in Mullah Omar's House and they blindfolded my eyes and made me sit on a chair for a few hours. After a moment of silence suddenly lashes of cable struck my head and back very hard from behind, they beat me for one hour. They wanted me to tell them who I had relations with. They were all Afghans beating me, though the beating took place in the presence of Americans. Afghan forces beat me with the Americans there."[311] It should be noted that researchers received no other claims of U.S. forces present during abuse of detainees, and this account could not be independently verified.

Another detainee reported being arrested by U.S. forces during a raid on his home and taken to a location that he guessed was Mullah Omar's House, and beaten by Afghan officers there. They took me blindfolded to somewhere, my guess is that it was Mullah Omar's house, where I was beaten and tortured badly by Afghan soldiers and officials. They beat me on the feet, legs and back by something like a cable. The beating continued for a few hours until I felt numb in my back and legs, and it burned with pain on my feet and on the soles of my feet. They punched and kicked me also, and the next day I was transferred to the NDS."[312] The detainee stated that he had not been mistreated while in NDS custody, and at the time of the interview, there were marks consistent with beatings visible on the detainee's back and feet. Some detainees report being treated well while in U.S. custody for 1-2 nights, before being transferred to NDS Kandahar.

Four detainees transferred to NDS officials in Kandahar by U.S. forces reported being subsequently tortured by NDS. According to one detainee, "I was severely beaten by cable in the head and neck. I was shackled and they connected the shackles to an electrical current and shocked me until I was unconscious. They also beat me on the

world/asia/28intel.html?pagewanted=all; Amnesty International, Getting Away with Murder? The Impunity of International Forces in Afghanistan, February 2009 (Dalwa 1387), http://www.es.amnesty.org/uploads/media/Kandahar. Getting_away_with_murder_01.pdf, p. 7-10; Julius Cavendish, "After the US Pulls Out, Will CIA Rely More on Afghan Mercenaries?," The Christian Science Monitor, November 16, 2011 (25 Aqrab 1390), http://www.csmonitor.com/World/Asia-South-Central/2011/1116/After-the-US-pulls-out-will-CIA-rely-more-on-Afghan-mercenaries/(page)/2.
310 Id.
311 Interview with Detainee 61
312 Interview with Detainee 63

back and waist very hard. As a result, my left hand is still hurting and even my tongue is severely damaged from the electric shock."[313] Three other transferred detainees also alleged that they were abused in NDS Kandahar, including being subjected to beatings with cables.

In response to queries regarding these cases, U.S. military officials have stated that there are no ISAF or USFOR–A forces transferring detainees to NDS Kandahar, and that the order suspending transfers to NDS Kandahar among other facilities in RC-South remain in full effect.[314] Interviews with detainees as well as responses by U.S. officials to queries from the AIHRC and the Open Society Foundations indicate that there may be U.S. forces or personnel, perhaps including C.I.A. or other U.S. intelligence officials, operating outside ISAF and USFOR-A commands in Kandahar that are detaining individuals and transferring them to NDS Kandahar.

These transfers are occurring despite widely held and long-standing concerns about torture and detainee abuse at NDS Kandahar. ISAF and U.S. forces first prohibited transfers to NDS Kandahar in July 2011 (Saratan 1390), and had received reports of abuse from independent monitors for several years prior. The United Kingdom suspended transfers to NDS Kandahar in January 2011 (Jadi 1389). AIHRC monitors received 10 credible allegations of abuse in NDS Kandahar as recently as January 2012 (Jadi 1390), indicating that detainee abuse continues to be a serious problem. Yet there is compelling evidence that at least some U.S. forces or personnel continue to transfer individuals to NDS Kandahar despite not only a widely acknowledged risk of torture but also evidence that detainees transferred to NDS Kandahar by U.S. forces have been subjected to torture.

It is important that the transfer policies of all U.S. forces and agencies are made clear, and that they meet their obligations to refrain from transferring detainees to facilities where they face a real risk of torture. It is unclear whether and under what circumstances U.S. policy permits detainee transfers from JSOC-run and other temporary detention facilities or from U.S. forces and personnel operating outside ISAF and USFOR-A chains of command to the NDS.

Lack of U.S. Detainee Monitoring Program

Despite the high number of detainees transferred by U.S. forces to Afghan custody, the United States has yet to implement a detainee monitoring program to ensure detainees are free from a real risk of torture. While the U.S. has a role in ISAF's proposed detainee

---

313 *Interview with Detainee 62.*There is some ambiguity as to whether this detainee was being held at NDS Kandahar headquarters or another NDS facility in Kandahar city near to NDS Headquarters when he was allegedly abused.
314 *Interview with ISAF/U.S. officials, Kabul city,* Kabul province, December 11, 2011 (20 Qaws 1390)

monitoring program, this monitoring element of the ISAF program will not cover detainees transferred by U.S. forces outside ISAF — a significant gap, particularly with respect to U.S special forces under the Combined Forces Special Operations Component Command-Afghanistan (CFSOCC-A), which carry out a significant number of detention operations. The AIHRC is also not informed of U.S. forces 'detainee transfers, leaving such detainees largely uncovered by a specific detainee monitoring program.

The United States remains the only ISAF nation with a long-term detention facility, the Detention Facility in Parwan (DFIP). In recent years, the United States has made significant improvements in its detention policies and practices, particularly by ensuring proper confinement conditions at DFIP and ensuring detainees are free from abuse.[315] Due process for detainees has been slightly improved through the adoption of Detainee Review Boards (DRBs), though serious concerns remain, including detainees still not being afforded a meaningful opportunity to challenge the grounds for their arrest and continued detention. Both the AIHRC and Open Society have welcomed the opportunity to conduct visits been to DFIP and DRBs, when the U.S. government has granted access, and the AIHRC and Open Society have engaged productively with U.S. officials on a range of detention issues.[316]

However, the United States has made disappointingly little progress on ensuring the rights of transferred detainees are protected. Creation of a U.S. monitoring program to ensure transferred detainees are not subjected to torture has proceeded at a disappointing pace. As early as 2009, a U.S. Inter-Agency Task Force on Interrogation and Transfer Policies recommended physically monitoring the status of transferred detainees.[317] In February 2010 (Dalwa 1388), the U.S. State Department proposed adopting a detainee monitoring program, noting not only the significant number of detainees being transferred

---

315 There have been significant improvements in treatment of detainees in U.S. custody over the past 10 years. While there are still denials of basic rights in terms of due process flaws, there have been very few allegations received regarding mistreatment at DFIP, particularly in recent years. This contrasts with serious reports of abuse and deaths in custody occurring in U.S. detention facilities in earlier days of U.S. detentions in Afghanistan, particularly at the Bagram Theater Internment Facility (BTIF) pre-2006. See Tim Golden, "In U.S. Report, Brutal Details of Two Afghan Inmates' Deaths," The New York Times, May 20, 2005 (30 Saur 1384), http://www.nytimes.com/2005/05/20/international/asia/20abuse.html?pagewanted=all; Hilary Andersson, "Afghans 'Abused at Secret Prison' at Bagram Airbase," BBC News, April 15, 2010 (24 Saur 1389)

316 Jonathan Horowitz, "New Detention Rules Show Promise and Problems," April 20, 2010 (31 Saur 1389), http://blog.soros.org/2010/04/new-detention-rules-show-promise-and-problems/; Open Society Foundations, Confinement Conditions at a U.S. Screening Facility on Bagram Air Base, supra note 4.

317 U.S. Department of Justice, "Special Task Force on Interrogations and Transfers Policies Issues Its Recommendations to the President," August 24, 2009 (2 Sunbola 1388), http://www.justice.gov/opa/pr/2009/August/09-ag-835.html.

from U.S. to Afghan custody, but also NGO reports of torture and ill-treatment of detainees in Afghan custody.[318]

U.S. government officials informed the AIHRC and Open Society that the United States is currently in negotiations with the Afghan government to create a U.S. Embassy-led monitoring program to monitor transferred detainees.[319] Negotiations are ongoing and progressing, according to officials.[320] The United States has also signed agreements with the Afghan government on post-transfer monitoring in the past, yet ultimately failed to follow through on implementation.[321] While an agreement between the U.S. and Afghan governments on a detainee monitoring plan would be welcome, implementation is what matters most.

The United States clearly faces challenges in implementing such a program, many of which are substantially different from those faced by other ISAF nations. The United States detains and transfers far more individuals than any other nation, and transfers to a large number of Afghan facilities, located in many different areas of the country. Many detainees are also subsequently transferred between different Afghan government institutions and facilities. Nevertheless, the United States, like every other ISAF nation, has a strict and absolute legal obligation not to transfer any detainee into circumstances in which he or she will be exposed to a real risk of torture.

That the United States is moving forward with plans for implementing some form of detainee monitoring is a welcome step, as is its involvement in the creation of an ISAF detainee monitoring program. However, concerns remain as to whether a U.S. monitoring program, be it specific to the United States or part of an ISAF program, will be capable of satisfying its legal obligations. The proposed U.S. program will not monitor every detainee transferred into custody, as other nations do. Instead, the proposal envisions conducting interviews with select samples of detainees.

There are also concerns of monitoring giving rise to a two-tier system in which U.S. transferred detainees are given preferential treatment, the same risk raised by ISAF monitoring or any detainee monitoring program that only assesses the treatment and conditions of transferred detainees. Given the sheer number of detainees and facilities that must be monitored as well as the frequency of visits required, significant resources are needed to properly engage in detainee monitoring, including an appropriate number of experienced monitors as well as the transportation and security resources necessary to conduct regular visits.

---

318 *U.S. State Department, Cable,* "Proposed Afghanistan Detainee Monitoring Strategy," supra note 108
319 *Interview with U.S. State Department Official, Kabul city, Kabul province,* December 11, 2011 (20 Qaws 1390)
320 Id.
321 Id.

Given widespread reports of torture and ill-treatment, as well as the documented failings of other detainee monitoring programs, it remains unclear whether even a robust, well-resourced U.S. monitoring program will be sufficient to ensure that transferred detainees are free from torture. Furthermore, having committed to playing such an integral role in working with the Afghan government to improve rule of law, the United States has a broader obligation to try to ensure that the wider prison population is not subjected to torture. To this end, the United States should also take steps to ensure the AIHRC, which has a national, constitutional mandate to monitor all detainees, is afforded full, unfettered access to detention facilities. Any U.S. detainee monitoring program should also engage cooperatively with the AIHRC to ensure all detainees are free from abuse.

The cases of abuse and torture documented in this report underscore the urgent need for such efforts to ensure that the United States meets its legal obligations and never subjects detainees to a real risk of torture.

VII. Due Process Violations

Research shows that NDS officials regularly violate the due process rights of conflict-related detainees, subjecting individuals to prolonged, incommunicado detention without charge and without access to counsel.[322] The violation of these fundamental due process rights significantly increases the risk of torture. Addressing these due process violations, particularly lack of access to counsel and family members, could greatly reduce the vulnerability of detainee to torture, and should be a priority for the Afghan government and international forces.

The NDS reportedly operates under a number of presidential decrees that are not public and unpublished, despite repeated requests from national and international human rights organizations. In general, the opacity of the legal authority of the NDS frustrates effective oversight and accountability, and increases the likelihood of abuse. Despite the secretive nature of some of the rules governing the NDS, there are fundamental rights that are afforded all detainees under applicable Afghan law, including the constitution, the Afghan Penal Code, and the Interim Criminal Procedure Code (ICPC), as well as under international conventions to which Afghanistan is a state party.[323]

---

322 *Interviews with detainees in Kandahar* indicate that ANP is also responsible for violating due process rights of conflict-related detainees in that province. Incommunicado detention means that the detainee cannot communicate with anyone other than his or her captors and perhaps his co-detainees, and is permitted no contact with the world outside his place of detention or incarceration. See Nigel Rodley, Treatment of Prisoners under International Law, 2nd edition, Oxford: Clarendon Press (ed, 1999), p.334.
323 See also *International Covenant on Civil and Political Rights* (ICCPR), to which Afghanistan became a state party in April 1983 (Hamal 1362), http://www2.

Researchers of this report have reviewed an unpublished copy of the National Security Law, which reportedly governs the authority of NDS.[324] Though the National Security Law grants the NDS the power to organize, arrest, and detain in accordance with the provisions of the Law of Crimes against Internal and External Security, there is no provision in the law that grants NDS the authority to detain individuals beyond 72 hours, hold individuals incommunicado, deny access to counsel, or violate any other due process rights afforded individuals under the ICPC and the Constitution.

Interviews for this report with detainees and Defense lawyers, as well as UNAMA's findings, confirm that NDS officials regularly retain custody of detainees beyond the 72-hour time limit established by the ICPC, and prevent individuals from notifying family members, and accessing counsel.[325] Defense lawyers are also consistently prevented from participating in investigations and are sometimes subject to intimidation.

The NDS exercises the power to both investigate and detain, which, in an environment where the rule of law is already weak, increases the risk of abuse. The conduct of investigations is a responsibility that under Afghan law normally belongs to prosecutors. In general, having both detention and investigative authority resting with the same state officials increases the risk that detainees 'rights will be violated and that they will be tortured while in custody.[326]

Pre-Trial Detention in Violation of Legal Time Limits

Interviews with detainees and defense lawyers, in addition to documentation by other organizations, clearly establish that NDS regularly holds detainees for purposes of interrogation well in excess

---

ohchr.org/english/law/ccpr.htm.

324 National Security Law, issued by an unpublished Presidential decree (Decree no. 89, 13/12/1380), Art. 6.See also *UNAMA, Conflict-Related Detainees in Afghan Custody, supra note 3*, p. 41. See also Amnesty International, Afghanistan: Detainees Transferred to Torture, supra note 102.

325 Interim Criminal Procedure Code, Official Gazette, No. 820 (25 February 2004; 6 Hoot 1382) *hereinafter "ICPC"+, Art. 31, 34, and 36. Another major issue is the inability of detainees to challenge the lawfulness of their detention before a judge, and unclear legal grounds for pre-indictment and pre-trial detention. *UNAMA, Arbitrary Detention in Afghanistan, Vol. II, supra note 45.*

326 General Recommendations *UN Special Rapporteur on Torture*, (g), http://www. ohchr.org/Documents/Issues/SRTorture/recommendations.pdf; UNAMA, Conflict Related Detainees in Afghan Custody], supra note 3. See also, Open Society Justice Initiative, Pre-Trial Detainees and Torture: Why Pre-Trial Detainees Face the Greatest Risk, Open Society Justice Initiative,http:// www.soros.org/initiatives/justice/articles_publications/publications/pretrial-detention-and-torture-20110624/pretrial-detention-and-torture-06222011.pdf *hereinafter "Open Society Justice Initiative, Pre-Trial Detainees and Torture"

---

of the 72-hour time limit established by Afghan law.[327] The vast majority of detainees interviewed were held by NDS beyond 72 hours — many for several weeks or months. Such prolonged periods of pre-trial detention not only are in clear violation of Afghan law but also put detainees at greater risk of torture.[328] Under the Interim Criminal Procedure Code (ICPC), suspects can be held by police for no more than 72 hours before they must be handed over to a prosecutor (also known as the Saranwal).[329] Suspects must be informed of the reason for their arrest within 24 hours. Only prosecutors and courts may extend pre-indictment detention beyond the initial 72 hours, and in all cases suspects should be transferred from NDS or police custody to a MOI facility after 72 hours.[330]

The detention of suspects beyond the 72-hour time limit is a widespread, well-documented problem in the criminal justice system in Afghanistan.[331] Whereas lack of capacity and delay on the part of prosecutors are the most common causes of prolonged police detention of ordinary criminal suspects, for conflict-related detainees, the NDS has deliberately used its power to retain custody of suspects to conduct investigations and interrogations, and prosecutors have delegated or abdicated their investigative responsibilities in such cases.[332]

One detainee was first arrested by international forces in December 2010 (Qaws 1389) and soon after handed over to NDS Kabul. "I spent 30 days in Department 90, and was tortured for 21 days of that month. They said to me, if you are not tortured you will never tell us the truth." He remained in NDS custody for a total of three months

---

327 ICPC Art.15, 25; Interim Criminal Procedure Code, Official Gazette, No. 820 (25 February 2004; 6 Hoot 1382), Art 31, 34., [hereinafter ICPC], http://www.asianlii.org/af/legis/laws/icocpfcogn820p2004022513821206a675/.
See also UNAMA, Conflict-Related Detainees in Afghan Custody, supra note 3.
328 UNAMA, Conflict-Related Detainees in Afghan Custody, supra note 3, p. 44. See also Open Society Justice Initiative, Pre-Trial Detainees and Torture, supra note 173. Martin Schönteich, "The Scale and Consequences of Pretrial Detention around the World," in Justice Initiatives: Pretrial Detention (New York: Open Society Institute, 2008).
329 170 Police Law, Official Gazette No. 862 (2005), http://www.rolafghanistan.esteri.it/NR/rdonlyres/94667686-6B09-4E6E-9972-905E21EEC1E4/0/PoliceLaw.pdf. Art. 15, 25; ICPC Art.31, 34.15, 25; Interim Criminal Procedure Code, Official Gazette No. 820 (25 February 2004), Art 31, 34, [hereinafter ICPC], http://www.asianlii.org/af/legis/laws/icocpfcogn820p2004022513821206a675/
330 ICPC, Art. 36. Prosecutors must file an indictment within 15 days of initial arrest. This period can be extended by the court at the request of the prosecutor for an additional 15 days. For further details on the procedural time limits imposed by Afghan law, see UNAMA, Arbitrary Detention in Afghanistan, Vol. II, supra note 44.
331 United States Assistance Missionin Afghanistan, Arbitrary Detention in Afghanistan: A Call for Action, Vol. I, UNAMA, January 2009 (Jadi 1387) [hereinafter UNAMA, Arbitrary Detention in Afghanistan, Vol.I], http://www.ohchr.org/Documents/Countries/ADVC_Vol_I_UNAMA.pdf.See also, UNAMA, Conflict-Related Detainees in Afghan Custody, supra note 3.
332 UNAMA, Arbitrary Detention in Afghanistan, Vol. II, supra note 45, p. 55.

before he was transferred to MOJ custody. While in NDS custody, the detainee was subjected to beatings as well as sexual abuse, after which he signed a confession.[333] Such prolonged, pre-trial detention by the NDS, apparently for the purpose of continuing investigations, was regularly reported by detainees.

Defense lawyers also complain about prolonged periods of detention by the NDS, and say that when challenged, NDS officials contend that they have the legal authority to detain individuals beyond the 72-hour time limit. As one Defense lawyer stated: "The law is 72 hours, but they will keep them for many months. They should be charged after 72 hours and handed to prosecutors. But if you say it's illegal, the NDS says it has the right under the law — we ask to see this law and the directorate can't show it. To our knowledge it has no such authority."[334]

There is no publicly available evidence, executive order, or law that grants the NDS legal authority to detain individuals beyond the legally mandated 72-hour time limit. If the Afghan government or NDS officials defend such detention practices as legal, then they must make public those laws or presidential decrees that grant the NDS such authority.

Regardless of the legal authority of the NDS, numerous defense lawyers alleged that the NDS retains custody of detainees in order to ensure that any evidence of physical abuse and torture is no longer apparent—so that injuries such as marks, cuts, and bruises caused by physical abuse have healed. One lawyer interviewed said, "They need to keep them in detention for a longer time to treat the injury, and for it to heal. If the injury is not visible, the court is not likely to believe the detainee."[335]

Incommunicado Detention

Holding detainees in detention incommunicado, primarily by preventing family notification, is a violation of detainees 'rights under Afghan law and contravenes international human rights standards.[336] Most detainees were also unable to communicate with

---

333 *Interview with Detainee 6*
334 *Interview with Defense Lawyer 1*
335 *Interview with Defense Lawyer 16.* See also interview with Defense Lawyer 18
336 Detainees have the right to family contact and visits under the Law on Prisons and Detention Centers, Official Gazette No. 923 1 July 2007; 10 Saratan 1386), Art. 31, http://www.unodc.org/documents/afghanistan//Government_of_Afghanistan_LAW_ON_PRISONS_AND_DETENTION_CENTERS_2010.pdf. See also, *International Covenant on Civil and Political Rights, Art. 7 and 10* (1). Other international standards include Rules 37, 38(1) and (2), and 92, UN Standard Minimum Rules for Treatment of Prisoners(1955); Principles 15, 16(1), 16(4) and 19, Body of Principles for the Protection of All Persons under Any Form of Detention(1988). For the finding of the Human Rights Committee that denial of right to contact family members is inconsistent with standards of humane

defense counsel, which is discussed in the following section. Based on interviews with detainees, family contact for detainees in NDS custody, particularly in the first days after their initial arrest, appears to be the exception rather than the rule, a practice that increases the risk of mistreatment and torture.[337] In some cases, NDS officials appear to have held individuals in incommunicado-detention and only after obtaining confessions through the use of torture were detainees transferred to MOI facilities, where they were allowed to contact their families.

One detainee reported spending three weeks in NDS custody in Kandahar, where he was subjected to suspension, beating, and electrocution. —They said confess, confess. Then they would beat us more; whatever they wanted us to say, we did. A human is very weak and so we confessed, we had no choice. The beating stopped after we confessed. All of us then moved here to Sarposa [Kandahar Central Jail]. The detainee's family attempted to locate him throughout his time with the NDS. —It was 20 days after arresting me before my family found me. They went to many sources, AIHRC, NDS, ANP, and asked all of them where I was, but no one gave them any information. When I arrived at the central jail they were able to find me.[338]

Another detainee had been at NDS Nangarhar for almost two weeks and was still unable to contact his family when monitors interviewed him. "Please send me to the regular jail. At least...at least at the regular jail I could be visited by my family, and it's an open place."[339]

A number of detainees were unable to notify family members of their detention, and therefore had to rely on released prisoners to pass on word to their relatives. "They didn't let my family meet me, or send me food, or anything. My family did not know about my situation at all or where I was. I was there for 37 days when another prisoner who was released was able to tell my family where I was." The detainee alleged he was beaten regularly by NDS officials during his first week of detention in NDS Kandahar. "My family found out about me when I got into Sarposa [Kandahar Central Jail] and then they were able to meet me."[340]

International forces also hold individuals for substantial periods of time without permitting family contact or notifying family members of detainees 'whereabouts, a situation which may be prolonged by

---

treatment, see Communication No/ 577/1994, Espinoza de Polay v. Peru (Views adopted November 6, 1997; 15 Aqrab 1386), in UN doc. CCPR/C/61/D/577/1994, para. 8.6, http://www.worldcourts.com/hrc/eng/decisions/1997.11.06_Espinoza_de_Polay_v_Peru.htm.

337 Human Rights Commission, Resolution 1997/38, para. 2. *Report of the Special Rapporteur on Torture*, UN Doc.A/56/156, July 2001 (Saratan 1380), para. 39(f). See also, *UNAMA, Arbitrary Detention in Afghanistan*, Vol. II, supranote44, p. 60.

338 *Interview with Detainee 55*

339 *Interview with Detainee 22*

340 *Interview with Detainee 52*

transferring them to the NDS. One detainee told interviewers that he was held in U.S. custody at "Bagram" for approximately six months without contact with his family. According to the detainee, he was then transferred to NDS Kabul, where he faced an additional three months without family contact, as well as torture before being released. "My family had no news, no information at all; they didn't know where I was, if I was at Bagram, NDS, or Kabul, or wherever." When he was finally released after nine months in captivity, he reported that he was dropped off on a road in Kabul and given 1,000 Afghanis [approximately $20] to find his way home. "I called my brother and I told him to come and find me...He started crying. My whole family was so happy to hear from me. My wife, children, all of them were crying from their happiness."[341] U.S. forces at DFIP, however, do permit individuals to contact family members through the ICRC, including through a video conference link.

The burden of locating detainees often falls on family members, who may undertake frantic searches to locate loved ones after their arrest. "My father started searching for me as soon as I was arrested," explained one detainee. "He went to the provincial police, then to Laghman, Jalalabad, Kabul, then to the AIHRC office, then to Bagram. At Bagram they gave him a list of prisoners they had handed over to the NDS. After one and a half months my father found me and came to visit me at the NDS." During his detention at NDS Kabul, the detainee alleged that he was subjected to severe beatings and threatened with electric shock. "My father paid the prosecutor about 80,000 Afghanis [approximately $1600]. We sold two cows and borrowed money to pay the prosecutor. My father also spent a lot of money on travel, going back and forth everywhere trying to find me."[342]

Interviews with defense lawyers confirm that conflict-related detainees are particularly likely to be held in incommunicado-detention. As the head of an Afghan legal aid organization explained, —No there is no notification, but families should be notified when individuals are initially detained. Once they feel like it is time, the NDS will allow family members to come and visit. But if families are not influential, and have no connections, then they can't find out about detainees. They can't even find out if they are in custody and they don't know about their fate.[343]

Denial of the Right to Defense Counsel

The right to counsel is guaranteed in Article 31 of the Afghan Constitution, as well as in the ICPC. It is a fundamental procedural protection that mitigates the risk of abuse and other violations of

---

341 *Interview with Detainee 98*
342 *Interview with Detainee 10*
343 *Interview with Defense Lawyer 2*

detainees 'rights. The vast majority of detainees interviewed were unable to contact or see a lawyer while in NDS custody.

Authorities do not typically inform detainees of their right to counsel, and detainees are often unaware that they have this right.[344] As one detainee in NDS Kandahar stated, —I was never told anything about a defense lawyer, and no lawyer was ever offered to me. But this is because I am still under investigation and it is too soon for me to have a lawyer.[345]

It is often family members who must contact defense lawyers on behalf of detainees. However, even when families succeed in hiring defense counsel, lawyers are often unable to meet with detainees. Family members of a detainee in Kandahar were told by a defense lawyer that he would not be able to provide representation while the detainee remained in NDS custody. "He said we would have to wait until they were transferred to the central jail."[346] The detainee was tortured in ANP custody and then transferred to the NDS, where he subsequently died from his injuries.

Partly because it is families, not detainees, who are usually able to contact defense lawyers, it can take a substantial amount of time for lawyers to locate and meet with their clients. "We find clients through their families, but when we go to the NDS they say, 'we have no one by that name.' We have to go back and forth searching for them, sometimes it can take up to a month before we can eventually get the information," explained the head of the Legal Aid Organization of Afghanistan.[347]

While lack of access to counsel is a problem in the Afghan justice system as a whole, interviews with defense lawyers indicate that the problem is particularly significant for conflict-related detainees and that NDS officials deliberately and systematically deny access to counsel. According to defense lawyers and legal aid organizations, it usually not until after the NDS has completed its investigation or detainees have been transferred to MOI detention facilities that defense lawyers are able to access detainees.

As a result of this access to detainees in NDS custody is generally denied while officials are conducting investigations and interrogations — the precise period in which detainees are at the greatest risk of abuse. "Lawyers face great difficulties interviewing clients," according to the head of one Afghan legal aid organization. "The NDS doesn't allow lawyers to come talk to clients freely. Not until the NDS finishes its investigation do they allow the lawyer to be involved. We can see clients, but not before the investigation is complete."[348] The statement of one NDS director seemed to confirm that the NDS denies access

---

344 185 *See also* UNAMA *Arbitrary Detention in Afghanistan, Vol. II, supra* note 44.

345 *Interview with Detainee 41*

346 *Interview with family member of Detainee 58*

347 *Interview with Defense Lawyer 20*

348 *Interview with Defense Lawyer 2*

to counsel as a matter of policy: "When the detainee's investigation is complete and when the report is with the prosecutor, then the suspect can have a defense lawyer. Otherwise, it would not be clear for the defense lawyer whether the suspect is guilty or innocent."[349]

Almost every defense lawyer interviewed claimed the NDS denied access to clients during investigations. "There is no chance for the detainee to see the defense lawyer in the initial investigations; in this primary stage they do not let them call a defense lawyer," said a lawyer from Jalalabad. A lawyer in Kandahar stated, "No defense lawyer in Kandahar has ever met with a detainee in NDS. NDS officials say things like you are against the NDS, and therefore you are against our constitution and the law of Afghanistan. You are like the friends of the detainees."[350]

The findings of this report contradict official NDS statements that were issued in response to the 2011 UNAMA report on detainees.[351] In its response to the UN report; the NDS asserted that, —NDS has not limited the appointment of defense attorneys. The main challenge is the insufficient number of defense attorneys which makes it difficult to cover all cases. Defense attorneys do not show interest in cases of crimes against internal and external security...and do not provide services in insecure provinces.[352]

The shortage of defense lawyers in Afghanistan is a very serious challenge, but this does not explain situations in which detainees 'lack of access to counsel results directly from deliberate acts by NDS officials. Interviews for this report with defense attorneys confirm that many work in provinces suffering from significant levels of insecurity — including Kandahar, Kunar, Laghman, and Nangarhar —undermining NDS's claim that detainees lack counsel because defense lawyers will not work in insecure areas.

Defense lawyers also expressed willingness to take on cases of conflict-related detainees, and many have done so. But it is often the NDS's own practices and policies that deter lawyers from representing conflict-related detainees. As discussed below, practices such as excluding defense lawyers from investigations, preventing lawyers from meeting with their clients, and intimidating defense lawyers, all work to dissuade attorneys from taking national security cases and greatly undermine detainees' right to counsel.

Investigations Conducted by NDS Interrogators Instead of Prosecutors

In the Afghan justice system, prosecutors are primarily responsible for conducting investigations.[353] Interviews with conflict-related

---

349 *Interview with NDS Herat Dir. Herat city, Herat Province, July 31, 2011 (9 Asad 1390)*
350 *Interview with Defense Lawyer 16*
351 *UNAMA, Conflict-Related Detainees in Afghan Custody, supra note 3, p. 63.*
352 *Id.*
353 *ICPC, Art. 23, 34, 35, and 37*

detainees and defense lawyers confirm that in political or national security cases, NDS investigators, rather than prosecutors, often assume responsibility for conducting investigations and interrogations.[354] The assumption of investigative authority by NDS officials, and the delegation of this authority by prosecutors, is a key reason for systematic due process violations and increased risk of detainee mistreatment and torture.[355]

As a defense lawyer in Kandahar explained, —Our biggest problem is that the police or the NDS don't have rights to do investigations of detainees; this is only the right of the prosecutor or judges, but unfortunately they do it illegally and send their findings to the court. They keep a detainee for a long time without any reason; they only have the right to keep him for 15 days and not more but they keep them for months.[356]

194 While the National Security Law does contain a provision that grants the NDS authority to "investigate and organize arrests in accordance with the provisions of the Law on Crimes against Internal and External Security," it is unclear what the precise scope of that investigative authority is, and to what extent this provision displaces the investigative responsibilities typically granted to prosecutors. There are no specific provisions in the National Security Law that exempt NDS from adhering to the due process rights granted under the ICPC, which grant detainees the right to have counsel present during various phases of investigation, including line ups, interrogations, and searches. There is also no provision of the National Security Law that permits NDS officials to hold detainees beyond 72 hours in order to conduct investigations. Numerous defense lawyers interviewed claimed that it is during this initial investigatory period that detainees are subjected to mistreatment and torture, claims consistent with accounts provided by detainees.[357]

---

354 UNAMA, Conflict-Related Detainees in Afghan Custody, supra note 3, p. 46
355 Individuals are at greater risk of torture if they remain in the custody of state officials that are also responsible for investigating and interrogating such individuals. "Those legally arrested should not be held in facilities under the control of their interrogators or investigators for more than the time required by law to obtain a judicial warrant of pre-trial detention which, in any case, should not exceed a period of 48 hours. They should accordingly be transferred to a pre-trial facility under a different authority at once, after which no further unsupervised contact with the interrogators or investigators should be permitted." General Recommendations, UN Special Reporter on Torture, (g), ttp://www.ohchr.org/Documents/Issues/SRTorture/recommendations.pdf. See also Open Society Justice Initiative, Pre-Trial Detainees and Torture: Why Pre-Trial Detainees Face the Greatest Risk, Open Society Justice Initiative,http://www.soros.org/initiatives/justice/articles_publications/publications/pretrial-detention-and-torture-20110624/pretrial-detention-and-torture-06222011.pdf [finding greatest risk of torture for detainees in pre-trial stages when in custody of police attempting to obtain information and confessions from detainees].
356 Interview with Defense Lawyer 10
357 Interviews with Defense Lawyers from Kabul, Nangarhar, Kandahar, Laghman, Kunar.UNAMA also found that the vast majority of complaints of torture and

In effect, the NDS has become a —one-stop shop in which arrest, detention, investigation, and interrogation all take place under the authority of NDS officials, without prosecutorial oversight or judicial review.[358] Only upon completion of its investigation does the NDS typically forward the case to prosecutors for formal indictment, which is often based solely on the findings of NDS investigators. The vesting of both investigative as well as detention authority exclusively with the NDS, particularly without any independent judicial review or oversight, greatly increases the vulnerability of detainees to mistreatment and torture.

Denial of Defense Lawyers' Right to be Present and Participate in Investigations

The most significant challenges identified by legal aid organizations and defense lawyers in representing conflict-related detainees were the exclusion of defense lawyers from investigations and their inability to review findings and case files prior to trial. By excluding defense lawyers from participating in investigations, NDS officials not only undermine detainees' rights to counsel and to a fair trial, but they also remove a key procedural protection that helps ensure that confessions are not coerced and that detainees are free from torture.

In the Afghan justice system, the presence and participation of defense lawyers in the investigation of suspects play important roles in the judicial process. Under the ICPC, defense counsel has the right to be present during any interrogations of suspects, searches, examination of experts and witnesses, and line-ups. The defense lawyer also has the right to access the findings of the investigation and the case file compiled by the prosecutor prior to trial.[359] Defense lawyers 'presence and engagement with prosecutors during investigations enable them to ensure that detainees 'rights are respected, to learn of the evidence against their clients, and to assist their clients in preparing a defense. Detainees also have a basic right to understand the grounds for their arrest, and a meaningful opportunity to challenge their detention, which requires both access to legal counsel and the evidence against them.

As discussed above, investigations in political or national security cases are conducted not by prosecutors—generally the proper

---

mistreatment occurred while detainees were in NDS or ANP custody, before being transferred to MOI facilities. See UNAMA, *Conflict-Related Detainees in Afghan Custody, supra note 3, p. 44.*

358 200 There is no provision in Afghan law that requires prompt, periodic judicial review of detention, nor do detainees have the right to challenge the legality of their detention. See, UNAMA, *Arbitrary Detention in Afghanistan, Vol. I, supra note176* , p. iv.http://www.ohchr.org/Documents/Countries/ADVC_Vol_I_UNAMA.pdf.

359 ICPC, Art. 38

investigating authorities under Afghan law — but by NDS officials.[360] Almost every defense lawyer interviewed pointed to the inability to participate in investigations as the central challenge in representing conflict-related detainees, particularly the NDS denial of access to clients during investigation phase and interrogations, and NDS refusal to share findings of investigations or information compiled in case files.[361] —In normal cases the police and prosecutors will cooperate—but with the NDS we may be able to visit the client, but only to visit — not to participate in the investigation, one Defense lawyer stated.[362]

As another lawyer explained, "If it's a regular police case, a murder case for example, the other prosecutors allow us to take part in investigation. Sometimes they will even call us and say we're looking at this case today and he's your client. But with NDS, all we are allowed to do is to have the initial agreement with the client. They just do that so they can hold it before the court and say they allowed access. But then after that we never see our client again. They don't even let us study the file. We only get to study the case once we arrive in court to defend them. The law says that the lawyers have the right to take part in investigation, but they don't allow us."[363]

Intimidation of Defense Lawyers

A number of defense lawyers reported that they or their colleagues have faced intimidation and pressure by NDS officials because of their decisions to represent conflict-related detainees. Such intimidation undermines detainees' right to counsel and may inhibit the ability and willingness of defense lawyers to document and report abuse of their clients.

As the head of one Afghan legal aid organization explained, — The power is in the hands of the NDS and sometimes they use it to threaten lawyers. This is a big challenge. Lawyers fear they will be arrested. Some are arrested simply for calling certain phone numbers or being in the call history of someone arrested. The NDS will claim that they are helping terrorists get in touch with each other and implement their plans.[364]

---

360 Whether the NDS has been granted such investigative authority by presidential decree is unclear given the confidential nature of applicable law. The refusal of the Afghan government to make public laws governing the NDS greatly undermines the ability to assess the legality of NDS actions, protect detainees' rights, and ensure accountability for violations.
361 Defense lawyers' characterized participation in investigations as including access to case files, evidence obtained by the NDS or other authorities, and presence during questioning, line-ups, and other phases of NDS investigations.
362 *Interview with Defense Lawyer 20*
363 *Interview with Defense Lawyer 8*
364 *Interview with Defense Lawyer 2*

One defense lawyer in Kabul described how he was detained by the NDS for merely speaking with individuals seeking legal assistance for detainees in NDS custody: —Last year I was detained by NDS for two nights. I was working with [a legal aid organization] at the time. Two people came to me and asked me to take cases in Zabul and Helmand provinces for NDS detainees. The next day I was leaving my home and NDS was waiting for me, they arrested me and took me away.[365] NDS officials interrogated the lawyer, asking him why he would consider representing detainees and pressuring him not to take on such cases. —Eventually a government Minister intervened and I was released, thank God! But they were planning on taking me to some place to torture me. They told me to sign a paper saying I will never defend any insurgents or Taliban.[366]

Such pressure also deters lawyers from taking cases of conflict-related detainees. —Another problem we have with the NDS is that they are threatening the defense lawyer during the trial. For example, if our client is beaten by them, then indirectly they will attack our lawyers. Why would an ILF lawyer complain of an NDS person? How dare you?' It happens often when the lawyers of [our legal aid organization] work on NDS cases. That's why our lawyers sometimes do not take these cases. In Afghanistan, this is a dangerous job.[367]

VIII. Accountability and Transparency

Afghan Government Efforts to Prevent Torture and Mistreatment of Detainees

In recent years, the Afghan government has taken a number of positive steps to address weaknesses in the justice sector, which has consistently lagged behind the security sector in terms of efforts and resources dedicated to reform.[368] The Afghan government has also introduced measures which it hopes will help prevent torture and abuse in detention facilities, including improved training for prison officials, and a multiyear program that has so far educated 4,600 prison authorities, staff, and guards on best practices for the treatment of detainees.[369]

---

365 *Interview with Defense Lawyer 19*
366 Id
367 *Interview with Defense Lawyer 8.*
368 *Congressional Research Service*, "Afghanistan: U.S. Rule of Law and Justice Sector Assistance," November 9, 2010 (18 Aqrab 1389), http://www.fas.org/sgp/crs/row/R41484.pdf.
369 *Afghanistan Independent Human Rights Commission*, the Situation of Detention Centers and Prisons in Afghanistan, June 25, 2010 (3 Asad 1389),http://www.aihrc.org.af/media/files/Reports/Thematic%20reports/rep_25_jun_2010.pdf, p. 15.

Several measures have been taken to improve detainee treatment at the NDS in particular. In December 2010 (Qaws 1390), the NDS created an oversight commission charged with monitoring detention facilities and responding to allegations of mistreatment.[370] In response to the UNAMA detentions report, the Afghan government has also created a government committee to assess the allegations, and a Human Rights Unit in the NDS Office of Legal Affairs, which has access to detainees and is responsible for protecting detainee rights.

The Afghan government also renewed its commitment to protecting conflict-related detainees from torture and mistreatment.[371] It expressed its determination —to abide by the provisions of the enforced laws of the country, particularly Article 29, Chapter Two of the Constitution which deals with the prohibition of torture.[372] The NDS has committed to convene a seminar for interrogative and reconnaissance departments, and implemented trainings on interrogation for 80 officials with the support of the UK government.[373] The NDS acknowledged that —reform is feasible and has committed to ensuring accountability for torture by investigating allegations of abuse, suspending officials responsible, and prosecuting perpetrators where appropriate.[374]

In a January 2012 (Jadi 1390) meeting with a commissioner of the AIHRC, Dr. Sima Samar, and the head of the NDS, Rahmatullah Nabil, President Hamid Karzai made a commitment that AIHRC monitors would be given unlimited access to NDS facilities. While the Afghan government's stated commitment to reform is welcome, and it has taken positive steps to end torture, the government has failed to take some of the most basic steps toward addressing detainee abuse, including holding individuals responsible for torture accountable and ensuring transparency by making findings of investigations public, publishing all laws relevant to the legal authority of the NDS, and ensuring independent monitors have access to all NDS detention facilities.

---

370 UNAMA, *Treatment of Conflict-Related Detainees in Afghan Custody, supra note 3, p.* 42. There are significant concerns regarding the effectiveness of the detention oversight commission, given that it has failed to uncover torture and abuse documented by the AIHRC, the Open Society Foundations, and UNAMA.

371 In a statement to the media, the Afghan government said: "Torture methods such as electric shock, threat of rape, twisting of sexual organs etc. are methods that are absolutely non-existent in the NDS." See Martin Petty, *"Torture Rife in Afghan Detention Facilities: U.N.," Reuters,* October 10, 2011 (18 Mizan 1390), http:// www.realclearworld.com/news/reuters/international/2011/Oct/10/torture_rife_ in_afghan_detention_facilities_u_n_.html. Joshua Levs, "U.N.: Torture in Afghan Prisons," *CNN, October 10, 2011* (18 Mizan 1390),http://articles.cnn.com/2011-10-10/asia/world_asia_afghanistan-torture-prisons_1_afghan-prisons-torture-methods-torturing-detainees?_s=PM:ASIA; see also UNAMA, *Treatment of Conflict-Related Detainees in Afghan Custody, supra note3, p. 61.*

372 *Id. p. 58*

373 *Id. p. 68*

374 *Id. p. 70*

Failure to Hold NDS Officials Accountable for Torture

The first steps in ensuring accountability for torture are the suspension, investigation, and if justified, removal of officials responsible for torture. The Afghan government has largely failed to hold NDS officials implicated in detainee abuse accountable. Though several NDS officials have been removed from their positions, most have simply been transferred to different detention facilities where they retain responsibility for detainee treatment.

The Afghan Government has removed several officials implicated in torture.[375] However, in many of these cases; officials were not removed from the NDS but instead shifted or reassigned from one facility to another. The head of NDS Khost, where UNAMA found systematic torture, was installed as the head of NDS Gardez. The head of NDS Gardez was, in turn, made head of NDS Khost. Similarly, the head of NDS Laghman, a facility where AIHRC, Open Society, and UNAMA have all found significant evidence of torture, was made deputy head of NDS Nangarhar, with the head of NDS Nangarhar taking over NDS Laghman. In these cases, individuals implicated in serious allegations of torture were not even demoted or subject to other disciplinary action. Instead, they were simply reassigned to new positions of leadership within the NDS.

According to NDS officials, investigations of individuals are ongoing and after investigations are complete, the NDS will decide whether to discipline or remove officials.[376] However, despite requests by the researchers, NDS officials have not provided any additional information regarding which, if any individuals are currently under investigation, or have been removed, transferred, or disciplined as a result of allegations of detainee abuse.[377]

Actions Taken against Government Officials Implicated in Detainee Abuse[378]

- Head of NDS Kandahar, General Muhammad Naeem
  ◇ Removed September 2011 (Sunbola 1390), remains within the NDS
- Deputy Head of NDS Kandahar, Col Abdul Wahab

---

375 UNAMA, *Treatment of Conflict-Related Detainees in Afghan Custody, supra note 3, p.* 62, 69.

376 *Meeting with NDS officials, Kabul City, Kabul Province, December 11, 2011 (20 Qaws 1390)*

377 Id.

378 Id. See also *Interview with UNAMA official, Kabul City, Kabul Province*, December 12, 2011 (21 Qaws 1390). See also Comments and Responses of the National Directorate of Security to the United Nations Assistance Mission in Afghanistan (UNAMA)'s Report, *UNAMA Detentions Report, p. 62, 69. See also interviews with foreign government officials*, February 19, 2012.

◊ Removed September 2011 (Sunbola 1390), remains within the NDS
- Head of NDS Khost, Akhtar Mohammad Ibrahimi
  ◊ Reassigned, currently Head of NDS Gardez
- Head of NDS Laghman, Noor Khayder
  ◊ Reassigned, currently Deputy Head of NDS Nangarhar
- Head of NDS Nangarhar
  ◊ Reassigned, currently Head of NDS Laghman
- Head of NDS Farah
  ◊ Suspended
- Director of JCC Helmand, Abdullah Khurram
  ◊ Reassigned as director of JCC Uruzgan; has since left that position

In response to criticisms regarding the failure to hold individuals accountable, NDS officials have contended that they cannot "ruin a person's career" based on mere allegations, and investigations are necessary to determine whether removal or other disciplinary action is justified.[379] Investigations are certainly necessary and proper when allegations of abuse are made. But investigations must be genuine, findings made public, and action taken against those responsible. So far, there is little indication that the NDS has taken such steps. No findings of any NDS investigations have been made public, and despite credible evidence of torture provided to the NDS by UNAMA, including findings of torture in 16 detention facilities, no officials appear to have been permanently dismissed from the NDS, nor have any officials been prosecuted for abusing detainees.

Transferring individuals into new positions is not meaningful accountability, which requires subjecting individuals to appropriate disciplinary measures, including permanent removal from positions if they are responsible for detainee abuse. Failing to hold individuals accountable for torture not only robs victims of justice, but permits perpetrators to continue abusing detainees, and sends a signal to other officials that torture will go unpunished.

Denial of Access to NDS Facilities

Denial of access to the detention facilities is another challenge faced by AIHRC monitors. Such denials are not always direct or explicit, and AIHRC staff has encountered several forms of restrictions and constraints on access that compromise the effectiveness of monitoring. These restrictions on access are inconsistent with the NDS's previous statements that —all the detention centers and investigation sub-directorates of the NDS are open to inspections [by

---

379 Id

AIHRC and a group of other institutions] and they have full access to [the facilities].[380]

Over the research period for this report, AIHRC monitors were explicitly denied access to two NDS facilities: NDS Kunar and NDS Department 90/124. In February 2011 (Dalwa 1390), the director of NDS Kunar denied AIHRC access to the facility stating that NDS Kabul had not granted them permission to grant access to AIHRC monitors. The AIHRC has also repeatedly requested access to NDS Department 90/124, most recently on December 19, 2011 (28 Qaws 1390), and has yet to be granted access.[381]

Significantly, the NDS does not generally permit the AIHRC to conduct unannounced visits to any NDS facilities, which seriously undermines the ability of AIHRC to fulfil its legal mandate and conduct effective monitoring. Before visiting detention facilities, NDS officials usually require the AIHRC to submit a formal letter requesting access at least 1-2 days in advance. NDS officials also prohibit AIHRC monitors from bringing cameras into NDS facilities, which prevents AIHRC monitors from properly documenting physical evidence of abuse such as bruises, scars, and other injuries.[382]

AIHRC monitors have encountered a range of additional difficulties in gaining full, unfettered access to NDS facilities. On numerous occasions, NDS officials have abruptly cancelled AIHRC visits — sometimes even while the monitors are on the way to the facility— and insisted that the visit must be postponed because another monitoring group is visiting the facility. AIHRC monitors have been prevented from visiting facilities under such circumstances multiple times, even when visits were arranged and approved well in advance. Other times, detention officials would simply deny that any visit had been arranged, even if monitors had the proper documentation and approval. The AIHRC also observed during several facility visits that certain protocols and practices of NDS officials, such as official meetings and excessive and prolonged facility tours, resulted in significant delays and time constraints that affected the quantity and quality of detainee interviews AIHRC monitors were able to conduct.

In general, the persistent uncertainty AIHRC monitors face in gaining full, unfettered access to NDS facilities, and the apparent

---

380 UNAMA, *Treatment of Conflict-Related Detainees in Afghan Custody, supra note 3*, pp. 59-60.

381 In its official written response to *AIHRC's* request to visit Department 90/124, dated December 31, 2011 (10 Jadi 1390), the NDS stated that the AIHRC could visit Department 17/40 where it could interview individuals that have been detained in Department 90/124.

382 The use of cameras and other means of documenting conditions and treatment of detainees are standard methods of investigation for the AIHRC. If security concerns exist regarding the possession and use of such equipment by AIHRC monitors in NDS facilities, the AIHRC would welcome the opportunity to address such concerns, particularly through the adoption of protocols and practices that would address security concerns while allowing the AIHRC to properly document evidence of abuse.

discretion of local NDS officials in granting access, undermines AIHRC's ability to fulfill its mandate to conduct rigorous and effective monitoring of the conditions and treatment of detainees.

IX. Recommendations

National Directorate of Security

- Investigate all credible allegations of torture, including reports of torture at the NDS facilities identified in this report.
- Investigate and hold to account all those who are responsible for torture including commanding officers. End the practice of moving rather than removing officials responsible for torture and make public or provide to AIHRC the results of investigations and actions taken.
- Ensure AIHRC has full, unfettered, and confidential access to all NDS detainees and facilities, including NDS Kabul Department 90/124, as legally mandated under the Constitution of Afghanistan. Ensure NDS officials permit AIHRC monitors to conduct unannounced visits to all NDS facilities.
- Ensure the NDS Human Rights Unit immediately inspects and investigates NDS detention facilities where the AIHRC alerts the government that it has been denied access.
- investigate all credible allegations of —off-site or undisclosed facilities being used by NDS interrogators, and end the use of such facilities or locations for interrogations, to which independent monitors have no access.
- Provide the NDS Human Rights Unit with the authority and resources necessary to effectively investigate allegations of abuse and ensure those responsible are held to account.
- Cease holding detainees incommunicado. Notify family members of detainee's arrest immediately or as soon as practicably possible, ensure access to legal counsel, and permit family members to visit detainees. Transfer all detainees to MOI custody within 72 hours, inform detainees of the reason for their arrest within 24 hours, and ensure all detentions beyond 72 hours are authorized by a prosecutor or judge.
- Ensure investigations are conducted by the proper authorities under Afghan law; permit prosecutors to conduct investigations of suspects.
- Ensure defense lawyers have access to detainees and all NDS detention facilities at all stages of detention as well as proper access to the findings of investigations and evidence against clients.
- Provide mandatory training for NDS interrogators and their superiors on lawful interrogation methods, alternative

investigative approaches (such as forensics), and legal obligations under Afghan and international law that prohibit torture and ill-treatment, in coordination with international partners.

Government of Afghanistan

- Make public all legislation and Presidential decrees governing the legal authority of NDS.
- Afghan Supreme Court
- Ensure judges do not permit confessions obtained through torture to be admitted in court, as required by the Afghan Constitution and the Interim Criminal Procedure Code.
- Issue guidance to all judges to require them to investigate allegations made by detainees of confessions under duress.
- Ensure that AIHRC monitors can testify in court and make available other evidence relevant to a detainee's allegation of torture, ill-treatment, and other forms of abuse.
- Afghan Parliament
- Reform the ICPC to provide detainees the right to have their detention promptly and periodically reviewed by a court and the right to challenge the lawfulness of their detention before a court, consistent with Afghanistan's obligations under the ICCPR.
- Create a mechanism to ensure proper compensation for victims of abuse and torture suffered as a result of acts by state officials.
- **ISAF Command and Troop Contributing Nations**
- Support the NDS and the Afghan government to ensure all detainees are free from torture. Work with the NDS to identify critical deficiencies in resources, and provide appropriate technical and financial assistance to help ensure detainee treatment and interrogations comply with Afghan and international law.
- Enhance the capacity of Afghan officials to conduct lawful and effective interrogations, evidence-based investigations and prosecutions, and strengthen the effectiveness of internal monitoring and accountability mechanisms.
- Make use of ISAF suspension and remediation policies to work with the Afghan government to adopt measures that will protect all detainees from abuse, such as full, unfettered access by AIHRC, detainee access to defense counsel, and accountability for detainee abuse.
- Ensure no detainee is transferred into facilities where there is real risk of torture. Where detainee transfers have been suspended by ISAF due to credible allegations of torture, ensure resumption of transfers to a facility occur only when there is sufficient information to determine that there is no real risk of torture at that facility.

- Ensure the detainee monitoring program has the resources, civilian expertise, and authority necessary to effectively monitor all detainees transferred to Afghan custody.

United States

- constructively engage with the NDS to ensure it provides guarantees of lawful detainee treatment, and holds officials accountable for abuse.
- Support the NDS and the Afghan government to ensure all detainees are free from torture. Work with the NDS to identify critical deficiencies in resources, and provide appropriate technical and financial assistance to help ensure detainee treatment and interrogations comply with Afghan and international law.
- Enhance the capacity of Afghan officials to conduct lawful and effective interrogations, evidence-based investigations and prosecutions, and strengthen the effectiveness of internal monitoring and accountability mechanisms.
- Ensure all U.S. forces, including U.S. Special Operations Forces and intelligence agency personnel, comply with U.S. detainee transfer policies and international law and are covered by the AIHRC monitoring program.

Courtesy: **Afghanistan Independent Human Rights Commission** (AIHRC), *Open Society Foundations, 17 March, 2012).* The AIHRC is a national human rights institution working in the area of protection and promotion of human rights. This Institution was established based on the Bone Agreement and Presidential Decree and afterwards, pursuant to Article 58 of the Afghan Constitution, it found a legal base to monitor the observance of human rights as well as to protect and promote human rights in the country, "Every individual shall complain to this Commission about the violation of personal human rights. The Commission shall refer human rights violations of individuals to legal authorities and assist them in defense of their rights.

Open Society Foundations (OSF), formerly the Open Society Institute, is an international grant making network founded by business magnate George Soros. Open Society Foundations financially support civil society groups around the world, with a stated aim of advancing justice, education, public health and independent media. The OSF has branches in many countries encompassing a group of country and regional foundations, such as the Open Society Initiative for West Africa, and the Open Society Initiative for Southern Africa. The Open Society Foundations work to build vibrant and tolerant societies whose governments are accountable and open to the participation of all people. The OSF seeks to strengthen the rule of law; respect for human rights, minorities, and a diversity of opinions; democratically elected governments; and a civil society that helps keep government power in check. The society help to shape public policies that assure greater fairness in political, legal, and economic systems and safeguard fundamental rights. The OSF implements initiatives to advance justice, education, public health, and independent media. The OSF builds alliances across borders and continents on issues such as corruption and freedom of information. Working in every part of the world, the Open Society Foundations place a high priority on protecting and improving the lives of people in marginalized communities.

Postscript

The elephant failed to defeat the lion as Washington paid a steep price for its political and military mistakes. The country invested more than $800 billion in Afghanistan without any political and military gain. Thousands Americans were killed injured, and mentally tortured in this longest and toughest war against terrorism, but large swath of territory is still under Taliban control. The emergence of Russian Taliban and the deployment of MGB intelligence units across the country may further complicate the US war game. The game has totally failed and now Washington and its allies may face the wrath of Russia and China proxy war in Afghanistan. In reality, the US and NATO have failed to deliver in case of peace, security and state building as the war now become boring and irksome. Today, Afghanistan is sinking back into a quagmire of chaos.

Fifteen years after the US war on terrorism, Afghanistan still remains one of the worse places for journalist, NGOs, Doctors, businessmen and women. The Unity Government hardly controlled 30% percent territory of the state in 2016, while Daesh and Taliban posed bigger challenge to the ANA and its associated private militias. The perceptualization of the altercation in Afghanistan by the United States and its allies was based on contradictory approach to the exponentially growing insurgency in the country. The years 2015 and 2016 saw several record low points at once. Taliban gained control over larger swath of territory, and it was the first time Taliban conquered Kunduz province. Russian intelligence established its networks and deployed secret units across the country and continues to train and equip its fighters. In December 2015, Washington Post reported Mr. Zamir Kabulov, President Vladimir Putin's special representative for Afghanistan, told the Interfax news agency that "the Taliban interest objectively coincides with ours" in the fight against the Islamic State.

"I have already said earlier that we and the Taliban have channels for exchanging information," Kabulov added.

On 29 December 2016, Samuel Ramani critically highlighted relations between Russia, Taliban and China. Russian support to Taliban he says is in fact, the denial of the legitimacy of the Afghan government: "Critics of Russian foreign policy argues that Putin's outreach to the Taliban is a cynical ploy to undermine the legitimacy of President Ashraf Ghani's U.S.-backed government. Some Afghan policymakers and General John Nicholson, a leading US military commander in Afghanistan, publicly given credibility to this contention. The Russian government has responded to these criticisms by insisting that its support for Taliban participation in peace negotiations will not necessarily result in the Taliban becoming an Afghan government coalition partner. Containing the Taliban's influence will be more difficult for Moscow to achieve than its rhetoric suggests, however, as major Russian strategic partners, China and Iran, have also supported the Taliban's participation in the Afghan government".

Moscow returned to the country with a strong Taliban group, and the incarnated KGB (MGB) network to intercept the US and NATO expansion towards Central Asia, and eliminate the ISIS terrorist organization in Afghanistan. To complete its mission, Russia may possibly deploy strong intelligence units along the Afghan-Tajik, and, Pak-Afghan borders. However, China also wants to ensure the security of its borders by deploying security and intelligence unites along the Afghan and Pakistan's borders to intercept the infiltration of Uyghur separatists inside the country. Beijing and Moscow fear that there are serious grounds to expect that security situation in Afghanistan may rapidly deteriorate as the Unity Government's legitimacy is in spike.

On 14 January 2017, Pajhwok News reported Moscow asked warring factions in Afghanistan, primarily the Taliban movement, to renounce violence and take urgent action to launch intra-Afghan dialogue. The Russian foreign Ministry spokesperson told a media briefing that security situation in Afghanistan remained challenging and number of terrorist attacks is on the rise. Maria Zakharova noted the armed opposition had somewhat scaled back its offensive, a usual tactic in the winter. While condemning the heinous terrorist attack on 10 January 2017, she said there was no justification for such acts. "Our sympathy goes out to all victims, families of the deceased and colleagues, foreign diplomats. "We hope that the masterminds and perpetrators of these terrorist attacks will receive the punishment they deserve," Maria said.

On 04 January 2017, Long War Journal reported the Moscow conference between Chinese and Pakistani emissaries to discuss the war in Afghanistan. However, the trio of nations urged the world to be "flexible" in dealing with the Taliban, which remains the Afghan government's most dangerous foe. The Russian courtship of the

Taliban began some time prior to Taliban's dramatic 15-day takeover of the northern Afghan city of Kunduz, which was reportedly facilitated by the delivery of Russian weapons to the group via Tajikistan. Russia and China have the opportunity to use the platform of Shanghai Cooperation Organization, which included all of the Central Asian republics, Pakistan and India.

Now, the emergence of Russia with a strong military might, more than fifty nations and their intelligence agencies in Afghanistan have failed to effectively counter Russian and Chinese secret agencies? The Putin administration has invested heavily in Afghanistan and continues to reduce the political and military space of the United States and its NATO allies who neither stabilized the war torn country nor established a strong army. This inattention of international community resulted in the resentment of Afghan population towards their presence. China helped the United States in its war against the Soviet Union, and now helps Russia in its war against the United States. However, Pakistan and Russia are moving towards an embrace, but looking at each other with suspicion. Chinese involvement in Afghanistan is growing, and it has established good contacts with Afghan and Pakistani extremist organizations. However, in 2014, China introduced its own special envoy to Afghanistan and Pakistan.

The recent Pentagon China-phobia policy, its containment of China, the emergence of new military and intelligence alliance among China, Pakistan and Russia, has become a hot debate in electronic and print media in South Asia. The increasing Chinese influence in Pakistan, Afghanistan and Central Asia and its strong presence in European and African market together with the aggrandizement of Russian economy and military industry have caused an unending torment for the United States and its European allies. The Pentagon authorities didn't sleep a wink since the commencement of recent joint Russia-China-Pakistan rapprochement. The recent establishment of a new military intelligence agency, 'Defence Clandestine Intelligence Service' (DCIS) and its focus on China raised many questions about the US presence in Afghanistan. The emergence of China as an economic and military power is no doubt irksome for Pentagon that wants to contain and confine both China and Russia to specific regions.

The Defence Clandestine Service, according to Pentagon's report, will be working closely with both Pentagon and CIA, recruiting spies from Defence Intelligence Agencies and deploying them in most part of South Asia to closely watch the military and economic movements of communist China in South and Southeast Asia. The agency is struggling to maintain a strong presence in Afghanistan. In Xinjiang province, Uyghur Islamic Movement and other minor ethnic and political groups have established their secret networks, recruit and invite young people to their groups. Beijing is already facing constant threats from Tibet and Taiwan, the low-key conflict which has been simmering in the region since long. These ethnic and religious challenges are very serious for China's expanding economic and military role in both Asia and Africa. The Obama administration wants to switch US national security focus away from Middle East to address long-term issues such as the rise of China, Russia and North Korea.

The Unity Government is not lessoning to the Chinese and Russian demand that Taliban should be accommodated in the political set up to bolster the fight against the ISIS terrorist group. The United States and its allies are increasingly worried that any deepening of ties between Russia, China and their own Taliban group, their supply of modern weapons, and the deployment of their intelligence units across Afghanistan may cause further intensification of civil war in the country. The US policy of killing and torture has now failed to draw on the cultural and historical lessons of local governance in the country. Undoubtedly, there are thousands innocent civilians who get killed in the US bombing in Afghanistan. The US army killed 42 people including 14 innocent patients and doctors in Kunduz hospital, and then argued that the $5 billion intelligence computer system was failed. This was, in fact, an ignominious joke with an occupied country like Afghanistan, where they are free to kill, torture, and kidnap civilians with impunity.

The rise and fall of Afghan intelligence agencies, and the way they operated during the last three decades left reams of bloodstained and heartbreaking stories in newspapers, journals and books. The KHAD killed thousands in its secret prisons, in broad daylight, and in its torture cells, the NDS killed, tortured and forcefully disappeared numerous innocent Afghan men, women and children. International human rights organizations and Afghanistan's Independent Human Rights Commission in their research papers deeply criticized the National Directorate of Security (NDS) for its brutal ways of retrieving information from detainees. These illegal tactics alienated the citizens from the state, and forced young people to take arm against the government and its international partners.

The NDS demonstrated in an unprofessional way, and failed to counter the Taliban and ISIS's geographical expansion. The chiefs of the intelligence agencies have been unlawfully critical of Afghan Presidents, parliamentarians and neighbouring states in their print and electronic media statements, since 2001. They criticized former President Hamid Karzai's approach towards Pakistan, criticized President Ashraf Ghani's visit to Islamabad, and criticized NATO and Pakistan for failing to stabilize the teetering state. The chief of National Directorate of Security (NDS), Mr. Rahmatullah Nabil hammered Prime Minister Nawaz Sharif for his remarks about Afghanistan. His precursor, Amrullah Saleh acted like an ethnic politician.

This controversial and unprofessional role of the Afghan intelligence agencies caused irksome for the government of

Afghanistan and international community. Despite scads of tips, the NDS failed to prevent an attack on Kabul that was billed as one of the largest in the entire war. Conflicts between Pashtuns and the Panjshiri Tajik-dominated officer corps of the NDS have been cited as among the main reasons that information about the attack did not reach the right people at the right time in Kabul. The spy agency was severely criticized by parliamentarians after a brazen prison break in Kandahar and the fall of Kunduz to Taliban insurgents.

In fact, during the last 15 years, the US and its NATO allies failed to substantially improve governance and intelligence sharing systems or recruit the NDS officers. A strong centralized intelligence infrastructure remained a dream. The Americans took no interest in establishing a strong Afghan intelligence system, and at the provincial level, the intelligence networks no longer exist. The ability of the Afghan state to establish its rule in rural areas has been completely undermined. For an ordinary Afghan, insecurity of all types destabilizes any attempt to rebuild a life. Corruption is rife in the justice system, and Afghans are completely fed up.

The matrix of the Islamic State was expanding towards the northern parts of the country. Terrorist groups are pledging allegiance to the ISIS struggle to establish their units in the Jalalabad province. In an exclusive interview with Pajhwok Afghan News Agency, NATO spokesman Brigadier General Charlie Cleveland confirmed the existence of more than 1,000 Daesh fighters in the Jalalabad province. On 19 April 2016, Russian diplomat, Zamir Kabulov warned that more than 10,000 trained terrorists of the Islamic State were preparing to enter Central Asia. Last week, Abdul Rashid Dostum expressed the same concern and warned that some internal (government) and foreign circles want to transport more than 7,500 Daesh fighters (Chechen, Uzbeks, Tajiks, Iraqi, Syrians, Lebanese, and Libyans) to parts of Northern provinces.

On 11 January 2017, unknown terrorists attacked important government installations and diplomatic compound in Kabul and Kandahar, which prompted huge fatalities and the killing of more than 100 Afghans and five diplomats of the United Aran Emirate (UAE). Terrorists also targeted Parliament in which 34 employees were injured. This was a clear message of those who recently became strong stakeholders in the country. Some Afghan experts view it as foreign intelligence-led attacks-facilitated by some wolves within the Unity Government, some affixed to sweeping generalization that Russian and Chinese intelligence agencies are behind it, and some blamed Pakistan based Quetta Shura and the Haqqani network for their involvement. There are many stakeholders who want to show their power and create space for them, but one cannot deny the fact that Afghan war criminals, Ministers and member parliament also support terrorist groups, purveying them with weapons and money and transport their fighters to their destinations. This issue has already been taken seriously in Afghan parliament so many times, but no law has been passed to bring these state sponsor terrorists to justice, or remove them from their posts.

Dr. Mohammad Najibullah Ahmadzai

Muhammad Najeebullah became the President of Afghanistan in 1987. He was the Director General of KHAD as he gained the attention of several leading Soviet officials, such as Yuri Andropov, Dmitriy Ustinov and Boris Ponomarev. In 1981, Dr. Najibullah was appointed to the PDPA Politburo. In 1985, Dr. Najibullah stepped down as state security minister to focus on PDPA politics; he had been appointed to the PDPA Secretariat. Mikhail Gorbachev, the last Soviet leader, was able to get Karmal to step down as PDPA General Secretary in 1986, and replace him with Dr. Najibullah.

Mr. Amrullah Saleh

In 1997, Mr. Amrullah Saleh was appointed by Ahmad Shah Massoud as the head of his intelligence, and also entrusted the task to serve as Northern Alliance's liaison office inside the Afghan Embassy in Dushanbe, Tajikistan, handling contacts to international non-governmental (humanitarian) organizations and intelligence agencies. After the September 11, 2001 attacks in the United States, Mr. Saleh participated in leading intelligence operations of the United Front on the ground during the toppling of the Taliban regime.

In December 2004, Mr. Amrullah Saleh was appointed as head of the National Directorate of Security (NDS) by President Hamid Karzai. In 2005, Mr. Saleh engaged several NDS agents infiltrating the Pakistani tribal areas to search for bin Laden and other al-Qaeda and Taliban leaders. After the 2009 Afghan presidential election, Afghan President Karzai's views about the security issues confronting

Afghanistan and how best to deal with them reportedly changed. Both Mr. Saleh and Interior Minister Hanif Atmar subsequently had strong disagreements with Karzai on how to proceed against the Taliban, who Karzai began referring to as "brothers." In early 2010, an Afghan man approached the NDS claiming to represent senior Taliban commander Mullah Akhtar Muhammad Mansour.

On June 6, 2010, Mr. Saleh resigned from the NDS while Atmar resigned from his position as interior minister after a militant attack against the national peace jirga, although nobody had been killed or wounded and the attackers had been arrested. The resignation of Saleh and Atmar came amidst heavy disagreement between Hamid Karzai and Amrullah Saleh on how to proceed against the Taliban.

Mr. Assadullah Khalid

In August 2012, the nomination of war criminals and corrupt officials for key posts in Afghanistan enraged the entire population. Every section of society, government officials, politicians and parliamentarians expressed deep concern on the decision of the president. War Criminal Mr. Assadullah Khalid was appointed as the head of the National Directorate of Security (NDS) in September 2012, but after a few days, he was seriously injured in an assassination attempt by a suicide bomber in December 2012, and in August 2013, his predecessor, Mr. Rahmatullah Nabil, was appointed acting NDS head. Sources close to the NDS report that Khalid retains some influence within the NDS. Khalid previously served as Minister of Border and Tribal Affairs (2008-2012) Governor of Kandahar (2005-2008), Governor of Ghazni (2002- 2005), and the security commander for the Southern Zone (2011-2012). Immediately after the fall of the Taliban government in late 2001, he served as commander of Directorate 5 of the NDS.

Mr. Assadullah Khalid and his rogue Brigade 888 stand accused of human rights abuses, including rape and torture, during his governorship. Canada supported the Brigade 888 and considered it a trusted ally protecting Canadian outposts in Kandahar. The military and financial support of the Canadian government encouraged the criminal Brigade 888 to torture, rape and murder civilians in Kandahar. Canadians who knew said they witnessed no abuse by the Brigade 888. Nevertheless, common Afghans ask why the Canadian army was abetting the crimes of the Brigade 888. A Canadian newspaper, The Globe, reported that the Canadian soldiers "lived beside" Brigade 888 personnel in the governor's palace in Kandahar, and "helped train Afghans, who routinely committed torture."

In 2008, Khalid was removed from Kandahar and appointed as the minister of frontier and tribal areas. During Khalid's brutal tenure in Kandahar, from 2005 to 2008, the palace became a microcosm of

Canada's moral dilemma. Another heartrending story of the Canadian army relates to the use of Brigade 888 against the civilian population. The war criminal, Mr. Assadullah Khalid, is a known human rights violator. He ran a private detention facility for torturing detainees, but Canada never repudiated him or reported his crimes to the ISAF command. Mr. Assadullah Khalid was born in the Ghazni Province of Afghanistan in 1969 into a Taraki Ghilzai Pashtun family.

In April 2010, CBC News revealed the existence of top-level Canadian government documents reporting the personal involvement of Khalid in serious human rights abuses in his own private dungeon. Multiple sources report that the private detention center was located under Khalid's guest house while governor of Kandahar. Documents also said that Christopher Alexander, a top Canadian official working with the United Nations, alleged that Mr. Assadullah Khalid had ordered the killing of five United Nations workers by bombing, presumably to protect his narcotics interests.

CNN reported Richard Colvin, Canada, a former deputy ambassador to Afghanistan, who worked directly with Khalid while he was governor of Kandahar from 2005 to 2008. Colvin described evidence of torture by Khalid's subordinates and testified that:

> "[h]e was known to us very early on, in May and June 2006, as an unusually bad actor on human rights issues. He was known to have had a dungeon in Ghazni, his previous province, where he used to detain people for money, and some of them disappeared . . . He was known to be running a narcotics operation. He had a criminal gang. He had people killed who got in his way." Rather than arrest Khalid, Karzai wants to give him the almost limitless power as intelligence chief.

However, in 2015, Human Rights Watch reported the direct involvement of Mr. Assadullah Khalid in the acts of sexual violence against women and girls. A well-placed and credible source who sought anonymity because of security concerns told Human Rights Watch that while Khalid was governor of Ghazni, forces under his command used a false pretext to bring a group of several young women and at least one girl of 16 to a residence where the governor and several other men were present.263 The source said that Khalid offered the women and girls money to have sex with him and the other men, which they refused. The men were drinking alcohol, and Khalid pressured the women to drink as well. When they refused, the men, including Khalid, raped the women and girls. "Until morning they were doing those things," the source said, in reference to the rapes. At least one of the victims was reportedly left with blood on her clothes. Afterwards, Khalid allegedly told them that "they would be killed and their families destroyed if they told anyone what had happened." Human Rights Watch reported.

Letter from Human Rights Watch to President Ashraf Ghani, October 9, 2014

Dr. Ashraf Ghani, President-elect, Islamic Republic of Afghanistan
Re: Senior National Security Officials and Human Rights Concerns
Dear President Ghani and Chief Executive Abdullah,

As you begin the selection process for key government posts in your new averment, we would like to wish both of you success in carrying out your duties as President and Chief Executive of the Islamic Republic of Afghanistan.

Human Rights Watch would like to remind you of the opportunity – and the responsibility –you and your new national unity government now have to address the continuing human rights concerns in Afghanistan. One of the most crucial ways you can do so in these early days of your administration is by carefully vetting your appointments to key government posts to ensure that those appointees do not have a documented history of human rights abuses.

Over the last 13 years, Human Rights Watch has documented serious and widespread human rights violations by members of the Afghan National Police (ANP), the Afghan Local Police (ALP), and the National Directorate of Security (NDS), including systematic torture and other ill-treatment, enforced disappearance, and extrajudicial executions. Human Rights Watch has informed Afghan government officials about these abuses, as have the United Nations Assistance Mission to Afghanistan (UNAMA) and the Afghanistan Independent Human Rights Commission. However, we remain deeply concerned that to date no member of the security forces has been prosecuted for such violations.

We urge you to carefully consider these concerns in the coming days as you make appointments to the Ministries of the Interior and Justice, the National Directorate of Security, the Attorney General, and other critical official positions. We understand that the Afghan National Security Forces are under great pressure at this time due to a rise in insurgent attacks on frontline national police and ALP units over the past few months. We are aware that the national police, in particular, have suffered the heaviest losses in its history. However, it is precisely under such conditions that it is critical for security forces to adhere to Afghan and international law. In this regard, there are several measures that your government can undertake immediately to promote respect for human rights.

As you are aware, after the publication of UNAMA's 2013 report on the treatment of detainees, President Hamid Karzai issued a decree in February 2013 ordering anti-torture measures, including prosecution of officials responsible for torture. However, there have been no prosecutions for such abuses against detainees. While UNAMA reported that torture had been reduced in some facilities, it has continued in others. Lawyers have told Human Rights Watch that some detainees are shifted among detention centers to conceal the prevalence of torture. Without prosecutions, there is no real deterrent to torture.

The police and NDS continue to carry out torture and summary executions with impunity. They have also been cited in reports of sexual violence and enforced disappearances, and reportedly maintain secret detention centers to which UNAMA and international humanitarian organizations have no access. The paramilitary ALP and other militia forces have been responsible for extrajudicial executions, kidnappings, assaults, and other abuses against local civilians.

In some cases, the role of commanding officers in these abuses is evident. In others, where a police or paramilitary unit has been implicated in numerous abuses, commanders will at least be responsible for crimes committed as a matter of command responsibility –that is, when a commander knows or should have known about abuses by forces under his control, but failed to take action to stop them or punish those responsible.

President Ghani, during your election campaign, you committed publicly to ensuring that members of the Afghan security forces who have been responsible for torture and other human rights violations would be prosecuted. Chief Executive Abdullah, you pledged to strengthen disciplinary frameworks and elevate the level of accountability in the security forces. Out of our concern that due process and emphasis on individual accountability contribute to the rule of law in Afghanistan, Human Rights Watch makes the following recommendations:

Appoint as heads of the Ministries of Interior and Justice, the National Directorate of Security, and the Afghan National Police, individuals who are committed to ensuring that Afghanistan abide by Afghan and international law in the treatment of detainees, prisoners, and the local civilian population. People in positions of authority in public institutions should not only bear no taint of involvement in human rights abuses, but should be proponents of respect for human rights.

Establish an independent oversight and accountability mechanism empowered to conduct investigations into all allegations of torture and other mistreatment in custody.

Create a national civilian complaints mechanism covering all Afghan security forces, including the armed forces, national police, the Afghan Local Police, and other government-backed militias that would recommend cases for criminal investigation, and assist in vetting security force personnel.

Remove, discipline, and punish (including by referral to civilian and military prosecutors) all ANP, NDS and ALP officers and their superiors found responsible for committing or condoning torture and other ill-treatment, enforced disappearances, and extrajudicial executions. Measures should include suspension, loss of pension and other benefits, and criminal prosecution where appropriate.

Publicly denounce human rights violations by government officials and security forces and take action against counter-insurgency measures that rely on the unlawful use of force, extrajudicial killings, torture, and enforced disappearances.

Disband irregular armed groups and hold their commanders accountable for abuses they have committed.

Human Rights Watch thanks you for your attention to these issues. We would welcome your response and the opportunity to meet with members of the cabinet to discuss our recommendations.

Sincerely,

Brad Adams

Executive Director, Asia division

Human Rights Watch. Courtesy: (Human Rights Watch).

Engineer Rahmatullah Nabil

On August 29, 2012, President Karzai removed the intelligence chief, Rahmatullah Nabil, and said he wanted to limit the term of an intelligence chief to two years. However, the case is different here. Nabil with his non-professional conduct and political inclinations had failed to counter the Taliban insurgency and their infiltration into the rank and file of the police and Afghan National Army. There are reports that President Karzai was unhappy with his politicized approach to intelligence work. Mr. Nabil's removal from office is a clear proof of his non-professional methods of information gathering and processing. The main reason behind his removal was his inability to prevent the Taliban attack on the Afghan peace council in the capital last year.

The president accused him of power abuse. Like his predecessor, Mr. Nabil's tactics of investigation against detainees included electric shocks, threats of rape, beatings, extrajudicial killings, torture, humiliation, prolonged pre-trial detention, discrimination against ethnic opponents and sexual abuse of children. He is responsible for the killings of innocent Afghans during his brutal investigation tactics in Khost and other secret prisons. As we all understand, security is worsening in the country. As each day passes, the country moves closer to an unending civil war. Insurgent attacks, IEDs, suicide attacks, target killings, drug trafficking and corruption has triggered concern among all players in Afghanistan.

Mr. Rahmatullah Nabil lacks required intelligence skills and is not a well-known person for the post. President Karzai had intended to reshuffle so that he will not face major problems from NDS. Nabil was an unexpected choice to lead the intelligence service and initially not one of the front-runners considered for the job. The head of the

National Directorate of Security (NDS), Mr. Rahmatullah Nabil, resigned over policy disagreements with President Ashraf Ghani. In his resignation letter, Nabil alleged that Ghani had "verbally" asked him to resign.

Mr. Muhammad Masoom Stanekzai

Mr. Masoom Stanekzai was born 1958 in Mughul Khel village of Mohammad Agha District of Logar Province. As a young man, Stanakzai served in the Afghan army for a decade, rising through the ranks to end as a colonel, still, it seems, in communications. An adviser to Afghan President Hamid Karzai and vice chair of the Demobilization and Reintegration Commission, a group responsible for the disbandment of illegal armed groups, Stanekzai's research focuses on security, reconstruction and reconciliation in Afghanistan.

The defense nominee Mr. Masoom Stanekzai failed to win a vote of confidence from Wolesi Jirga. In May 2016, Mr. Masoom Stanekzai was appointment as chief of the NDS is likely to elicit a favorable response from USA and China due to his long association in peace process.

Courtesy: (Afghan Bios is a searchable Database for VIP's like Afghan Ministers, Governors and other Politicians e.g. members of Jirga, search for military and police commanders the data have been compiled from international media, Web research and author's personal contacts with people from Afghanistan). Last Modified in 2016-05.

Appendix 1. Presidential Decree No. 129 of the Islamic Republic of Afghanistan, 16 February 2013

1. The Attorney General of the Government of Afghanistan is in charge of prosecuting the violators of article 51 of the Law on Prisons and Detention Centers in light of the findings of the delegation's report which has reported torture and mistreatment of detainees and prisoners, and to prevent any torture, mistreatment and conviction of any innocent detainee in the future.

2. According to the Constitution of Afghanistan, the discovery of crime is the responsibility of the police, investigation and prosecution are the responsibility of the Attorney General's Office, despite the fact that there are [other] security and discovery organizations that detain detainees for more than 72 hours and do the work instead of the crime investigation agencies. Accordingly all organizations are obliged to do their duties as conferred according to the applicable laws of the country and prevent interference in others' duties and should send cases to responsible prosecution offices within the timeframe prescribed by law.

3. According to article 29 of the Constitution, the torture of human beings is prohibited. All the discovery and investigation departments of the Ministry of Interior, NDS and Attorney General's Office are ordered not to torture or mistreat any suspect or detainee during detention and interrogation.

4. The Ministry of Justice is instructed to regularly organize meetings of the Legal Aid Board in cooperation with the Faculty of Sharia and Law of Kabul University to monitor the lack of access of detainees and prisoners to legal assistance and Defense lawyers, and to discuss methods and possibilities of offering legal assistance in a widespread manner to all detainees and prisoners as per Article 31 of the Constitution. The Ministry of Justice is obliged to revise the

current structure of the Legal Aid Department, so that it provides for the actual numbers of detainees and prisoners.

5. The Ministry of Interior and NDS are duty bound to facilitate access of the detainees and prisoners by legal aid providers and Defense lawyers in the supervision and detention centers and prisons since their arrest.

6. The Ministry of Interior and Ministry of Public Health are duty bound to provide as soon as possible medical treatment and cure to the detainees who are suffering from illness and those who have been complaining from illnesses arising from beating during the interrogation process as stated in article 27 of the Law on Prisons and Detention Centers.

7. The Office of the Attorney General of the Islamic Republic of Afghanistan in coordination with the General Directorate for Prisons and Detention Centers of the Ministry of Interior are obliged to assess the cases of those prisoners and detainees who are acquitted by the court, and those who completed their period of imprisonment, but are still in prison. The responsible bodies (Attorney General and General Directorate for Prisons and Detention Centers) in light of article 50 of the Law on Prisons and Detention Centers should take legal steps for their release after assessment, within two months.

8. The Supreme Court is instructed to assess the cases of those detainees/prisoners who spent a long time in detention and for which the courts have not issued any timely decision/s on their cases and for whom procedural timeframes are over; the Supreme Court shall appoint expert judges to assess and issue decisions as soon as possible on the aforementioned cases. Otherwise, the officials in charge of liberty deprivation centers (detention centers/prisons) have the authority, in accordance with Section 4 of article 20 of Law on Prisons and Detention Centers, to release such prisoners; in case of failure to do so, detention/prison officials shall be prosecuted by the relevant prosecutorial office for the commission of negligence within the course of duty in relation to such cases.

9. The Supreme Court, the Ministry of Justice and the AGO are responsible, within the limits of what is possible to the Government, for establishing courts, prosecution offices and Huqooq offices and with preference to the super-scale, CBR and other privileges, in districts where these institutions do not exist in order to prevent the human rights violations of citizens and to pave the way for the sustainability and development of the system based on the rule of law.

10. The Ministry of Interior, Attorney General's Office and NDS are instructed –for professional capacity building purposes- to conduct training courses for their employees working in law enforcement, protection of the law and conduct of investigation, for learning human rights and other relevant professional and job-related subjects in order to increase their capacity to discover, investigate and collect evidence of crimes.

11. The responsible institutions are instructed to equip/mobilize their investigation and interrogation administrations with modern instruments –used in the proof of crime-, the investigation proceeding should be video-recorded to avoid any complaints from other persons. The criminal police and judicial police are ordered to collect material sources of crime, including the scientific and technical criminal pictures of the criminals on the spot. Once the documents have been collected within the legally prescribed period of time, the cases should be referred to the relevant prosecution office for further judicial process. The responsible organs must seriously avoid any arrest without proof, evidence and documents.

12. The Chief Justice, Attorney-General, Minister of Justice, Minister of Interior and the Director of the NDS must seriously observe the enforcement of this Decree and the progress on implementation of this Decree should be reported to the Presidential Office every three months, through the Office of Administrative Affairs & Council of Ministers' Secretariat. Hamid Karzai, President of the Islamic Republic of Afghanistan

APPENDIX 2. AGREEMENT BETWEEN THE TWO CAMPAIGN TEAMS REGARDING THE STRUCTURE OF THE NATIONAL UNITY GOVERNMENT, SEPTEMBER, 21, 2014

Agreement between the Two Campaign Teams Regarding the Structure of the National Unity Government This period in Afghanistan's history requires a legitimate and functioning government committed to implementing a comprehensive program of reform to empower the Afghan public, thereby making the values of the Constitution a daily reality for the people of Afghanistan. Stability of the country is strengthened by a genuine political partnership between the President and the CEO, under the authority of the President.

Dedicated to political consensus, commitment to reforms, and cooperative decision-making, the national unity government will fulfill the aspirations of the Afghan public for peace, stability, security, rule of law, justice, economic growth, and delivery of services, with particular attention to women, youth, Ulema, and vulnerable persons. Further, this agreement is based on the need for genuine and meaningful partnership and effective cooperation in the affairs of government, including design and implementation of reforms.

The relationship between the President and the CEO cannot be described solely and entirely by this agreement, but must be defined by the commitment of both sides to partnership, collegiality, collaboration, and, most importantly, responsibility to the people of Afghanistan. The President and CEO are honor bound to work together in that spirit of partnership.

A. Convening of a Loya Jirga to amend the Constitution and considering the proposal to create the post of executive prime minister

1. On the basis of Article 2 of the Joint Statement of 17 Asad 1393 (August 8, 2014) and its attachment ("...convening of a Loya Jirga in

two years to consider the post of an executive prime minister"), the President is committed to convoking a Loya Jirga for the purpose of debate on amending the Constitution and creating a post of executive prime minister.

2. After the inauguration ceremony, the President will appoint in consultation with the CEO by executive order a commission to draft an amendment to the Constitution.

3. On the basis of Article 140 of the Constitution, the national unity government is committed to holding district council elections as early as possible on the basis of a law in order to create a quorum for the Loya Jirga in accordance with Section 2 of Article 110 of the Constitution.

4. The national unity government is committed to ratifying and enforcing a law on the organization of the basic organs of the state and determination of the boundaries and limits of local administration by legal means.

5. The national unity government commits to completing the distribution of electronic/computerized identity cards to all the citizens of the country as quickly as possible.

6. The above issues and other matters that are agreed to will be implemented on a schedule which is appended to this agreement

B. The position of the Chief Executive Officer

Until such time as the Constitution is amended and the position of executive prime minister is created, the position of Chief Executive Officer (CEO) will be created by presidential decree on the basis of Article 50 of the Constitution and Article 2 of the attached Joint Declaration and its annex. The CEO and his deputies will be introduced in the presidential inauguration ceremony.

The appointment of the CEO with the functions of an executive prime minister will take place through a proposal by the runner-up and the agreement of the President. The CEO will be answerable to the President.

A special protocol for the CEO will be authorized in a presidential decree.

The President will delegate by a presidential decree specific executive authorities to the CEO with a view to Articles 60, 64, 71, and 77 of the Constitution. Key elements of authorities will include the following:

1. Participation of the CEO with the President in bilateral decision-making meetings.

2. Carrying out administrative affairs and executive affairs of the government as determined by presidential decree.

3. Implementing the reform program of the National Unity Government.

4. Proposing reforms in all government agencies and decisively combating official corruption.

5. Exercising specific administrative and financial authorities, which will be determined in a presidential decree.

6. Establishing working relationships of the executive branch of the government with the legislative and judicial branches within the framework of defined functions and authorities.

7. Implementing, monitoring, and supporting the policies, programs, and budgetary and financial affairs of the government.

8. Submitting necessary reports and proposals to the President.

9. The President, as the head of state and government, leads the Cabinet (Kabina), which meets at his discretion on government policy, strategy, budgeting, resource allocation, and legislation among its other functions and authorities. The Cabinet consists of the President, Vice Presidents, CEO, Deputy CEOs, the Chief Advisor, and ministers. The CEO will be responsible for managing the Cabinet's implementation of government policies, and will report on progress to the President directly and in the Cabinet. To that end, the CEO will chair regular weekly meetings of the Council of Ministers (Shura-e-Waziran), consisting of the CEO, Deputy CEOs, and all ministers. The Council of Ministers will implement the executive affairs of the government. The CEO will also chair all the sub-committees of the Council of Ministers. Based on this article of the agreement, a presidential decree will introduce and define the new Council of Ministers as distinct from the Cabinet.

10. Providing advice and proposals to the President for appointment and dismissal of senior government officials and other government affairs.

11. Special representation of the President at the international level as deemed necessary by the President.

12. The CEO is a member of the National Security Council.

13. The CEO will have two deputies, who will be members of meetings of the cabinet and meetings of the National Security Council. The functions, authorities, and responsibilities of the CEO's deputies, in line with the CEO's functions and authorities, as well as an appropriate protocol for them, will be proposed by the CEO and approved by the President through presidential decree.

C. Appointment of senior officials

On the basis of the principles of national participation, fair representation, merit, honesty, and commitment to the reform programs of the national unity government, the parties are committed to the following:

* Parity in the selection of personnel between the President and the CEO at the level of head of key security and economic institutions, and independent directorates. As a consequence of this parity, and the provisions of Sections B (12) and (13) above, the two teams will be equally represented in the National Security Council at the leadership level, and equitably (Barabarguna) represented at the membership level.

* The President and the CEO will agree upon a specific merit-based mechanism for the appointment of senior officials. The mechanism will provide for the full participation of the CEO in proposing nominees for all applicable positions and for full consideration of all nominations. In conformity with the intent of the Joint Declaration and its annex (Article 5), the President and the CEO will consult intensively on the selection of senior appointees not covered by the Civil Service Commission through the above mechanism, which can lead to equitable (Barabarguna) representation from both parties, and with attention to inclusivity and the political and societal composition of the country, with particular attention to women and youth, and persons with disabilities, for state institutions and agencies, including key judiciary and local administrative posts. The two parties are committed to early reform of the Civil Service Commission. Enabling broad participation of meritorious personalities and personnel of the country at various levels of the system, using these opportunities for securing enduring peace and stability and building a healthy administration.

Creation of the position of leader of the runner-up team In line with the Joint Declaration of 17 Asad 1393 (August 8, 2014) and its annex, and with the goal of strengthening and expanding democracy, the position of the leader of the runner-up team, referred to in the mentioned document as the opposition leader, will be created and officially recognized within the framework of the government of the Islamic Republic of Afghanistan on the basis of a presidential decree. The responsibilities, authorities, and honors of this position will be spelled out in the decree. After the formation of the national unity government with the presence of the runner-up team on the basis of this agreement, this position will act as an ally of the national unity government.

E. Electoral reform

To ensure that future elections are fully credible, the electoral system (laws and institutions) requires fundamental changes. Immediately after the establishment of the government of national unity, the President will issue a decree to form a special commission for the reform of the electoral system in accordance with Article 7 of the Political Framework. Members of the special commission will be agreed between the President and the CEO. The special commission will report to the CEO on its progress and the Cabinet will review its recommendations and take the necessary steps for their implementation. The objective is to implement electoral reform before the 2015 parliamentary elections.

F. Implementation

Any divergence in views or dispute regarding the interpretation or application of this agreement shall be resolved through consultation between the parties. The parties express appreciation for the role played by the international community in facilitating the political and technical agreements, and welcome the assurances the parties have received of its support for the implementation of this agreement and its engagement with the government of national unity.

G. Entry-into-force

Honoring their commitments to the Technical and Political Frameworks of July 12, 2014, and the Joint Declaration of August 8, 2014, as reflected throughout this agreement, the parties reaffirm their commitment regarding the outcome of the election and implementation of this agreement to establish the national unity government, which will enter into force upon signing by the two candidates in the presence of Afghan and international witnesses.

Dr. Mohammad Ashraf Ghani Ahmadzai

Dr. Abdullah

The foregoing signatures were witnessed by:

H.E. Jan Kubis, Special Representative of Ambassador, the Secretary General of the United Nations H.E. James B. Cunningham, of the United States of America

AI Index: ASA 11/015/2012

4 September 2012

Afghanistan: Defer parliamentary vote on appointment of National Security Director

The Parliament of Afghanistan is due to vote on President Karzai's proposal to appoint Assadullah Khalid as the new Director of Afghanistan's intelligence service, the National Directorate of Security (NDS). Amnesty International urges all parliamentarians to defer voting on this appointment until all acts of torture and other serious human rights violations allegedly committed by Assadullah Khalid are fully investigated.

On 2 September (12 Sunbulla 1391, in the Afghan calendar), President Karzai nominated Assadullah Khalid for the post of NDS Director. The Afghan parliament is required to approve or reject nominations by the President for senior government positions including for Ministers, the NDS Director, and Supreme Court judges.

There have been numerous reports of Assadullah Khalid's alleged involvement, both directly and in a supervisory role, in the commission of crimes under international law, including torture and unlawful killings in particular during his service as Governor of Ghazni Province between 2001- 2005 and the Governor of Kandahar Province between 2005–2008.

In 2007 Amnesty International reported on cases of torture including at the Kandahar NDS detention facility, while Assadullah Khalid was serving as Governor of Kandahar and had oversight of all provincial departments including the NDS.

There are also credible allegations that Assadullah Khalid was involved in the bombing of a UN vehicle in Kandahar that killed five UN workers in April 2007. As Kandahar Governor, Khalid supervised

Brigade 888, which comprised tens of armed men, who are alleged to have arbitrarily arrested and tortured individuals, perceived as having links with the Taliban and other insurgent groups in Kandahar. It is widely reported that detainees were tortured on the Kandahar governor's premises.

Afghanistan government as a state party to the UN Convention Against Torture and Other Cruel, Inhuman or Degrading Treatment or Punishment has obligation to investigate all the allegations of torture committed by Afghan government officials or institutions and to make sure the victims are protected and provided with justice, compensation or reparation and to remove and prosecute individuals responsible for torture.

Amnesty International urges President Karzai, the Afghan Parliament and all other Afghan authorities to guarantee that all individuals suspected of having committed serious violations of human rights law and humanitarian law violations, including war crimes, are held to account for their actions.

Amnesty International also calls upon the Afghan president and all members of the Afghan parliament to make sure that the human rights records of every nominee for a senior government position including for the NDS Director, the Minister of Defense and the Minister of Interior – all now before parliament – have been fully assessed by the President's Advisory Panel on Senior Appointments, as required. Any credible allegations of links to serious human rights violations should be fully and openly considered by parliament before any voting on the proposed appointments.

Amnesty International once again also urges international partners of the Afghan government to ensure that rule of law, accountability and access to justice are meaningfully delivered to the Afghan people as promised at the Tokyo Conference in July 2012 declaration. Courtesy: Amnesty International and Afghanistan Independent Commission of Human Rights.

BIBLIOGRAPHY

Abbas Hassan, 2004, *Pakistan's Drift into Extremism: Allah, the Army and America's War on Terror*, M. E, Sharp.

Abbaszadeh, Nima. 2008. *Provincial Reconstruction Teams: Lessons and Recommendations*, Princeton University Woodrow Wilson School

Adair, Jason T. 2008. Learning on the run: company level counter-insurgency in Afghanistan, *Canadian Army Journal, Vol. 10, No. 4.*

Afsar, Shahid, Chris Samples, and Thomas Wood, The Taliban: An Organizational Analysis, *Military Review, May-June 2008.*

Ahmad, Irfan. 2009. Role of Airpower for Counterinsurgency in Afghanistan and FATA (Federally Administered Tribal Areas). *NPS master's thesis*

Ali, Imtaz. 2008. 'Preparing the Mujahidin: The Taliban's Military Field Manual', *CTC Sentinel, Vol. 1, Issue 10.*

Afghanistan Independent Human Rights Commission (AIHRC), 2012, *From Arbaki to Local Police: Today's Challenges and Tomorrow's Concerns. Kabul Afghanistan*

Atran, Scott. 2010. 'A Question of Honor: Why the Taliban Fight and What to Do About It. *Asian Journal of Social Science, Vol. 38.*

Abramowitz, Morton, *United States and Turkey: Allies in Need.* New York: Century Foundation Press, 2003.

Adamec, Ludwig W. *Afghanistan's Foreign Affairs to the Mid-Twentieth Century: Relations with the U.S.S.R., Germany and Britain.* Tucson: University of Arizona Press, 1974.

Adas, Michael. *Dominance by Design: Technological Imperatives and America's Civilizing Mission.* Cambridge: Belknap Press of Harvard University Press, 2006.

Alexiev, Alexander R. "The Soviet Strategy in Afghanistan." *Global Affairs, Volume 2, Winter 1987:*

Alexiev, Alexander R. "U.S. Policy and the War in Afghanistan." *Global Affairs, Volume 3, Winter 1988*

Alin, Erika. *The United States and the 1958 Lebanon Crisis.* Lanham, MD: University Press of America, 1994.

Allison, Robert. *The Crescent Obscured: The United States and the Muslim World, 1776-1815.* University of Chicago Press, 2000.

Arlinghaus, Joseph T. 1988. *The Transformation of Afghan Tribal Society: Tribal Expansion, Mughal Imperialism and the Roshaniyya Insurrection, 1450-1600.* PhD Dissertation, Department of History, Duke University.

Azerbaijani Moghaddam, Sippi. 2009. *Northern Exposure for the Taliban,* Antonio Giustozzi

Azoy, Whitney. 2003, Masood's Parade: Iconography, Revitalization and Ethnicity in Afghanistan. *Expedition, Vol. 45, No. 1.*

Aziz Khalid, 2013, Five Pillars of a Successful Transition in Afghanistan Post 2014, *DIS Policy Brief,* Danish Institute for International Studies, Copenhagen.

Barakat, Sultan and S. Zyck. 2010. 'Afghanistan's insurgency and the viability of a political solution *Studies in Conflict and Terrorism, Vol. 33, No. 3.*

Barfield, Thomas. 2005. 'Afghanistan is Not the Balkans: Ethnicity and its Political Consequences from a Central Asian Perspective', *Central Eurasian Studies Review, Volume 4, Number 1, winter 2005.*

Bayly, C. A. 1996. *Empire and Information: Intelligence Gathering and Social Communication in India, 1780–1870.* Cambridge: Cambridge University Press.

Bar-On, Mordechai. *Gates of Gaza: Israel's Road to Suez and Back, 1955–1957.* New York: St. Martin's Press, 1994.

Bar-Siman-Tov, Yaacov, with commentary by David Schoenbaum and Peter Hahn. The United States and Israel since 1948: A 'Special Relationship'? *Diplomatic History. Vol. 22,*

Bass, Warren. *Support Any Friend: Kennedy's Middle East and the Making of the U.S.-Israel Alliance.* Oxford University Press, 2003.

Bayne, E.A. and Richard V. Collin. *Arms and Advisors: Views from Saudi Arabia and Iran.* Hanover, American University Field Staff, 1976.

Beckwith, Col. Charlie A., *with Donald Knox. Delta Force: The U.S. Counter-terrorist Unit and the Iran Hostage Rescue Mission.* New York: Harcourt, Brace, and Jovanovich, 1983.

Bennett, G. H. *British Foreign Policy during the Curzon Period, 1919–24.* New York: St. Martin's Press, 1995.

Beley, Mathieu, and Barnett Rubin. 2004. The Benefits and Drawbacks of doing Business in Afghanistan. *Afghanistan Investment and Support Agency Media Magazine*

Bell, Marjorie Jewett. 1948. *An American Engineer in Afghanistan:* From the Letters and Notes of A. C. Jewett. Minneapolis: The University of Minnesota Press.

Bentley, G. Carter. 1987. "Ethnicity as Practice." *Comparative Studies in Society and History* 29.1

Bergh, Gina et al. 2009. 'Conflict analysis: Jaghori and Malistan districts, Ghazni province', CPAU.

Basso, John A. 2004 *America's last battles: organizing brigades to win the peace 14 lessons from East Timor, Afghanistan, and Iraq.* U.S. Army CGSC

Bebber, Robert J. 2009. Developing an IO Environmental Assessment in Khost Province: Information Operations at PRT Khost in 2008', *Small Wars Journal, February 2009.*

Behr, Timo. 2011. *Germany and Regional Command-North: ISAF's Weakest Link? in State building in Afghanistan: Multinational Contributions to Reconstruction.* Edited by Nik Hynek and Péter Marton. Routledge.

Bell, Kevin. 2009. 'Pulling Teeth: An Infantry Platoon Leader's Perspective on a Year in Afghanistan *Army Magazine, May 2009.*

Betz, David and Anthony Cormack, 2009. Wars amongst the People: Iraq, Afghanistan and British Strategy', *Orbis, Spring 2009, Volume 53, Number 2.*

Betz, David. 2008. 'The virtual dimension of contemporary insurgency', *Small Wars & Insurgencies, Vol. 19, No. 4.*

Berman, Eli, et al. 2011. 'Do Working Men Rebel? Insurgency and Unemployment in Afghanistan, Iraq and the Philippines', *Journal of Conflict Resolution, March 2011*

Brown, Vahid, 2013, *Fountainhead of Jihad: The Haqqani Network 1973–2012,* C. Hurst & Company, London, UK

Brown Vanda Felbab, 2013, *Aspiration and Ambivalence: Strategies and Realities of Counterinsurgency and State Building in Afghanistan.* Brooking Institution Press, Washington, USA

Banuazizi, Ali and Myron Weiner, 1986. *The State, Religion, and Ethnic Politics: Afghanistan, Iran, and Pakistan.* Syracuse: Syracuse University Press.

Barfield, Thomas. 2010. *Afghanistan: A Cultural and Political History.* Princeton University Press.

Barry, Michael. 2006. *A History of Modern Afghanistan.* Cambridge University Press.

Bashir, Shahzad and Robert D. Crews, 2012. *Under the Drones: Modern Lives in the Afghanistan-Pakistan Borderlands.* Harvard University Press.

Bhatia, Michael and Mark Sedra. 2008. *Afghanistan, Arms and Conflict: Armed Groups, Disarmament and Security in a Post-war Society.* Routledge.

Bayley, D.H., Perito, R.M. 2010. *The Police in War: Fighting Insurgency, Terrorism and Violent Crime.* London

Byrd, W. and S. Guimbert, 2009, Public Finance, Security, and Development, A Framework and an Application to Afghanistan, Policy *Research Working Paper, Washington, D.C., World Bank*

Caldicott, Helen. 2002, *The New Nuclear Danger: George W. Bush's Military-Industrial Complex.* New York: The New Press

Cassidy M. Robert, 2012, *War, Will and Warlords: Counterinsurgency in Afghanistan and Pakistan*, Marine Corps University Press

Centlivres, P. and M. Centlivres-Demont. 2000. State, National Awareness and Levels of Identity in Afghanistan from Monarchy to Islamic State, Central *Asian Survey, Vol.19*

Chandra, Vishal. 2011. The Evolving Politics of Taliban Reintegration and Reconciliation in Afghanistan', *Strategic Analysis, Volume 35, Issue 5.*

Chorev, Matan and J. Sherman. 2010. *The Prospects for Security and Political Reconciliation in Afghanistan: Local, National, and Regional Perspectives*, Institute for Global Leadership.

Chaudhuri, Rudra and Theo Farrell. 2011. 'Campaign disconnect: operational progress and strategic obstacles in Afghanistan, 2009–2011', *International Affairs, Vol. 87, No. 2.*

Chin, Warren. 2010. 'Colonial Warfare in a Post-Colonial State: British Military Operations in Helmand Province, Afghanistan', *Defense Studies, Vol. 10, No. 1.*

Chin, Warren. 2007. 'British Counter-Insurgency in Afghanistan', *Defense & Security Analysis, Vol. 23, No. 2*

Choharis, Peter Charles and James A. Gavrilis. 2010. 'Counterinsurgency 3.0. *Parameters, Spring 2010.*

Clark, Kate. 2011. *The Takhar attack: Targeted killings and the parallel worlds of US intelligence and Afghanistan* Afghanistan Analysts Network.

Clukey, David S. 2010. 'A District Approach in Afghanistan? *Small Wars Journal, April.*

Coffey, Luke. 2009. 'Detainee Operations in Counterinsurgency Operations Lessons from Afghanistan 2005–2006', Small Wars Journal, September 2009.

Coghlan, Tom. 2009. *The Taliban in Helmand: An Oral History', in Antonio Giustozzi. Decoding the New Taliban: Insights from the Afghan Field.* Hurst/Columbia.

Crews D. Robert and Tarzi Amin, 2009, *the Taliban and the Crisis of Afghanistan*, Harvard University Press

Donini Antonio, Niland Norah and Wermester Karin, 2004, *Nation Building Unravelled: Aid, Peace and Justice in Afghanistan*, Kumarian Press Int.

Dorronsoro, Gilles. 2005. *Revolution Unending: Afghanistan, 1979 to the Present.* New York: Columbia University Press.

Edwards, David B. 2002. Before *Taliban: Genealogies of the Afghan Jihad.* Berkeley, CA: University of California Press.

Edwards, David B. 1996. *Heroes of the Age: Moral Fault Lines on the Afghan Frontier.* Berkeley, CA: University of California Press.

Emadi, Hafizullah. 2010. *Dynamics of Political Development in Afghanistan: The British, Russian, and American Invasions.* Palgrave Macmillan.

Ewans, Martin. 2005. *Conflict in Afghanistan: Studies in Asymmetric Warfare.* Routledge

Giustozzi, Antonio. 2009. *Empires of Mud: Wars and Warlords of Afghanistan.* Hurst/Columbia University Press

Eveland, Wilbur Crane. *Ropes of Sand: America's Failure in the Middle East.* New York: W.W. Norton, 1980.

Eamon Murphy, 2012, the *Making of Terrorism in Pakistan: Historical and Social Roots of Extremism*, Routledge.

Englehart A Neil, 2010, *Tale of Two Afghanistan: Comparative Governance and Insurgency in the North and South*, Bowling Green State University.

Forsberg, Carl. 2010. *Politics and Power in Kandahar.* Institute for the Study of War.

Forsberg, Carl. 2009. *The Taliban's Campaign for Kandahar', Afghanistan Report.* Institute for the Study of War.

Fingar, T. 2011 *Reducing uncertainty: intelligence analysis and national security*, Stanford, CA: Stanford University Press

Friedrichs J, 2008, *Fighting Terrorism and Drugs. Europe and international police cooperation*, London and New York: Routledge

Frederic Volpi, 2008. *Transnational Islam and Regional Security*, Routledge, London.

Fair C. Christine. 2007. Militant Recruitment in Pakistan: A New Look at the Militancy-Madrasa-Connection, *Asian Policy.*

Ganguli Sumit and Devin T. Hagerty. 2006. *Fearful Symmetry: India-Pakistan Crisis in the Shadow of Nuclear Weapons.* Seattle, W.A, University of Washington Press.

Ganguli Sumit and S. Paul Kapur. 2009. *Nuclear Proliferation in South Asia: Crisis Behavior and the Bomb.* Routledge, New York.

Goodson, Larry P. *Afghanistan's Endless War: State Failure, Regional Politics, and the Rise of the Taliban* University of Washington Press, 2001

Gregorian, Vartan , *The Emergence of Modern Afghanistan: Politics of Reform and Modernization, 1880–1946*, Stanford University Press, 1969.

Griffin, Michael , Reaping the Whirlwind: *The Taliban Movement in Afghanistan* , Pluto Press, 2001.

Gall Calotta, 2014, *the Wrong Enemy: America in Afghanistan, 2001–2014*, Houghton Mifflin Harcourt, New York, USA

Giovacchini, Tommaso, August 2011, *Governance and Representation in the Afghan Urban Transition*, Afghanistan Research and Evaluation Unit Research for a better Afghanistan

Giustozzi, Antonio, Justice and State Building in Afghanistan: State VS Society VS Taliban, *Occasional Paper No-16 August 2012, Asia Foundation*

Grau, Lester W. and Dodge Billingsley, 2011. *Operation Anaconda: America's First Major Battle in Afghanistan.* University Press of Kansas

Grau, Lester W. 2003. *The Bear Went Over the Mountain: Soviet Combat Tactics in Afghanistan.* Routledge.

Gress, Michael A. and Lester W. Grau, *Russian General Staff.* 2002. *The Soviet-Afghan War: How a Superpower Fought and Lost.* University Press of Kansas

Goodhand Jonathan, Hakimi Aziz, 2014, *Counterinsurgency, Local Militias, and State Building in Afghanistan,* United States Institute of Peace

Goodhand Jonathan, February, 2014, *Winning Hearts and Minds? Reconstruction, Governance and Counterinsurgency in Afghanistan,* Mount Holyoke College South Hadley Massachusetts, USA

Harvey Frank P. 2008. The Homeland Security Dilemma: Fear, Failure, and the Future of American Insecurity. *Contemporary Security Studies*

Howie, Luke. 2012. *Witnesses to terror: understanding the meanings and consequences of terrorism.* Basingstoke: Palgrave Macmillan

Hanifi, M. Jamil. 2004. Editing the Past: Colonial Production of Hegemony through the Loya Jerga in Afghanistan, *Iranian Studies 37 (2)*

Howitt, Arnold M. 2003. *Countering terrorism: dimensions of preparedness.* Cambridge, Mass.: MIT Press.

Ibrahimi, Niamatullah. 2009. 'Divide and rule: State penetration in Hazarajat from monarchy to the Taliban', *Working Paper No: 42. Series 2*

Ibrahimi, Niamatullah. 2009. 'At the sources of Factionalism and Civil War in Hazarajat', *Working Paper No. 41 series 2*

Ilan, Amitzur. 1996. *Origin of the Arab-Israeli Arms Race: Arms, Embargo, Military Power and Decision in the 1948 Palestine War*. New York: New York University Press,

Jalalzai, Musa Khan, 2014, *Whose Army? Afghanistan Future and the Blueprint for Civil War*, Algora Publishing, New York, USA

Johnson, Thomas H. and M. Chris Mason. 2008. No Sign until the Burst of Fire: Understanding the Pakistan-Afghanistan Frontier. *International Security, Vol. 32, No. 4.*

Johnson, Thomas H. 2007. On the Edge of the Big Muddy: The Taliban Resurgence in Afghanistan *China and Eurasia Forum Quarterly, Vol. 5, no. 2.*

Johnson, Thomas H. and M. Chris Mason. 2007. Understanding the Taliban and Insurgency in Afghanistan. *Orbis, Vol. 51, No. 1.*

Johnson, Thomas. 2004. Ismail Khan, Herat and Iranian Influence. *Strategic Insights, Vol. 3(7).*

Jones, Seth G. 2008. The Rise of Afghanistan's Insurgency: State Failure and Jihad', *International Security, Vol. 32, No. 4*

Kenneth Katzman, 2006, *Afghanistan: Post War Governance, Security, and US Policy,* CRS Report for Congress, Washington DC Library of Congress, USA

Khan, M.O. 2009. Don't Try to Arrest the Sea: An Alternative Approach for Afghanistan. *Small Wars Journal, October 2009.*

Keating, Michael, Women's Rights and Wrongs. *The World Today, Vol.53, January 1997*

Khalilzad, Zalmay, "Afghanistan in 1995: Civil War and a Mini-Great Game. *Asian Survey, Vol. 36, February 1996*

Khalilzad, Zalmay, "Afghanistan in 1994: Civil War and Disintegration", *Asian Survey, Vol. 35, February 1995*

Khalilzad, Zalmay, Anarchy in Afghanistan. *Journal of International Affairs, Vol.51, summer 1997*

Kinnunen, Eero and Lester W. Grau. 2011. Two Tours in Afghanistan: Twenty Years and Two Armies Apart. *Military Review, May-June.*

Kiss, Zoltan Laszlo. 2009. Hungarian experiences from peacekeeping in Afghanistan. *Contributions to Conflict Management, Peace Economics and Development, Vol. 12. 1*

Kolenda, Christopher. 2010. Winning Afghanistan at the Community Level. *Joint Forces Quarterly, Issue 56..*

Kotkin, Jeremy. 'Is the War in Afghanistan in the Interests of the United States and its Allies? *Small Wars Journal, August 2009.*

Kenneth Katzman, April 2015, *Afghanistan: Post Taliban Governance and Security and US Policy*, Congressional Research Service

Lamb D. Robert, 2012, Political Governance and Strategy in Afghanistan, *A Report of the CSIS Program on Crisis, Conflict and Cooperation*, Center for Strategic and International Studies

Larry P. Goodson, 2001, *Afghanistan's Endless War: State Failure, Regional Politics and the Rise of the Taliban*, University of Washington Press

Lafraie, Najibullah. 2008. 'Resurgence of the Taliban insurgency in Afghanistan: How and why?', International Politics, Vol. 46, 1.

Lieven, Anatol. 2009. The war in Afghanistan: its background and future prospects', Conflict, *Security & Development, Vol. 9, Issue 3.*

Maley, William, Editor. 1998. *Fundamentalism Reborn? Afghanistan and the Taliban.* New York: New York University Press.

Malik, Hafeez. 2008. *US Relations with Afghanistan and Pakistan: The Imperial Dimension.* Oxford University Press.

Maroof, Mohammad Khalid, 1990. *Afghanistan and Super Powers, New Delhi: Commonwealth*

Matinuddhin, Kamal, 2000. *The Taliban Phenomenon: Afghanistan 1994–1997,* New Delhi: Lancer

Moghadam, Valentine M 1990. *Revolution En-gendered: Women and Politics in Iran and Afghanistan,* Toronto: York University

Moghadam, Valentine M. 1999, Revolution, Religion, and Gender Politics: Iran and Afghanistan Compared, *Journal of Women's History, Vol. 10, No.4, winter*

Marsden, Magnus and Benjamin Hopkins. 2012. *Beyond Swat: History, Society and Economy along the Afghanistan-Pakistan Frontier.* Columbia University Press.

Marsden, Magnus and Benjamin D. Hopkins. 2012. *Fragments of the Afghan Frontier.* Columbia University Press

Maloney, Sean M. 2011, *Fighting for Afghanistan*, Annapolis: Naval Institute Press

Mursal Mansoory, 2 June 2013 Afghan Forces to Lead All Military Operations in Few Weeks. *TOLOnews Kabul Afghanistan*

Mir Amir, 2009, *Talibanization in Pakistan*, Pentagon Security International, India

Murshed Iftikhar, 2006, *Afghanistan: The Taliban Years*, Bennett & Bloom, UK

Montgomery John, D, 2004, *Beyond Reconstruction in Afghanistan*, Palgrave Macmillan, USA

Najumi Neamatollah, 2002, *the Rise of the Taliban in Afghanistan*, Palgrave Macmillan, USA

Nawid, Senzil K. 1999. *Religious Response to Social Change in Afghanistan, 1919–1929: King Aman-Allah and the Afghan Ulama*. Costa Mesa, Calif.: Mazda Publishers.

Nebenzahl, Kenneth. 2004. *Mapping the Silk Road and Beyond: 2,000 Years of Exploring the East*. London: Phaidon.

Noelle, Christine. 1997. *State and Tribe in Nineteenth-Century Afghanistan: The Reign of Amir Dost Muhammad Khan (1826–1863)*. Richmond, Surrey: Curzon Press.

O'Hanlon, M. 2009. 'Towards Reconciliation in Afghanistan', *Washington Quarterly, Vol. 32, No. 2*.

O'Loughlin, John, Frank D. W. Witmer, and Andrew M. Linke. 2010. The Afghanistan-Pakistan Wars, 2008–2009: Micro-geographies, Conflict Diffusion, and Clusters of Violence. *Eurasian Geography and Economics, Vol. 51, No. 4.*

Oren, Michael. *Six Days of War: June 1967 and the Making of the Modern Middle East*. New York: Oxford University Press, 2002.

Omrani, Bijan, and Matthew Leeming. 2005. *Afghanistan: A Companion and Guide*. Hong Kong: Odyssey Books & Guides

Ollapally Deepa, 2003, *Unfinished Business in Afghanistan: Warlordism, Reconstruction and Ethnic Harmony*, the United States Institute of Peace

Patrick Hannessey 2012, *Kandak: Fighting with Afghans*, the Penguin Group, and USA.

Peters, Gretchen. 2010. *Crime and Insurgency in the Tribal Areas of Afghanistan and Pakistan'*, Combating Terrorism Center.

Phillips, Andrew. 2009. The Anbar Awakening: Can It Be Exported to Afghanistan? *Security Challenges, Vol. 5, No. 3.*

Radnitz, Scott. 2004. Working with the Warlords: Designing an Ethnofederal System for Afghanistan', *Regional and Federal Studies, Vol. 14, No. 4, Winter 2004*

Rahimi, Roohullah. 2008. *Afghanistan: Exploring the Dynamics of Socio-political Strife and the Persistence of the Insurgency*. Pearson Peacekeeping Center..

Rashid Ahmad, 2010, *Taliban: The Power of Militant Islam in Afghanistan and Beyond*, IB Touris &Co, London

Roy, Olivier. 1995. *Afghanistan: From Holy War to Civil War*. Princeton: Darwin Press.

Rubin. Barnett R. 2006. Peace Building and State-building in Afghanistan: Constructing Sovereignty for Whose Security? *Third World Quarterly, 27(1)*

Rubin, Barnett R. 2000. 'The Political Economy of War and Peace in Afghanistan', *World Development, Vol. 28, No. 10*

Rubin, Barnett R. and Helena Malikyar, 2003. *The Politics of Center-Periphery Relations in Afghanistan* Center on International Cooperation.

Ruttig, Thomas. 2011. 'Negotiations with the Taliban: History and Prospects for the Future, New America Foundation.

Ruttig, T. 2010. *How Tribal Are the Taliban? Afghanistan's Largest Insurgent Movement between its Tribal Roots and Islamist Ideology'*, Afghanistan Analysts Network.

Ruttig, Thomas. 2010. 'The Ex-Taliban on the High Peace Council: A renewed role for the Khuddam ul-Furqan? Afghanistan Analysts Network

Roy, Olivier. 1990. *Islam and Resistance in Afghanistan*. Cambridge University Press

Rubin, Barnett R. 2012. *Afghanistan in the Post-Cold War Era*, Oxford University Press

Rubin, Barnett. 1995. *The Search for Peace in Afghanistan: From Buffer State to Failed State*. New Haven, CT: Yale University Press.

Rubin, Barnett. 1995. *The Fragmentation of Afghanistan: State Formation and Collapse in the International System*. New Haven, CT: Yale University Press.

Saikal, Amin. 2004. *Modern Afghanistan: A History of Struggle and Survival*. I. B. Tauris.

Sreedhar, Sinha Rakesh, Nilesh Bhagat, and O.N. Mehrotra, 1997, *Taliban and the Afghan Turmoil: The Role of USA, Pakistan, Iran and China*, Mumbai: Himalaya

Sreedhar, Sinha, and Mahendra Ved, 1998. *Afghan Turmoil: Changing Equations*, Mumbai: Himalaya

Stobdan, P. 1998. *Afghan Conflict and India*, New Delhi: Institute for Defense Studies and Analysis, 1998.

Shahrani, M. Nazif and Robert L Canfield, 1984. *Revolutions and Rebellions in Afghanistan: Anthropological Perspectives*. Berkeley: University of California.

Saltmarshe Douglas and Medhi Abhilash, 2011, Local Governance in Afghanistan: *A view from the Ground, Afghanistan Research and Evaluation Unit Synthesis Paper*

Sedra Mark, 2014, An Uncertain Future for Afghanistan's Security Sector, *International Journal of Security &Development.*

Sedra Mark, 2005, Security Sector Reform in Afghanistan: A Continued March towards Implementation, *Research Paper No-22 July-August*, NATO Defense College, Italy

Sexton Renard, April 21 2015, *Aid, Insurgency and the Pivotal Role of Control: Evidence from Afghanistan, Department of Politics*, New York University

Saikal, Amin. 2000. The Role of Outside Actors in Afghanistan, *Middle East Policy, Vol. 7(4).*

Saikal, Amin. 1998. *The Rabbani Government, 1992–1996, in William Maley Fundamentalism Reborn? Afghanistan and the Taliban*. New York University Press

Saikal, Amin. 1998. 'Afghanistan's Ethnic Conflict', *Survival, Vol. 40, No. 2.*

Sajjad. Tazreena. 2010. *'Peace at all Costs?* Reintegration and Reconciliation in Afghanistan AREU

Sakhi, Farishta. 2009. What is needed to Enhance National Security? *Swedish Committee for Afghanistan Conference: Peace Building in Afghanistan.*

Schetter, C. 2006. 'Geopolitics and the Afghan Territory', *Geographische Rundschau International Edition,*

Schetter, Conrad. 2005. 'Ethnoscapes, National Territorialization, and the *Afghan War Geopolitics, Vol. 10, pp. 50-75.*

Shahzad Saleem, 2011, *Inside Al-Qaeda and the Taliban: Beyond Bin Laden and 9/11,* Pluto Press, and London

Stricl Alex Van Linchuten, Kuehn Flix. 2012, *An Enemy we created: The Myth of the Taliban, Al-Qaeda Merger in Afghanistan, 1970–2010,* Hurst & Company, and London

Shahrani, M. Nazif. 2009. Afghanistan Since 1919: From Failed Modernization and Failed-State to a Post-Taliban Militia-State', in The Islamic world in the age of Western dominance. *Volume 5 of the New Cambridge History of Islam. Francis Robinson*

Shahrani, M. Nazif. 2008. *Taliban and Talibanism in Historical Perspective', in R. D. Crews and A. Tarzi. The Taliban and the Crisis of Afghanistan.* Harvard University Press

Shahrani, M. Nazif. 2002. War, Factionalism, and the State in Afghanistan. *American Anthropologist, Vol. 104, No. 3. September 2002*

State-building in Afghanistan: a case showing the limits? Lucy Morgan Edwards, *International Review of the Red Cross, Volume 92 Number 880 December 2010*

Suhrke Astri, 2011, *when more is less: The International Project in Afghanistan,* Hurst & Company, London

Steinberg, Guido and Nils Wormer, 2010. 'Escalation in the Kunduz Region: Who are the Insurgents in North-eastern Afghanistan? *SWP Comments, No. 33*

Stenersen, Anne. 2011. 'Al Qaeda's Foot Soldiers: A Study of the Biographies of Foreign Fighters Killed in Afghanistan and Pakistan between 2002 and 2006. *Studies in Conflict & Terrorism, Vol. 34, No. 3*

Stenersen, Anne. 2010. The Taliban insurgency in Afghanistan – organization, leadership and worldview. *Norwegian Defense Research Establishment*

Stenersen, Anne. 2010. *Al-Qaeda's Allies: Explaining the Relationship between Al-Qaeda and Various Factions of the Taliban after 2001.* New America Found.

Stenersen, Anne. 2009. 'Are the Afghan Taliban Involved in International Terrorism? *CTC Sentinel, Vol. 2, No. 9.*

Strick van Linschoten, Alex and Felix Kuehn, 2012. *Islamic, Independent, Perfect and Strong": Parsing the Taliban's Strategic Intentions, 2001–2011'*, AHRC.

Suhrke, Astri, et al. 2009. Conciliatory Approaches to the Insurgency in Afghanistan. *An Overview', CMI Report.*

Taj Farhat, 2011, *Taliban and Anti Taliban*, Cambridge Scholars Publishing, UK

Thomson, William. 2012. Criminal Organizations, Competitive Advantage and State Failure in Afghanistan, *Small Wars Journal January*

Thomas, R. 2009. 'Origins of the Strategic Advisory Team: *Afghanistan'*, *On Track, Vol. 14(1)*

Thruelsen, Peter Dahl. 2010. *Fighting an insurgency without unity: NATO in Afghanistan, 2006 to 2010.* PhD thesis, University of Copenhagen

Thruelsen, Peter Dahl. 2008. Counterinsurgency and a Comprehensive Approach: Helmand Province, Afghanistan', *Small Wars Journal*

Thruelsen, Peter Dahl. 2007. NATO in Afghanistan: What Lessons are we learning and are we willing to adjust? *Danish Institute for Int. Studies Report No. 14.*

Turner, L.S. et al. 2010. Optimizing Deadly Persistence in Kandahar: Armed UAV Integration in the Joint Tactical Fight. *Canadian Army Journal, Vol. 13, No. 1.*

Thruelsen, Peter Dahl. 2010. 'The Taliban in southern Afghanistan: a localized insurgency with a local objective', *Small Wars & Insurgencies, Vol. 21, No. 2.*

TLO. 2009. Three Years Later: A Socio-political Assessment of Uruzgan Province from 2006 to 2009. *Tribal Liaison Office*

Upadhyay, R. 2009. Vigier, Corrina. 2009. *Conflict Assessment: Afghanistan.* American Friends Service Committee

Waldman, Matt. 2010. *The Sun in the Sky: The Relationship between Pakistan's ISI and Afghan Insurgents.* Crisis States Research Center

Waldman, M. 2010. Navigating Negotiations in Afghanistan. *USIP Peace brief, No. 52.*

Waldman, Matt. 2010. *Dangerous Liaisons with the Afghan Taliban: The Feasibility and Risks of Negotiations* United States Institute of Peace

Waldman, Matt. 2010. *Golden Surrender: The Risks, Challenges, and Implications of Reintegration in Afghanistan.* Afghanistan Analysts Network

Williams, Brian Glyn. 2008. Talibanistan: History of a Transnational Terrorist Sanctuary. *Civil Wars, Vol. 10, No. 1.*

Williams, Brian Glyn. 2008. Afghanistan's Heart of Darkness: Fighting the Taliban in Kunar Province', *CTC Sentinel, Vol. 1, Issue 11.*

Williams, Jason T. 2009. Understanding an Insurgency: Achieving the United States' Strategic Objectives in Afghanistan', *SAMS Monograph.*

Willis, Michael S. 2010. *Contrasts between American and Afghan warriors, a comparison between two martial cultures,* Master's thesis, U.S. Army Command and General Staff College

Wilner, Alex S. 2010. Targeted Killings in Afghanistan: Measuring Coercion and Deterrence in Counterterrorism and Counterinsurgency', *Studies in Conflict & Terrorism, Vol. 33, No. 4.*

Yetiv, Steven A. *Crude Awakenings: Global Oil Security and American Foreign Policy.* Ithaca: Cornell University Press, 2004.

Yetiv, Steven A. *Explaining Foreign Policy: U.S. Decision-making and the Persian Gulf War.* Baltimore: Johns Hopkins University Press, 2004.

Zelikow, Philip D., and Robert B. Zoellick, *America and the Muslim Middle East: Memos to a President.* Washington, DC: Brookings Institution Press, 1998.

Zabih Ullah. 2010. *A view from Kandahar: How Afghans View Coalition Military Operations in Kandahar,* Lowy Institute.

Zweibelson, Ben. 2010. The US in Afghanistan: Follow Sun Tzu rather than Clausewitz to Victory *Small Wars Journal, Vol. 6, No. 11.*

Printed in the United States
By Bookmasters